MW00380908

REVOLUTIONARY FREEDOMS

A History of Survival, Strength and Imagination in Haiti

Cécile Accilien, Jessica Adams,
and Elmide Méléance, editors

with the paintings of
Ulrick Jean-Pierre

For information, please contact
Caribbean Studies Press
7550 NW 47th Avenue
Coconut Creek, FL 33073

Telephone: 954 725-0701
www.caribbeanstudiespress.com

ISBN: 1-58432-293-4

Contents

Paintings

Section IV - Legacies of Vodou

Section V - Behind the Mountain Are More Mountains

Notes on Contributors

Cécile Accilien is assistant professor of French and Francophone Studies at Columbus State University, Columbus, Georgia. She has published work on Francophone literatures and cultures in *Revue française, Études francophones, Dalhousie French Studies* and *Diaspora in Caribbean Art*. She has co-edited a collection of essays, *Just Below South: Performing Intercultures in the Caribbean and the Southern United States,* for the University of Virginia Press (2007). Her research interests include representations of women in Francophone Caribbean and African literature and cinema and contemporary representations of plantations/*habitations* in Louisiana, Haiti, Martinique, and Guadeloupe.

Jessica Adams is a lecturer of English at the University of California-Berkeley. She has published articles on Southern culture in *Cultural Critique* and *TDR (The Drama Review)*, and is co-editor of *Just Below South: Performing Intercultures in the Caribbean and the Southern United States* (University of Virginia Press, 2007). Her book *Wounds of Returning: Race, Memory and Property on the Post-Slavery Plantation* is forthcoming from the University of North Carolina Press.

Margaret Mitchell Armand is a psychologist and mediator active in promoting Haitian culture through art, storytelling, and poetry.

Max Beauvoir has been a houngan for over 30 years and is well-known and respected in Haiti and beyond. His temple, "Le péristyle de Mariani," located in Mariani, Haiti was founded in 1974, and is visited by people from all over the world. Mr. Beauvoir conducts symposia and workshops and has participated in conferences on African traditional religions at M.I.T, Northwestern University, Hunter College, and Portland State University. He has participated in several international conferences on African cultures and religions as a representative of UNESCO. Beauvoir is also a biochemist with degrees from the Sorbonne and Cornell.

Charles L. Blockson is the author of 13 books, including *Pennsylvania's Black History, Black Genealogy, The Underground Railroad in Pennsylvania, The Journey of John W. Mosley: An African American Pictorial Album,* and *African Americans in Pennsylvania: Above Ground and Underground:An Illustrated Guide*. He donated his collection of rare books to Temple University in 1984, and The Charles L. Blockson Afro-American Collection contains more than 150,000 books, documents, and photographs and functions as a research center for scholars around the world. Mr. Blockson is also the co-founder of the African-American Museum in Philadelphia and a founding member of the Pennsylvania Black History Committee.

Kamau Brathwaite is an acclaimed poet, critic, and playwright. He is the author of numerous works, including *The Arrivants: A New World Trilogy* (Oxford University Press, 1973), *Black + Blues* (New Directions, 1995), *History of the Voice: The Development of Nation Language in Anglophone Caribbean Poetry* (New Beacon, 1984), and *Born to Slow Horses* (Wesleyan University Press, 2005). He is professor of comparative literature at New York University.

Camila is the pen name of Gladys Bruno. A staunch advocate for Caribbean refugees, Ms. Bruno serves as president and CEO of the Haitian Agricultural Renaissance Fund. Ms. Bruno is also the author of *The Common Dream,* a work of historical fiction. Several of her poems and a short story, "Journey," have been published by Forward Press in the United Kingdom, *Farsight Magazine*, and *Full Moon* magazine.

Emile Césaire is a poet who lives in New York.

Marc A. Christophe is a professor of French Language and Literature at the University of the District of Columbia, where he specializes in 18th-century French literature and black Francophone literatures and civilizations. In addition to scholarly articles, Dr. Christophe has published two collections of poetry and collaborated on an anthology of historical essays, *1492: Le viol du nouveau monde* (1996), which examined the racial, social, cultural impacts of the encounters between Europe, Africa, and America in 1492. More recently, he worked with Edwidge Danticat on *The Butterfly's Way: Voices from the Haitian Diaspora in the United States* (2001).

Edwidge Danticat became one of the leading voices in Haitian-American literature in 1995 when she became a finalist for the National Book Award for *Krik? Krak!* She received the 1995 Pushcart Short Story Prize and fiction awards from *The Caribbean Writer, Seventeen*, and *Essence* magazines. She has a BA in French literature from Barnard College, and a MFA from Brown University, where as her thesis she wrote the novel *Breath, Eyes, Memory* (Soho Press, 1994). Her other works include *The Farming of Bones* (1998), *The Butterfly's Way: Voices from the Haitian Dyaspora in the United States* [editor] (2001), *Behind the Mountains* (2002), *After the Dance: A Walk through Carnival in Jacmel* (2002), and *The Dew Breaker* (2004).

Lauren H. Derby is assistant professor of history at the University of California-Los Angeles. She has been awarded Fulbright, Fulbright-Hays, MacArthur Foundation, Newcombe Foundation, and Social Science Research Council grants. Her article on Dominican racial ideology in the Haitian-Dominican borderlands, "Haitians, Magic and Money: Raza and Society in the Haitian-Dominican Borderlands, 1900-1937," published in *Comparative Studies in Society and History* won the 1995 Conference on Latin American History award. Her book, *The Dictator's Seduction: Politics and the Popular Imagination in the Dominican Republic,* is forthcoming from Duke University Press.

Sallie Ann Glassman has been practicing Vodou in New Orleans since 1977. She is the owner of the Island of Salvation Botanica, a store and gallery specializing in Vodou and Haitian and local artworks. She traveled to Haiti in November, 1995 to undergo the week-long Couché initiation. During her initiation, Ms. Glassman was ordained as Manbo Asogwe, or Priestess of Vodou. She is the founder of *La source ancienne Ounfo* in New Orleans, where she presides over weekly Vodou ceremonies. Ms. Glassman is the author of *Vodou Visions* (Random House, 2000). She is co-creator and artist of *The New Orleans Voodoo Tarot,* published by Destiny/Inner Traditions, and is the illustrator of *The Enochian Tarot,* published by Llewellyn.

Gwendolyn Midlo Hall is Distinguished Research Fellow in the Southern University System. Her most recent book is *Slavery and African Ethnicities in the Americas: Restoring the Link* (UNC Press). Her other books include *Africans in Colonial Louisiana: the Development of Afro-Creole Culture in the Eighteenth Century* (LSU Press, 1992), which received nine prizes, and *Social Control in Slave Plantation Societies: A Comparison of Saint-Domingue and Cuba* (Johns Hopkins, 1971). She is the author of Louisiana Slave database and Louisiana Free Database 1719-1820 available at www.ibiblio.org/laslave.

Andrea Schwieger Hiepko is a doctoral candidate in the Latin American Institute at the Freie Universität Berlin and works with Project "European Forum" at the Academy of Sciences of Berlin-Brandenburg.

Régine Latortue is a native of Port-au-Prince, Haiti and holds a Ph.D. from Yale University. She is professor of comparative literature at Brooklyn College of the City University of New York (CUNY) in the Department of Africana Studies, and served as chair of that department for 15 years. Her publications include a co-translated bilingual edition of Louisianan poetry, *Les Cenelles: A Collection of Poems by Creole Writers of the Early Nineteenth Century,* and a co-edited monograph on Haitian women, *Femmes haïtiennes en diaspora*, as well as numerous articles in French and English on Haitian studies, Francophone literature, and women writers of the African Diaspora.

Michel-Philippe Lerebours was born in Port-au-Prince, Haïti, and holds a degree from l'École Normale Supérieure (lettres classiques), a law degree from l'Université d'Haïti, and a Ph.D. in Art History and Archeology from Université de Paris. He is a professor and general curator at the Musée d'Art Haïtien and a renowned Haitian art historian. He has published numerous articles on visual arts and theater in Haiti. Among his published works are a study on Haitian painting entitled *Haïti et ses peintres* and two dramatic texts, *Le roi* and *Temps mort.*

Valérie Loichot is assistant professor of French and Francophone studies at Emory University in Atlanta, Georgia. She is also affiliated with the university's Comparative Literature and Latin American and Caribbean Studies Programs. She has published articles on Edouard Glissant, Raphaël Confiant, Gisèle Pineau, Saint-John Perse, Derek Walcott, and on Creole folktales from Martinique and Louisiana. Her recent book is titled *Orphan Narratives and the Postplantation Literature of Faulkner, Glissant, Morrison and Perse* (University of Virginia Press, 2007).

Carolyn Long is a research associate at the Smithsonian Institution. She was educated at Auburn University, the University of Missouri, and the University of Mississippi in studio art and art history and employed for 18 years as a conservator of paper artifacts and photographs at the National Museum of American History, Smithsonian Institution. Her publications include *Spiritual Merchants: Religion, Magic, and Commerce* (University of Tennessee Press, 2001) and articles on New Orleans Voudou and Southern hoodoo in the journals *Pharmacy in History, Folklore Forum, The Louisiana Folklore Miscellany, Nova Religio,* and *Louisiana History.* She is completing a biography of the nineteenth-century New Orleans Voudou priestess Marie Laveau.

Elmide Méléance currently works for Montgomery County Public Schools at John F. Kennedy High School in Silver Spring, Maryland. She has presented papers on, among other subjects, "The Quest for (Cultural) Identity among Haitians: Through Africa, Europe, and the Americas," at the International Caribbean Conference in Vienna, and "Language Choice and Culture, Haitian-Creole: A Case Study." Her primary interests are in the fields of linguistics, second-language acquisition, and translation.

John T. O'Connor, professor emeritus of history at the University of New Orleans, specializes in French history as well as international relations during the *ancien régime.* He has written a book on a German diplomat who served Louis XIV, *Negotiator Out of Season: The Career of Wilhelm Egon Von Fürstenberg, 1629-1704* (University of Georgia, 1978), and has published numerous articles in scholarly journals in the United States and France.

Sue Peabody is associate professor of history at Washington State University-Vancouver. Her books, *"There Are No Slaves in France:" The Political Culture of Race and Slavery in the Ancien Regime,* and *The Color of Liberty: Histories of Race in France* (with Tyler Stovall), explore the development of racial ideology in France.

Catherine A. Reinhardt is a lecturer at Chapman University in southern California. She has given numerous talks and published on race, slavery, and memory in the French Caribbean and on French and Caribbean literature. Her book *Claims to Memory: Beyond Slavery and Emancipation in the French Caribbean* was published by Berghahn Books (2006).

Charles E. Siler is a program curator for the Louisiana State Museum. He has organized cultural events and assisted in the development of African American museums and festivals around the state of Louisiana. He served as programs coordinator for the Division of Black Culture at the Louisiana State Museum and created the first comprehensive exhibits of Louisiana artists in the early 1990s at the Museum of the Americas in New Orleans and the Masur Museum of Art in Monroe, Louisiana. He also created the successful "Music at the Mint" series for the Louisiana State Museum and curated the exhibit "Capturing The Flash: African American Photographers View the Black Indians of New Orleans." He has lectured on the Mardi Gras Indian tradition and Louisiana culture at a number of venues around the country, including the Smithsonian Institution.

Richard Turits is associate professor of history and Afroamerican and African studies at the University of Michigan-Ann Arbor. He is the author of *Foundations of Despotism: Peasants, the Trujillo Regime, and Modernity in Dominican History* (Stanford, 2004).

Ashli White is assistant professor of history at State University of New York-Stony Brook. She received her Ph.D. in history from Columbia University in 2003. Her dissertation about the impact of the Saint-Dominguan exiles on the United States won the Bancroft Dissertation Award for 2003.

Philippe Zacaïr is assistant professor of colonial Latin American and Caribbean history at California State University-Fullerton. His research interests include Caribbean nationalism in the nineteenth century, Caribbean expressions of identity, and inter-Caribbean migrations in the nineteenth and the early twentieth centuries. He recently published two articles, "Haiti on His Mind: Antonio Maceo and Caribbeanness" in *Caribbean Studies* and "Représentations d'Haïti dans la pensée française du dix-neuvième siècle" in *French Colonial Society*.

Foreword

The Book of Haiti

or/ the gift of words of dream shd nvr be taken to
the guillotine

When they come. early in the glow of the morning. at
the hitch of dawn. w/ the newes that le bom fils.
the liberator. is gone . has betrayed le cap. fled
for france on a swift fleet . left the kweyol
revolution behind for the alien sorcerers. for
dessalines to tatter the flag in a flutter of fury.
for christophe to bankrupt the treasury w/ his
masonic art at <la ferrière>. for pétion to refuse
ogou's okro soup hot from the anvil of the gods. for
défilée to petition the devil. for the <cacos> to
be shot like makak monkies by united states marines.
for charlemagne péralte to be left naked & mock(ed)
of his spirits. his ancestors apparently dead. for
philomé obin to have been a mistake négritude when
he encompass. when he encompassion(ed) him. that <le
nèg mawon.> uncouth & inconnu. has nothing to do w/
the <labiche> of our native narrative. that we are
nothing really but boat-people and refugees.
drowning off bimini & ocho rios. that we nvr
invented anything <chimera>. neither democracy nor

freedom from slavery. that nobody here dances into
the cosmos upon the very vèvè of revelation. that we
are not payin the bitterest price for being the
world's first harshest revolution. <men anpil. kòb
la kout.> when they come. late in the night.
trampellin w/ tom-tom boots & searchlights into our
dreams. telling you these repeated/these
unrepeatable parables. how lies can lower the whole
ship of the nation to a horizon of horrors. its true
story slipping off the water of the page into fear &
contempt & kalunga

Open therefore this testament of ulrick jean-pierre
of roseaux. accilien warrior vision & her scholars.
lighthouse & sacred palette of words & color of our
history. here resides a griot of time. one of a
dozen a hundred a thousand antecedents & ancestors
from before the <bois caiman > unto anacaona.
restoring the story now larger than life into longer
than death w/ the faces you know. w/ the features
you love. these new <manman nou> that are always
here. w/ the beautiful tortures you have undergrown
w/ the power & the glory of a struggle that we say
we sorry bout . <o crucified liberty. uprising. o
motherland depestre.> that you will overstand
preserve & persevere through cloud & drought &
hurricane & season(s). for i can tell you now that
water from the badman banyan outside will nvr reach
inside the culture of the <kokoye > w/ its three
all-seeing legba eyes of past doorway and future
makandal & boukman & the boukman xperianz. the
struggle and the revolution continuing continuing
continuing

from the pic of le cap where the citadel sits
the arawaks wait
the flèches of their headdress are stairs up the
montagne

the rings of the palm trees are bells up the montagne
toussaint is a zemi
he stares from the flesh of the stone

the white of the helmet . columbus conquistador
the bright of the sword
becomes lightning

the steel of the cutlass. the knife of the god
thongs of the whips
drink water like trees

africaines from the slave ships
dance out of the riflemen's loins
become dessalines dessalines

la crête-à-pierrot
the spangle of death from the hot
of the trees

and christophe columbus climbs up to his mountain top
w/ the face of his horse in the faith of his shadow
he stumbles on priest . on an African slave . on a
spaniard the places of pain become pig snouts
the black becomes white becomes black becomes rain
falling to plunder the roof

of the world

xvi

toussaint is a zemi
he stares from the stone . from the eye-
-lids of flame

at his fate

Kamau Brathwaite

1 August 05/ Slave Emancipation Day in the anglican
Caribbean

To the memory of my mother, Mrs. Melina Saint-Vil Jean-Pierre, my very first teacher of life, who ignited the first flame of my artistic inspiration.

To Mrs. Marie Thérèse Jérôme and in loving memory of Dr. Yves Jérôme.

To the memory of Lavorancy Exumé, my art teacher, and to the memory of Edouard and Marcel Wah.

Ulrick Jean-Pierre

To the memory of my mother, Monique Ste-Croix Méléance, who always wondered what I was working on this time.

Elmide Méléance

Acknowledgments

This book has been a long journey and, like most journeys, has involved many dedicated individuals. As the Haitian proverb states, "Anpil men, chay pa lou" [In unity there is strength]. We are grateful to Ulrick Jean-Pierre for sharing his unique genius and wonderful spirit with us, and for giving us permission to reproduce his work. We thank the contributors to this volume, who have focused their wide range of expertise on illuminating the history and culture of Haiti.

We also wish to extend our thanks to Adam Stone, for his constant support, energy, and help in so many ways; Serge and Chantal Déclama of the Association for Haitian American Development, Inc. (AHAD) for allowing us to use their website and for all their work and dedication to the cause of Haiti; Charles Blockson of the Charles Blockson Special Collection at Temple University in Philadelphia for allowing us to explore his wonderful collection of rare books and materials about Haiti; Raphael Cassimere, J. Michael Dash, Carole Demesmin, Yvelyne Germain-McCarthy, Joyce M. Jackson, Fehintola Mosadomi, Rose-Myriam Réjouis, Shelene Roumillat, Philippe Accilien, Barbara Trevigne, Felipe Smith, and Ina Fandrich for giving us access to their research and ideas; Marie Wendell of the University of New Orleans library for her enthusiastic support; Marivonne Jacques Méléance, Roseline Massé, Myriam Huet, Apricot Anderson Irving, Diana Pierre-Louis, Gladys Bruno, and Margaret Mitchell Armand for their encouragement and constant interest in the progress of the book; to Eric (Ti Yo-yo) and Eugene Goodman for their inspiration; Monique Méléance, our "Jill of all trades" while we traveled and researched in Haiti, particularly in Cap-Haïtien; Letroy and Véronique Accilien, Olga Accilien and Odile Accilien-Sorger for their encouragement; Isabel Fernandez Anta, our correspondent in Madrid, Spain; Myriam Francoeur-Cointre in France for her good faith efforts on our behalf; Gerda Ste-Croix for her help in providing resources and on-site references in Cap-Haïtien, Haïti; thanks to Louis Estiverne in Haiti; and Katherine Gracki for being one of the first to help imagine this project. Philippe Zacaïr generously shared his expertise in the history of the Caribbean, for which we will always be grateful. A special thanks to Kamau Brathwaite.

Mrs. Marie Thérèse Jérôme and her late husband Dr. Yves Jérôme, founder and president of the Haitian Cultural Society of Philadelphia, generously offered the initial support and effort that were instrumental in the creation of Ulrick Jean-Pierre's first historical painting series, which began in 1979. Their encouragement, kindness, and mentorship have long been invaluable. A special thanks also to Oméus Jean-Pierre, Louius Jean-Louis (Tonton Loulou), Claudette Dorvilier, Catherine Debrosse, Melia Jean-Pierre, Marie-Edith Nivose, Marie-Lourdes Jean-Pierre, Lina Jean-Pierre, Résia Jean-Pierre, Willio Jean-Pierre, Michelle Jean-Pierre, Kettely Jean-Pierre, Sandra Jean-Pierre and Immacula Michel.

We would like to recognize the following collectors and supporters of Jean-Pierre's art: Drs. Yvelyne and Henry McCarthy, Dr. and Mrs. Joseph Michel Lemaire, Mr. Louis Lapointe, Dr. and Mrs. Alix Bouchette, Dr. and Mrs. Daniel Bouchette, Mrs. Jacqueline Simon, Dr. and Mrs. Daniel Mompoint, Mr. and Mrs. Picard Losier, Dr. and Mrs. Ludner Confidant, the Honorable Marie Bookman, Drs. Edna and Farère Dyer, Dr. and Mrs. Jean-Philippe Austin, Dr. Jean Brierre, Dr. Fritz Fidèle, Dr. Denese Shervington, Dr. Sarah Moody-Thomas and Vernon Thomas, Dr. and Mrs. Patrick Roumer, Dr. and Mrs. Paul Nacier, Dr. Jean-Claude Compas, Dr. Serge Célestin, Mr. and Mrs. Gustave Renault, Dr. and Mrs. Reynold Dépestre, Mr. and Mrs. Gérard Fombrun of the Musée Colonial Ogiers-Fombrun in Montrouis, Haiti, Mrs. Marlène Pilet-Vilaire, Dr. Dwight Mckenna of the George and Leah Mckenna Museum of African American Art in New Orleans, Louisiana, Dr. and Mrs. Robert Nerée of *Haïtiens Aujourd'hui* magazine.

Thank you also to the following friends and supporters: Emile Viard, Dr. and Mrs. Fritz Darguillar, Kofi Moyo, Ernest Jones, Mary Day, Gaston Vilaire, Jonas Allen, Edgard and Joyce Wah, Patrick Wah, Patrice Piard, Shoubert Denis, Emmanuel Dostaly, Maryse Edouard, Maryse Dejean, Lolis Edward Elie Sr., Lolis Eric Elie, Lyonel Laurenceau, René Exumé, Lavorancy Exumé, Raynald Exumé, Eric Giaolt, Reynold Rolls, Patrick Chevalier, Diane Horne, Louius Jean-Louis, Jean-Claude Damas, Jean-Richard Coachy, Patricia and Jean-Joseph Brierre, Charles Brierre, Monique Aziz Brierre, Omar and Nicolas Aziz, Dr. and Mrs. Fréderic Helmke, Dr. and Mrs. Gérard Helmke, Jean-Paul Lafitte, Thelma Williams, Jessica Harris, Janée "G" Tucker, Owen Leroy, Edwidge Danticat, Kenna and Karl Franklin, John Hankins at the New Orleans Museum of Art, and Jeannette Hodge at BAND.

A musician remains a musician even without his instrument, and although Ulrick Jean-Pierre's historical painting series has been affected by one of the most devastating events in U.S. history, Hurricane Katrina, he has not lost his place in Haitian history as a troubador and guardian. In many ways, loss is a new beginning. Jean-Pierre has stated that as an artist he finds perfect beauty in the midst of life's imperfections. For him, New Orleans has been a place of inspiration, a magical place where he has had opportunities to kindle the flames of his artistic passion, and he will find new subjects, new dreams, and new ideas in the midst of change.

Ayibobo!

Introduction

Cécile Accilien

Dèyè mòn gen mòn.
Behind the mountains are more mountains
—Haitian proverb

Today is January 1. As I sit down to write on this symbolic date, the date that Haiti commemorates as its independence day, I am forced to wonder what the next century will bring. Without going into the details of the political situation in Haiti, I feel saddened by where Haiti stands as a nation economically, socially, and politically, but I remain hopeful about where it can be. The proverb "Dèyè mòn, gen mòn" is fitting to explain Haiti's complexity, ambiguity, and contrasts. I sometimes feel as if there are two or even three nations within Haiti: the one the media often portrays, with its slums and profound poverty; a rich Haiti where members of the upper-class drive new, expensive cars, live in nice houses, shop in supermarkets, and spend their leisure time at the beach; and a third Haiti that lies in the mind, in the possibilities that Haiti has embodied for the colonizers, for the slaves, for the revolutionaries, for those trying to realize democracy, for the artists in every medium whom Haiti inspires.

This project is very close to my heart, for I believe that art is one of the most important mediums through which to educate people about Haitian history and culture, and to dispel misrepresentations and widely held misperceptions of Haitian people and Haitian culture. Haiti is too often remembered solely as the poorest country in the Western Hemisphere. Although it might be poor in economic terms due to the lack of infrastructure, the centralization of its wealth, and the inability to adequately use its resources, it is enormously rich in culture and history. The painter Ulrick Jean-Pierre uses his brushes to re-create Haiti's wealth of culture and beauty, and to sensitize people to it. This project began to develop when I had the opportunity to work with Jean-Pierre on an exhibit at Tulane University in New Orleans. The exhibit was such a success in helping the public view Haiti from a new perspective, one that differs from what the typical media usually present.

As the African filmmaker Sembène Ousmane has remarked, "The artist must in many ways be the mouth and the ears of his people. In the modern sense, this corresponds to the role of the griot in traditional African culture. The artist is like a mirror. His work reflects and synthesizes the problems, the struggles, and the hopes of his people."[1] Artists, modern griots, tell stories and teach about the past. This is the legacy that Ulrick Jean-Pierre communicates on his canvases. He takes his role as an artist-griot seriously, and has been depicting his passion for Haiti and its history for over 30 years. He is full of energy, creativity, and hope for a better Haiti. And in Haiti, where reading and writing are privileges available only to a fortunate few, art, like music, is a medium to raise consciousness and a channel for self-expression.

In *Caribbean Discourse,* Martinican novelist and theorist Edouard Glissant describes the artist's commitment and his or her rapport with the community thus:

> La parole de l'artiste antillais ne provient donc pas de l'obsession de chanter son être intime: cet intime est inséparable du devenir de la communauté. Mais cela que l'artiste exprime, révèle et soutient, dans son œuvre, les peuples n'ont pas cessé de le vivre dans le réel. Le problème est que cette vie collective a été contrainte dans la prise de conscience; l'artiste devient un réactiveur. C'est pourquoi il est à lui-même un ethnologue, un historien, un linguiste, un peintre de fresques, un architecte. L'art ne connaît pas ici la division des genres. Ce travail volontaire prépare aux floraisons communes. S'il est approximatif, il permet la réflexion critique; s'il réussit, il inspire.

> [The artist's speech does not come from a desire to praise him- or herself. He or she is fully connected to the community. But what the artist expresses, reveals, and maintains in his or her work, the people are constantly living in their daily lives. The artist becomes a reactivator. This is why artists are at once ethnologists, historians, linguists, architects. Art does not know the division of genre. This labor of love allows for a sense of community to flourish. If it is close enough it allows for critical reflection; if it is successful it inspires.][2]

To see one of Jean-Pierre's historical paintings is to see and feel Haiti's history. Looking at his work is like listening to the story of the past, and in this sense his paintings convey this history as well if not better than most history books. Even in the midst of ongoing turmoil, he reveals the vibrancy of the Haitian people and Haitian history.

History still often belongs to those who were able to document it first. Christopher Columbus, for example, is still viewed by many as the glorious founding father of the Americas, and narratives of early Caribbean and "American" history often revolve around him because his record of the early contacts between Caribbean peoples and Europeans is essentially the only one we have. As an African proverb states, "Until the lion tells his own story, the tale of the hunt will always glorify the hunter." And so this book is an attempt to retell some old stories, and to tell some new ones.

Haiti shares the western third of the island of Hispaniola, between the Caribbean Sea and the Atlantic Ocean, with the Dominican Republic, which occupies the eastern two-thirds. Haiti is a country somewhat smaller than Maryland with a tropical climate and a population of about 7 million. After its independence from France in 1804, Saint-Domingue, as it was known during the centuries of slavery, reclaimed its Arawak name, Ayti, Ayiti, or Haiti, meaning "mountainous and high land." The story of Haiti is similar to that of many other islands in the Caribbean in the sense that slaves were imported here to provide forced labor to enrich European colonizers. However, what sets it apart is that it was the site of the only successful slave revolt in the history of the Americas, and the first independent nation of former slaves.

From the time of its independence in 1804, Haiti has experienced many forms of leadership, from dictatorship to so-called democracy to various forms of occupation. But Haiti's story is most of all one of survival and strength, of the people's desire to remain a free and independent nation in spite of exploitation by Haitians and non-Haitians alike. And with all its hardships, Haiti has been a powerful presence in the imaginations of historians, critics, and novelists in the Caribbean and elsewhere, from C.L.R. James's gripping analysis of the Haitian Revolution in *The Black Jacobins* to Alejo Carpentier's *El reino de este mundo*, William Faulkner's *Absalom, Absalom!*, Aimé Césaire's *La tragédie du roi Christophe*, Edouard Glissant's *Monsieur Toussaint*, and Maryse Condé's *Haïti chérie*, among others.

Although Haiti is in constant political and economic turmoil, the fact remains that the Haitian Revolution has been a crucial benchmark in the transatlantic world. Of all the revolutions in the Americas, it was the first of its kind, and it brought about tremendous social change. The Haitian Revolution is the only example of an enslaved country that seized its independence from its colonizers and created a free country--all this in an era when the Atlantic slave trade was at its zenith and slavery was commonly accepted, in terms of both the philosophy behind it and the practices necessary to maintain it. At the time of the Haitian Revolution, Haiti was, moreover, France's most important colony economically. Its independence led Napoleon to sell the 828,000 square miles of the Louisiana territory to the United States in 1803 for 15 million dollars—at less than three cents per acre, a transaction considered one of the greatest land bargains in American history. In spite of the turmoil that marks its history, however, Haiti remains a majestic country. It is filled with contrasts--wealth and poverty, beauty and darkness, despair and hope—and the images and texts throughout this book attempt to reveal rather than to simplify Haiti's complexity.

The book is divided into six sections. The first, "Beginnings of the 'New World'," starts with the period immediately after Columbus's arrival in Haiti; it depicts Arawak life before the intrusion of the Europeans, as well as the native revolt against European attempts at conquest. The second section, "What Is Freedom?," examines the evolution of the struggle for freedom across different periods of Haitian history; it also considers how Haiti's thirst for liberation has affected other sites in the Western Hemisphere. "Forgotten Women of Haitian Liberty," the third section, traces the instrumental role that Haitian women such as Anacaona, Cécile Fatima, Marie-Jeanne Lamartinierre and Catherine Flon played in bringing Haiti to freedom. Section Four, "Legacies of Vodou," looks at the role of spirituality, and Vodou in particular, during the Haitian revolution. It also examines the religious connections between Haiti and Louisiana. The fifth section, "Behind the Mountains Are More Mountains," considers links between Haiti and other parts of the Americas, particularly the United States. The sixth and final section contains the historical paintings of Ulrick Jean-Pierre.

This book does not pretend to offer a complete account of all the events in Haitian history; rather, through Jean-Pierre's art accompanied by commentaries and reflections from a wide variety of scholars and thinkers, it hopes to pique readers' interest and to inspire them to find out more about the history of the first black republic (see Appendix 3, Suggested Readings). The book presents heroines and heroes of Haiti's early history and independence. It describes the maroons who created their own society, defying colonial oppression. It examines the ceremony of Bois Caïman, one of the most controversial and misunderstood events of the Haitian Revolution and an event that has played a crucial role in Haitian consciousness. Through Jean-Pierre's images, this book offers a renewed vision of Haiti's possible futures.

<u>*Notes*</u>

1. See Ousmane Sembène, "Filmmakers and African Culture," *Africa* 71 (1977): 80.

2. *Le discours antillais* (Paris: Gallimard, 1997) 759. My translation.

SECTION I

Beginnings of the "New World"

Tout bèt jennen mòde
All animals that are cornered bite

—Haitian proverb

The pre-Columbian past in much of the Caribbean is elusive; traces of the early peoples who lived here before the influx of Europeans and Africans have, in many places, faded away or been obliterated during the process of colonization and the long history of slavery and its aftermath. But, although stories of Haitian life before Columbus are little-known outside Haiti and the Haitian diaspora, they are a crucial factor in understanding the reality of the "New World"—its newness grounded in an unprecedented series of contacts and conflicts between peoples and cultures rather than in the European conceit of discovery.

When Columbus landed in Haiti on December 6, 1492, in a bay now known as St. Nicholas, Haiti was organized in five *caciquats* or kingdoms, and each was governed by a monarch known as the cacique. The Higuey and Ciguay caciquats were populated by Caraïbes and Iguayos, and the Marien and Xaragua were populated by Tainos. The Magua and the Maguana caciquats were governed by the cacique Caonabo and were inhabited by both Caraïbes and Tainos (see the pre-Colombian map of Haiti, p. 197). Like the Portuguese, the first European colonists, and like the French who followed in Columbus's wake, the Spaniards believed it was their divine right to seize Arawak lands. They aimed both to convert and to enslave the natives, then use them to mine gold. In pursuit of this goal, they invaded, pillaged, and raped women and children. Slavery began in Haiti almost as soon as Europeans arrived. Abbé Raynal's *History of the East and West Indies* states that the Spaniards vowed to massacre twelve Indians per day in honor of the twelve apostles.[1] They believed that their God had ordered them to kill the Indians in order to "civilize" and "Christianize" them; thus the Spaniards themselves would become better Christians. It is estimated that between 1492 and 1514 more than 7 million Indians, or 92% of the population of Hispaniola (the island that comprises both Haiti and the Dominican Republic) died at the hands of the Spanish due to forced labor, slavery, and disease.[2]

By 1503, most of the natives were dead and the Europeans had begun importing Africans to replace them—the traffic in African bodies continued in Haiti for over two centuries, and by 1789, Saint-Domingue held more than 480,000 slaves. By the time thousands of Arawaks had been killed by harsh labor and disease, the Spanish fortunes from gold, exploitation, and sugar cane plantations were depleted. By 1545, most of the colonizers had abandoned the island for Peru, Cuba, and Mexico. In such accountings of devastation, however, we rarely hear about the resistance of the early peoples. Although many of their revolts are undocumented, and though the large majority of them were decimated, the legacy of their cultures is still alive.

Notes

1. *History of the Island of Santo Domingo from its First Discovery by Columbus to the Present Period* (New York: Negro U P, 1971) 12.

2. For more information see Jean Élie Barjon , Chapter IV of *1492: Le viol du nouveau monde,* "L'autre visage de la découverte" (Montréal: CIDIHCA Presse/Editions Indépendantes, 1996) 153-171.

Chapter 1

Christopher Columbus's First Landing
Jessica Adams

> They spoke…of the beauty of the lands that they saw; and said that the most beautiful and best lands of Castile could not be compared with them. And the Admiral also perceived this to be true because of the lands that he had seen and those that he now had before him…. They said that all these lands were cultivated, and that in the midst of the valley there passed a big and wide river which could water all the lands. The trees were green and full of fruit, and the undergrowth full of flowers and very high, and the paths were very wide and good. The breezes were like those of Castile in April. The nightingale and other small birds sang as in the said month in Spain, for he says that it was the greatest sweetness in the world.[1]

So Christopher Columbus's sailors reported, the first Europeans to set foot in the place that we now call Haiti. They spoke in Castilian Spanish, and their words were recorded by Columbus, Cristobal Colomb, or Cristoforo Colombo. But his *Diario* was lost centuries ago, and the sentences above, with their almost biblical rhythms, are translations of a paraphrase written by Fray Bartolomé de las Casas.

Loss, renaming, and translation were, of course, intrinsic to European society in the Middle Ages—evident in the fact that Columbus himself was known by different names as he traveled from Italy to Spain. But in the record of his first landing in Haiti, these terms also speak to the legacy of encounters in the Caribbean between peoples from different parts of the world, in which so much has been obliterated, transformed, and rendered in an entirely new set of signs, often to tell a story that legitimates the brutality of the teller. Yet evidence of the lives, stories, and beliefs of the first inhabitants of Haiti remain in legend, in myth, in performance. African language and culture traveled through the bodies of slaves and their descendants, becoming, indelibly, part of "America."

Jean-Pierre's painting "Christopher Columbus's First Landing" brings us to the brink of this new entity. As the two Spanish caravels, *Niña* and *Pinta,* and the larger *não,* the *Santa María,* sit at anchor with their softly billowed sails, sailors dipping their oars into the Caribbean Sea, Jean-Pierre invites us to consider, just for a moment, the possibility of other futures. He suspends the carnage to follow, allowing us to glimpse this landscape before European slavery took root in it. At the same time he traces for us the shock of this meeting between Columbus's expedition and early Haitians, a meeting that would have such profound and permanent consequences. It inaugurated an entirely new paradigm, one in which cultural collision, syncretism, and hybridity, effected first through native slavery and then the Atlantic slave trade, would eventually signify across the Americas, Europe, and Africa.

The Haitian natives were first wary of the strangers who broached their shores. Once their fears had been allayed by Columbus's captured native guides and by the gifts the Spaniards bestowed, they welcomed the expedition like polite and generous hosts—the hosts of a spontaneously arranged party of which they had had no warning, but which offered an opportunity for goodwill and potentially much of interest in the form of the newcomers' dress, manners, beliefs. Las Casas records: "The Christians said that later, when the Indians were without fear, they all went to their houses and each one brought them something to eat. They gave the Spaniards bread and fish of what they had, and because the Indians that he brought on the ship had understood that the Admiral wanted to have some parrots, it seems that the Indian who went with the Christians told the natives something about this, and so they brought parrots to them and gave as many as they were asked for without wanting anything for them."[2] Later, the natives were happy to trade what they valued for what the Europeans valued, apparently taking for granted that those bits and pieces the Spanish sailors sometimes offered—"pieces of broken crockery and pieces of broken glass and the ends of laces," in Columbus's words[3]—held the same value for the Spanish as the Arawaks' gold and bread and cotton held in their own culture. (Today, tourists from Europe and the United States happily bear home valueless plastic trinkets from their Caribbean travels—the Arawaks' revenge?)

The shores of "Hispaniola," or "Española," as the Europeans' name for it suggests, seemed to them to announce another Europe. The words of the exploring sailors, describing the island for us through a sinuous chain of translation, imagine it in terms of their own country—it is like Castile and Cordova, only more beautiful. But this initial act of colonization—renaming—was, perhaps like all such acts, profoundly nostalgic, an attempt to transport home into a new place very much like the old. Perhaps the most important difference between home and Española was that here sailors hoped to wield the power of gods, or kings. The moment that Jean-Pierre has suspended in his painting—a moment at which the "Old World" is fast becoming old as a new one emerges, but before the eruption of conquest—would be brief. The first physical contact between the early Haitians and the Spanish colonists apparently took place between a captured naked woman and a group of Spanish men—the metaphor of the (exploited) "breast of the new world" began with literal fact. [4] She was captured, Columbus said, because he planned to "treat [the natives] courteously and make them lose their fear, which would be something profitable, since it seems that the land cannot be other than profitable, judging by its beauty."[5] This bald equation of beauty and profit would lead inevitably, as we know, to desecration.

From the very beginning of his explorations, Columbus intended to introduce slavery into Haiti. Portugal and Spain were already rife with it. Portugal, in fact, was the site of plantations where Africans, Jews, and Muslims labored, enriching the "Christians." In an earlier voyage, Columbus may have even been to El Mina, the slave trading fort on the west coast of Africa. If this is true, he—and perhaps also his African pilot, Pedro Nino—had, in arriving in the Caribbean, already outlined what would become the main European trade routes of the eighteenth century.[6]

Doubtless with images of Europe's slaves in mind, during the course of his first voyage Columbus confidently wrote to his patrons Isabella and Ferdinand that the native peoples of Haiti "do not have arms and they are all naked, and of no skill in arms, and so very cowardly that a thousand would not stand against three. And so they are fit to be ordered about and made to work, plant, and do everything else that may be needed, and build towns and be taught our customs, and to go about clothed."[7]

This is the history that we know: colonization, slavery, unbearable waste. And, knowing this, Jean-Pierre's image gives us an answer to the loud voices of Columbus, his sailors, Las Casas—before renaming, before translation, before loss.

Notes

1. *The Diario of Christopher Columbus's First Voyage to America, 1492-1493*, trans. Oliver Dunn and James E. Kelley, Jr. (Norman, OK: Univ. of Oklahoma Press, 1989) 225. Las Casas, a contemporary of Columbus and a member of his third expedition to the Americas, produced the account of Columbus's voyage that survives today. Columbus's own account, to which Las Casas had access, vanished centuries ago. Las Casas is known today as the champion of the "Indians" (in quotes because the term reflects Columbus's confusion over where he had in fact made landfall— it was not India at all), but at the expense of the Africans. Moved by the desperate plight of enslaved Indians, who were dying in droves from European diseases as well as forced labor, Las Casas suggested that slaves be brought from Africa instead. He believed that Africans would be more suited to the harsh conditions.

2. Ibid, 223.

3. Christopher Columbus, "Letter to Santángel," *Letters from America: Columbus's First Accounts of the 1492 Voyage*, ed. and trans. B.W. Ife (London: King's College, 1992) 53. Columbus told Santángel that he put a stop to this type of exploitation.

4. Although here I'm appropriating F. Scott Fitzgerald's famous phrase from *The Great Gatsby* ("the fresh, green breast of the new world"), the concept of the New World as a (naked) woman is, of course, commonplace.

5. *The Diario*, 219.

6. Paul Gilroy has described this commercial route as "the triangular trade of sugar, slaves, and capital" (*There Ain't No Black in the Union Jack: The Cultural Politics of Race and Nation* [Chicago: U of Chicago P, 1987] 157).

7. Quoted in William Least-Heat Moon, *Columbus in the Americas* (John Wiley & Sons, 2002) 63.

Chapter 2

The Naked Migrants[1]

Régine Latortue

Translated by Jessica Adams and Cécile Accilien

It has been 500 years since they embarked from Guinea—after having traveled *le chemin de non retour*, after having gone around *L'arbre de l'oubli* seven times. Their feet and arms were bound, to ensure the security of the crew members. They knew neither the length nor the destination of the voyage. Abandoned to themselves, they had only their courage, will to survive, and faith in their gods. Some of them were former soldiers who fought for their king. But they did not have arms and they were defeated, and the conquerors, of the same race, of the same faith as they were, sold them as slaves to foreign merchants searching for livestock to cultivate stolen lands.

It was one of the first of thousands of crossings between Africa and America. The unfortunate passengers who were able to survive it found themselves in a strange world two months later, relegated to sordid huts where whites snatched a servile obedience through torture. They were obliged to work—work without ceasing. However, while they succumbed they resisted. They survived, implanting a culture whose richness and depth influenced a whole continent.

It is said by historians that the little island of Hispaniola received the first shipment of human cargo from Africa. Despite the fact that the slaves were often treated like animals, the *Code Noir*, the first regulation established by the colonizers in 1685, legally recognized their status as human, particularly by obliging them to be baptized in the new Roman Apostolic Catholic Church and take a new name.[2] But they nurtured their own faith. This was the source of their hopes, the object of their consolation, the strength behind their confidence in themselves, and also the blessed voice of salvation. Through Vodou they were unified spiritually and connected with their ancestors.

Haiti was the first place in the New World afflicted by European slavery, and the first to break its bonds. Haiti's sons ran to Savannah to fight along with the Americans during the Revolutionary War. They flew to the help of Miranda and Bolívar in their revolt against Spain, all the while knowing that this powerful kingdom could retaliate by destroying the city of Port-au-Prince. Anticipating the cause of Pan-Americanism, they gave their blood, having served the struggles of other countries with determination and unselfishness. Yet, even though they had helped their neighbors in so many occasions, they were not allowed to participate in the Congress of Panama in 1826.[3]

Yet Haiti continues its steps toward democracy and development, steps that have been considerably slowed by great political upheavals as well as the accruing deterioration of its economic situation. In a senseless effort to help Haiti find a way to reclaim the route to democracy, the Organization of American States (OAS) levied a complete embargo in 1991, violating the charter of that organization. This extreme measure compounded the abuses of an inefficient and corrupt government. Approximately 300,000 jobs were lost and the disastrous consequences of economic isolation that followed are still felt.[4]

Haiti continues to struggle, as if the struggle for liberty is its perpetual vocation. But still Haiti shines—in the many writings, the innumerable works of art, the beauty and magnificence of the paintings that her glorious history has inspired. This book is an invigorating testimony to the magical Haiti.

Notes

1. The term "naked migrants" (les migrants nus) is borrowed from Glissant, who uses it in *Le discours antillais* to refer to the slaves who came to the new world.

2. The Code Noir (Black Code) was an edict passed by Louis XIV in 1685. The Code Noir defined the "proper" conditions of slavery and provided a list of regulations of slave life and behavior.

3. The 1826 Congress of Panama was convened by Bolívar and attended by representatives of the recently liberated Spanish colonies. Haiti had helped Bolívar in his struggle for South American independence from the Spanish. Chapter 12, "President Alexandre Pétion," (in this volume) addresses the relation between the South American leader and Haitian President Alexandre Pétion.

4. For more information see Chapter 2, " Imposing International Sanctions: Legal Aspects and Enforcement by the Military," *Economic Sanctions Against Haiti (1991-1994)* by Richard E. Hull. http://www.ndu.edu/inss/books/Books%20%201997/Imposing%20International%20Sanctions%20-%20March%2097/chapter2.html>.

Chapter 3

Indian Revolt

Jessica Adams

If "Christopher Columbus's First Landing" shows us a moment before European colonialism and slavery entered the consciousness of native peoples, "Indian Revolt" presents the beginning of a long genealogy of resistance to European domination that would culminate in the emergence of Haiti as an independent nation three centuries later.

A group of native people were the first to be enslaved by Columbus in this New World—the members of "cannibal" groups captured from other islands were then shipped to Spain from Haiti. This human cargo was followed by at least two other groups—perhaps the only slaves who traveled east, rather than west, across the Atlantic. But Haiti itself would soon become a site of slavery imposed by Europeans, who forced the natives to perform hard labor and infected them with foreign diseases. By 1510, only about 25,000 of the approximately 1,500,000 original Haitians remained. This carnage did not discourage colonization; instead, the import of Africans began. As C.L.R. James recounts in *Black Jacobins,* his landmark study of the Haitian Revolution, Fray Bartolomé de las Casas, "haunted at the prospect of seeing before his eyes the total destruction of a population within one generation, hit on the expedient of importing the more robust Negroes from a populous Africa; in 1517, Charles V authorised the export of 15,000 slaves to San Domingo, and thus priest and King launched upon the world the American slave-trade and slavery."[1] But Jean-Pierre's painting recognizes that from the very beginning of their induction into "history," the prospect of freedom, however dim, would not cease to inspire the Haitian people.

It is common in records of exploration and colonization in the New World to find whites claiming that the natives they encountered believed that white men had "come from the sky," as Columbus did. ("Generalmente en quantas tierras yo aya andaya, creieron y creen que yo, con estos nauios y gente, venia del çielo," he tells Isabella and Ferdinand.)[2] Even if this was an accurate interpretation of the gestures and translations that passed between natives and Europeans, we have little means of knowing what such an origin might ultimately have meant to peoples who were not Christian. Columbus claimed that the first Haitians believed him to be heaven-sent—his captive translators, however, abducted from another island, had begun learning Spanish less than a month before. Although the only written records we have of these early days come from Columbus and Las Casas, whose *Historia de las Indias* was based on Columbus's now-lost *Diario,* the native peoples have left us with some remarkable object lessons.

One of these, as William Least-Heat Moon remarks in his book *Columbus in the Americas,* was a mask presented to Columbus by his Taino hosts shortly before he first returned to Spain. "To the man hiding his plan of enslavement," writes Moon, "a leader who now could see only auric metal and would listen only to tales about it, a captain blind and deaf, the Indians gave a large mask with gold for eyes and ears."[3] Another vivid, more violent communication from the natives about their views on European obsessions took shape in the destruction of the first outpost of colonization in the New World.

It began in this way: Columbus wanted more gold. Therefore he set sail along the northern coast of Haiti on Christmas Eve, 1492 to search out new territory to explore. Because of the mistakes of a junior crew member, his flagship, the *Santa María,* foundered in the dark on a reef near modern-day Cap Haitien. Columbus was distraught, but determined to make the most of his loss. He transformed the ship's timbers into a fort, which he intended as an unmistakable, intimidating manifestation of European power. He called the fort "La Navidad:" the birth of Christ, Christmas— the birth of a new colony, claimed for Spain.

Eager for the glory and rewards of "discovery," Columbus then departed Haiti to report his progress in person to the Spanish monarchs. He left behind 39 sailors because the loss of the *Santa María* meant that there was no room for them, but he took with him several captive Indians. The Spaniards who remained in Haiti that January of 1493 started to fight among themselves, greedy for gold and sex. They began to rape native women and to steal from a people who had, just days or weeks before, willingly shared what they had. Within a few months, a group of Indians led by the powerful *cacique* Caonabo decided to rid the land of these invaders. They began by killing the Spaniards, and ended by burning La Navidad. When Columbus returned to Haiti later that year, his sailors went ashore to scout for further sites to expand the colony—sites nearer the gold mines they believed were inland. But instead of more gold, they found bound and sometimes eyeless corpses.

Arriving at La Navidad in darkness, Columbus signaled to the shore with cannon fire; it was met with silence.

In Jean-Pierre's painting, the night is lit by the moon and by fire. But as native men and women fight the Spanish sailors, it is not always clear which side will prevail. Sometimes it seems that the Spanish might emerge victorious; then it is the natives who seem poised for victory. Viewing the painting, we exist in a breach—an uncertain, shifting, contested space opened up by the evolution of the old ways of precolonial Haiti, another "Old World." And this breach is the result of another, the breach of trust by the Spanish who have so carelessly discarded native good will. Jean-Pierre's work not only revises the notion of Haitian Indians as "incurably timid"[4] and pliable creatures, which has come down to us through Columbus's version of events; it also announces a tension that will henceforth be part of the culture and society of Haiti, and of the Caribbean as a whole. We find here the inception of a struggle between the colonial imagination and the force of resistance to it that has endured for over 500 years, moving through bodies of many different hues, becoming tangled in allegiances not always based on color, but always present.

Notes

1. (New York: Vintage [1938], 1963) 4.

2. "Letter to the Monarchs," *Letters from America: Columbus's First Accounts of the 1492 Voyage*, ed. and trans. B.W. Ife (London: King's College, 1992) 31.

3. (John Wiley & Sons, 2002) 72.

4. "Letter to Santángel," *Letters from America: Columbus's First Accounts of the 1492 Voyage*, ed. and trans. B.W. Ife (London: King's College, 1992) 51.

Chapter 4

Caonabo, the Intrepid
Cécile Accilien

In 1492, still stubbornly convinced that he had found a new route to China, Columbus made landfall in Haiti. There he was discovered by the native Arawak, who greeted him and his Spanish sailors with kindness. The five kingdoms on the island were ruled by caciques, each of whom was assisted by a wise elder from the kingdom who was dedicated to preserving cultural traditions, as the arts were an important element of Arawak culture. There were many poets called *sambas* who specialized in composing songs for a variety of occasions and for public festivities in honor of the reigning leaders.

When it became clear that the goals of the European expedition were not peaceful, one of the bravest caciques to resist the Spanish and defend his people and their lands was Caonabo, of the Maguana caciquat. Caonabo is believed to have come to Haiti during one of the Caraïbe invasions from the island of Ayay, known today as Guadeloupe. After he married Anacaona, sister of the powerful chief Bohechio and queen of the Xaragua kingdom, he became the caciquat of Maguana. Maguana was known as a cultural center. One well-known surviving *areyto* or dance is known as Caonabo's war song. It is not clear whether this was the song he sang to go to war against the Spaniards or a song for more general purposes:

> Je vais en guerre venger la mort de mes freres: je tuerai, j'exterminerai, je saccagerai, je brulerai mes ennemis: j'emmènerai des esclaves, je mangerai leur coeur, je ferai sécher leur

chair, je boirai leur sang, j'arracherai leur chevelure et je me serverai de leur crâne pour en faire des tasses....

[I am going to war to avenge my brothers' deaths. I will kill, I will exterminate, I will wreak havoc, I will burn my enemies, I will take slaves, I will eat their hearts, I will dry their flesh, I will drink their blood, I will tear out their hair and use their skulls to make cups....[1]

Another war song attributed to Caonabo goes as follows:

O fidèles nytainos, race noble et indépendante! Je suis né, vous le savez, dans l'île redou-tée qu'on nomme Ayay. Mes aïeux promenaient la terreur et la mort sur le lac sans rivages....Mon père était le plus vaillant chef de sa tribu!...J'ai sa force et son courage. En me choisissant pour votre Kacik, vous avez été bien inspirés par les Zémès (les dieux). Je tâcherai de me rendre digne du pouvoir que vous m'avez donné. Guerriers des tribus de la Maguana, levez-vous!...Malheur à celui qui, à l'heure du péril commun ne se lève pas! Mais celui qui meurt pour défendre les forêts sacrées où dormant les ancêtres, oh! Il vivra éternellement dans les areytos impérissables des sambas.

[O faithful Tainos, noble and independent race! As you know, I was born on the fierce island known as Ayay. My ancestors would spread terror and death on the lake without shores...My father was the most valiant chief of his tribe! I possess his strength and courage. By choosing me as your cacique, you were well inspired by the gods. I will endeavor to make myself worthy of the power that you have given me. Warriors of the Maguana tribe, rise! Woe to the one who does not rise during the time of common danger! But the one who dies defending our sacred forest where the ancestors rest will live on for-ever in the deathless dances of poets.][2]

When Columbus returned to Spain in 1493 leaving 39 of his men behind in Haiti, one of their missions was to evangelize the Indians. Yet instead of occupying their minds with holy mat-ters, they plotted to steal women from their husbands. When some ventured to the Maguana king-dom, they encountered the intrepid Caonabo, who killed about 11 of them. Frustrated and angered by the Europeans' audacity, the cacique led the destruction of the new Spanish fort of La Navidad. He met as well with Guarionex, another chief, and allied with him to fight the Spanish invaders. The Spaniards were particularly afraid of Caonabo because they believed he was preparing to kill as many of them as he could; moreover, he was aided by three of his brothers, valiant men unfazed by the prospect of war.[3] For these reasons, upon the return of Columbus, the Spaniards demanded that he rid the island of Caonabo. Alonso de Hojeda was given this task.

There are two versions of the capture of Caonabo by Hojeda.[4] In the first, it is said that Hojeda was sent to Caonabo's kingdom to tell him that he came on behalf of the Admiral

(Columbus), who wanted Caonabo to visit him in Isabela, which was located further north, to sign a peace treaty. Hojeda was told to persuade Caonabo to accompany him using any ruse he could devise. Hojeda used the ruse of a gift. It appears that the Indians called brass and other metals that the Spaniards brought from Spain by the term "turey" (meaning heaven). When his fellow Indians told him that the Admiral had sent a present—turey from Biscay—it is said that Caonabo was pleased. He had heard about the bells used in the Christian church in Isabela, which the Indians referred to as "speaking turey" because when the bell rang, all the Christians would follow its sound and attend mass in the church. Caonabo was curious about a piece of metal that had such power, and had requested on several occasions that the speaking turey be brought to his kingdom. Hojeda instead had brought well-crafted, polished shackles and handcuffs, and he led the cacique to believe that the Spanish kings would wear such adornments during special celebrations.

Hojeda supposedly knelt and kissed Caonabo's hands and made his Christian followers do the same. Impressed by this gesture of humility and by the "turey from Biscay," Caonabo softened a bit. The men went together to the river, and, after bathing, Caonabo wished to test the power of the Spaniard's shimmering gifts. Since he was in his own kingdom and Hojeda had only about nine Christians with him, Caonabo did not worry about danger to himself. But because many Indians were afraid of horses, Hojeda mounted his horse, telling the natives to step back. The other Christians then lifted Caonabo onto the horse's back and happily shackled and handcuffed him. Hojeda wheeled his horse around to hide the trick from Caonabo's people, and with the others took the road to Isabela, leaving the natives to think that the group was simply accompanying Caonabo to his village on horseback.

Thus Hojeda played his ruse and captured Caonabo. By the time Caonabo realized that he had been captured it was too late, and the Christians were ready to kill him with their swords if he did not allow himself to be bound with ropes. They went into the mountains and eventually arrived in Isabela, where the Spanish handed the cacique over to the Admiral.

In the other version of the story, the Admiral went to Vega Réal to fight the Indians who were gathered there and Caonabo, along with other caciques, was captured. Hojeda had been sent to Maguana to ask Caonabo to go see the Admiral. Caonabo decided to go with several of his armed men in order to kill Hojeda and the other Christians. Meeting him, Hojeda informed him that if he did not pay the Admiral a friendly visit unaccompanied by his army, he and the other Indians would be killed. It is said that Caonabo rebelled against this threat and mounted an armed resistance, in the course of which he was captured and taken prisoner by Hojeda.

It is not clear which of these stories is closer to the truth. It is believed that, when told that the Admiral wanted him go to Isabela to offer him turey from Biscay, Caonabo's response was: "Let the Admiral come here and bring me the bell of turey that speaks...."[5] It is also reported that the captured and chained Caonabo simply ignored the Admiral when he entered the room. However, when Hojeda entered, Caonabo rose up and wept, showing respect to the man who had captured him.

When asked by some Spaniards why he did not show respect to the Admiral, Caonabo told them that the Admiral did not have the courage to capture him himself. Hojeda, however, was brave enough to do so, and for this reason he felt that only Hojeda deserved his respect. Several months after his capture, he was deported to Spain, but the boat disappeared at sea. Thus ended the reign and the life of Caonabo, king of the Cibao. Even after his death, however, the Indians continued their fight against the Spanish. Caonabo's brother Manicatex became the new leader of the revolt. Caonabo's story of resistance and leadership remains in the Haitian imagination as one of the first recorded signs of resistance toward the Spanish invaders.

Notes

1. In Jean Fouchard, *Langue et littérature des aborigines d'Ayiti* (Paris: Editions de l'Ecole, 1972) 142. My translation.

2. For more information, see Fouchard, 142-143.

3. See "The Capture of Caonabo" in Samuel M. Wilson, *Hispaniola: Caribbean Chiefdoms in the Age of Columbus* (Tuscaloosa: U of Alabama P, 1990) 84-89.

4. For more information about the different versions of Caonabo's captivity, see "The Story of Hojeda and the Cacique Caonabó" in S. Lyman Tyler's *Two Worlds: The Indian Encounter with the European, 1492-1509* (Salt Lake City: U of Utah P, 1988) 162-165.

5. Ibid., 165.

Chapter 5

Bohechio

Cécile Accilien

Turehiguahobin Starei Huiho Doihyeniquan Bohechio, known more simply as Bohechio, was king of the Xaragua until his death. In the Indian tradition it was customary for friends and family to give a child the names they thought were appropriate. Thus, Bohechio's full name means "Plus brillant que l'or, Torche flamboyante, Grandeur, Fleuve fertile Bohechio" [More brillant than gold, blazing torch, greatness, fertile river Bohechio]. The word Bohechio itself means "chef d'un grand territoire" [chief of a great territory].[1] Bohechio was proud of his names. Las Casas noted, "Whenever Beuchios [Bohechio] publishes an order, or makes his wishes known by heralds' proclamation, he takes great care to have [his five] names and forty more recited."[2]

Bohechio was the brother of queen Anacaona, who shared with him the governing of the Xaragua kingdom, one of the last of the Indian kingdoms to be overtaken by the Spanish conquerors. The town in Haiti known as Léôgane is believed to have been the site of the capital of the Xaragua kingdom. Bohechio's birthplace and date are unknown, but it is believed that he was quite old when the Spanish invaded his kingdom. He is said to have had 30 wives; Las Casas wrote of one encounter between the Spaniards and Indians, "Out came thirty women, who were kept as wives of the king Bohechio, all completely naked, only covering their private parts with half-skirts of cotton…."[3] Bohechio was well-respected and neighboring caciques would seek him out for advice. He once occupied the Marien kingdom in the northwest of present-day Haiti to discipline Guacanagaric, a friend of the Spaniards whom he considered a traitor.

Beginning in 1495, all caciquats were required to pay an annual tribute to Columbus in the form of cotton, tobacco, grain, or gold depending upon what the region produced, but Bohechio's kingdom, Xaragua, was both the largest and the only one not paying the tribute to the Spaniards. When he heard news of the Spaniards invading other kingdoms, Bohechio prepared his army to defend Xaragua.[4] He had heard stories of the Spaniards' greed and obsession with gold and was distrustful and careful in his dealings with them. His main objective was to preserve Xaragua as a free kingdom. When Don Bartolomé Colón, Columbus's brother, came offering a peace treaty, Bohechio allowed himself to believe the Spanish were acting honorably. Because Bohechio shared the leadership of Xaragua equally with Anacaona, some critics, such as Fernando Colón, have made the sexist claim that Bartolomé Colón was able to mislead Bohechio simply because of the influence of a woman.[5]

To understand Bohechio's desire to keep Xaragua free at all costs, we must recognize its importance in Ayiti. Xaragua was situated in the center of the island, in the south and southwest of modern Haiti. This caciquat is believed to have extended all the way to present-day Môle Saint Nicolas and contained five provinces. One, Haniguayazo, was considered a paradise on earth:

> "Ce caciquat comprenait cinq provinces. L'Haniguayazo où les indiens logeaient le Paradis Terrestre. La légende fixait dans la région de Tiburon et des Abricots, le lieu des délices où les indiens …jouissaient d'une éternelle félicité, en savourant le soir des abricots juteux et parfumés."

> [This caciquat had five provinces. The (province of) Haniguayazo was where the Indians kept their paradise on earth. Legend has it that the region of Tiburon and des Abricots was a place of delights where Indians …enjoyed eternal happiness, luxuriating in evenings perfumed with juicy apricots.][6]

The fact that Xaragua was the only kingdom not paying tribute did not sit well with the Spaniards. Xaragua had thus far been protected against Spanish invasion by its geographic location. Unfortunately, its safety was temporary. Before Columbus returned to Spain in January, 1493, he ordered Don Bartolomé Colón, the "Adelantado" (a title given to him by his brother), to try to occupy Xaragua. Around 1496, many Indians were revolting against the Spaniards and they stopped cultivating the land, hoping to starve the Spaniards off the island. Colón knew that Xaragua was fertile, so he carefully planned his strategy. First he went to ask Bohechio for gold. The cacique is said to have responded, "How can I give tribute, for in all of my kingdom there is no place where gold can be found, nor do my people know what it is?"[7]

The Adelantado is said to have answered, "We do not want, nor is it our intention, to impose a tribute on anyone which they do not possess or know of, but only such things as they have in their lands and can easily pay. Of the things in your province and kingdom that we know to be abundant, such as much cotton and cassava bread, we want what you have the most of, not things that do not exist."[8] Colón made a pact with Anacaona and Bohechio: the Indians would plant cassava and cotton in large quantities to give to the Spaniards. It is believed that Bohechio accepted the terms of this demand to avoid conflict, reasoning that in so doing he could preserve the autonomy of Xaragua.

But this agreement would satisfy Bartolomé Colón only temporarily. When at last he entered Xaragua with his soldiers, Bohechio was quite old and no longer had the physical strength of a young warrior. In *Histoire des caciques,* Emile Nau, a Haitian historian, describes the event:

> L'attitude de Bohéchio était hostile à la vue des espagnols. Le vieux cacique croyait que les étrangers venaient s'emparer de ses Etats. Il les savait invincibles et peut-être n'avait-il pas beaucoup de confiance dans le succès des combats qu'il était décidé à leur livrer. Il pensa cependant qu'il valait mieux courir les chances incertaines de la lutte que de se laisser subjuguer sans réagir….Bartolomé Colón réussit à le persuader qu'il n'avait aucune intention de lui faire la guerre, qu'il venait au contraire visiter le Xaragua en ami et passer quelques jours avec lui et son frère…Bohéchio parut rassuré et se montra sans peine…satisfait de cette déclaration de paix….

> [Bohechio's attitude was hostile when he saw the Spaniards. The old caciquat believed that the strangers were coming to take over his kingdom. He knew them to be invincible and perhaps he did not have much confidence in the success of the battles that he planned to mount against them, but he believed that it was better to take the risk of fighting instead of giving up without a struggle.... Bartolomé Colón managed to persuade him that he had no intention of fighting, that he only came to visit him and his brother in Xaragua as a friend….Bohechio seemed reassured and showed that he was satisfied by this peace declaration….][9]

Bohechio believed this so-called peace declaration and naively allowed Colón into his kingdom. He hoped the Spaniards would finally leave the island once they had extracted all its gold. Because Xaragua did not have any gold, he wrongly assumed that the Spaniards would not remain there long. In this way, Xaragua was conquered.

It is believed that Bohechio died partly from chagrin and remorse for failing to protect Xaragua.[10] When he died, although he had a brother, Queen Anacaona became sole chief of the kingdom. Queen Anacaona interred Bohechio with Guanahattabenecheuá, one of his most beautiful wives, as custom required. He had a grand funeral and was mourned by his people, who loved him despite his mistakes.

A chain of mountains known as the Bahoruco in Xaragua were later made famous by the cacique Henri. Henri's father, the caciquat of Bahoruco, died in the battle of Xaragua, but Henri himself miraculously survived the fighting and was educated and Christianized by a certain Father Rémy. Later, however, he was enslaved by a Spaniard who mistreated him and insulted his wife, Mencia. Henri revolted and joined other Indian slaves as a maroon in the mountains of Bahoruco. When his master pursued him, Henri declared: "Renoncez à nous reprendre car jamais plus nous ne servirons les Espagnols: nous avons juré de vivre libres ou de mourir!" [Do not try to take us back because we will never serve the Spanish again: we have sworn to live free or die!][11] These words presage those that Boukman would proclaim during the Ceremony of Bois Caïman centuries later.

Henri and his fellow maroons captured the Spanish and his former master was now in his power, but Henri chose to pity him, saying, "Allez remercier Dieu de ce que je vous laisse la vie et ne revenez pas ici." [Go and thank God because I have let you live, and do not come back here again.][12] Henri spent over a decade in the Bahoruco and every year more Indian slaves would escape and join him. Eventually Henri had about 3,000 subjects and was proclaimed their cacique. It is said that Henri, who was related to Bohechio and Anacaona, wanted to avenge Xaragua. Although Xaragua was defeated, Henri would recapture its glory, if only in name.

Bohechio's downfall lay ultimately in his desire for peace and autonomy. Jean-Pierre portrays this king in all his majesty and glory, and, in so doing, he immortalizes the kingdom of Xaragua and the descendants of the Xaraguas who live in Haiti.

Notes

1. See Herman Corvington, *Deux caciques du Xaragua: Bohéchio et Anacaona* (Haiti: Librairie Samuel Devieux, 1954) 5-6. My translation.

2. Fray Bartolomé de Las Casas was a member of Columbus' third expedition to the Americas. He became a priest in 1512 after he experienced the traumas of New World colonization. He was, in fact, the first priest to be ordained in the Americas. Las Casas wrote extensively about the brutal treatment of Caribbean peoples by the Spanish (see his *Brief Report on the Destruction of the Indians*, also known as *Tears of the Indians*). This quotation is from Samuel M. Wilson, *Hispaniola: Caribbean Chiefdoms in the Age of Columbus* (Tuscaloosa: U of Alabama P, 1990) 120.

3. Ibid., 120.

4. See Corvington, 22.

5. Fernando Colón, Christopher Columbus's son, wrote an extensive biography of his father. See *General History and Collection of Voyages and Travels, Arranged in Systematic Order, Forming a Complete History of the Origin and Progress of Navigation, Discovery, and Commerce, by Sea and Land, from the Earliest Ages to the Present Time, Vol. 3*, trans. Robert Kerr (Edinburgh: William Blackwood, 1824).

6. Corvington, 15. My translation.

7. Wilson, 125.

8. Ibid., 125-126.

9. Quoted in Corvington, 19-20. My translation.
10. Ibid., 29.

11. *Histoire d'Haiti* (Haiti: Henri Deschamps, 1942) 31-32. My translation.

12. Ibid., 31

SECTION II

What Is Freedom?

Baton ou genyen se li ki pare kou pou ou
The stick that you have is what spares the blow for you

Se de dwèt ki manje kalalou
One can only eat callaloo with two fingers [because it's slippery]

—Haitian proverbs

Ginen yo desan yo pote yon fòs ki ban libète, libète-k delivre, libète-k libere...Libète e pran pou pran-l.... Se pou pran-l, ak tout fòs.... Se pou pran-l ak tout kè....

The [gods from] Guinen have come down and they bring a strength that gives freedom, freedom that delivers, freedom that delivers....Liberty must be seized....It must be seized forcefully....Take it wholeheartedly....

—Boukman Eksperyans

By 1789, the year of the French Revolution, Saint-Domingue was the site of over 6,000 plantations. Ships from Bordeaux, Nantes, La Rochelle, and Saint-Mâlo entered its ports, bringing wine and other merchandise. They left Saint-Domingue laden with sugar, coffee, cotton, and indigo. The city of Cap-Français, (now Cap-Haïtien) was known as the Paris of Saint-Domingue because of its theaters and monuments, as well as the luxuries filling its shops.

But the cause of freedom was percolating in the Atlantic world. When the American colonists revolted against the British, roughly 1,500 emancipated slaves from Haiti, including Henri Christophe, went to Savannah to help fight for the cause of independence. Then in 1789, the French people fought for the same rights as the nobility and the clergy. Haitian slaves knew of this revolution in France in the name of liberté, égalité, and fraternité. Some Haitians even fought alongside the French. The free blacks and free people of color hoped that the new French government would be true to its motto and give them the same rights as the white population. The slaves, for their part, wanted liberty as well. But both the French and American revolutions showed the limits of these ideologies of freedom. As president of the newly independent United States, Thomas Jefferson actively opposed the Haitian revolutionaries, and later refused to recognize the free Haitian state. The French revolutionary government did not want to recognize the Haitian government. The ideology of liberty, equality, and brotherhood that was preached in France did not apply to enslaved people. It was not until 1825 that the French King Charles X finally recognized Haiti's independence. Most people are not aware that upon its independence Haiti had to pay France reparations for its economic loss. The French Revolution and events that followed thus illuminated the prejudices of the time, both within Haiti and in the larger Atlantic world, even as they showed how powerfully the idea and reality of freedom lived in the hearts of Haitians. On August 14, 1791, slaves gathered to seal their commitment to fight.

Toussaint Louverture issued Haiti's first constitution in 1801. After Toussaint's arrest in 1802, Dessalines continued the fight. As Dessalines was leading the army to attack the French, it became clear to the revolutionaries that they needed their own song—they could no longer march to the tune of the enemy, "La Marseillaise." So, inspired by Dessalines, a courageous new military song was composed:

> Grenadie a laso
> Sa ki mouri zafè a yo
> Nan pwen manman, nan pwen Papa
> Grenadie a laso
> Sa ki mouri zafè a yo.

> [Grenadier, attack
> If you get killed, it is your loss
> Forget your mother, forget your father
> Grenadier, attack
> If you get killed, it is your loss.]

Decades after its official independence in 1804, Haiti continued to struggle for true independence. In 1915, under President Woodrow Wilson, the United States invaded Haiti. The U.S. Occupation lasted from July 28, 1915 through August 21, 1934. Before the U.S. Occupation, Haiti had been through a period of great political instability. For example, from May, 1913 until July, 1915, the country went through four presidents. This kind of instability was used by the United

States as a justification for playing policeman. The Marines arrived in Bizoton on July 28, 1915, and soon occupied Port-au-Prince. An "agreement" known as Convention Haïtiano-Américaine gave the United States power to "establish order" in Haiti and control the national finances and the army for a period of 10 years. The U.S. Marines were famous for their means of "establishing order." Among their crimes was the massacre of the peasants of Marchaterre on December 6, 1929.

President Wilson's troops murdered and destroyed, virtually reinstituted slavery, and demolished Haiti's constitutional system. An old forced-labor law called the corvée was reinstated. Haitians reacted with outright violence to this neo-slavery. Roped together, underfed, and brutally overworked, the corvée laborers were watched by overseers who gunned down any who attempted escape. Ultimately, the corvée sparked revolts leading to all-out war, and during the Caco Rebellion of 1918-1922, intellectuals, peasants, and students united and mobilized. Under the leadership of Charlemagne Péralte, the Caco movement, including over 5,000 peasants, became a great force of resistance to the occupation. Occupation forces killed thousands of Haitians who resisted. Charlemagne Péralte himself was murdered when two U.S. Marines in blackface infiltrated his camp and shot him, and then paraded his body on a cross like a slain Haitian Christ. Finally, on August 21, 1934, in a ceremony led by the new Haitian President Sténio Vincent, the Haitian flag again flew over the barracks in Port-au-Prince.

In the paintings in this section, Ulrick Jean-Pierre demonstrates the connections among the Haitian people—mulatto, freed slaves, and slaves in bondage. He depicts their resourcefulness in using their instruments, among them conch shells and drums, as well as machetes, as they invoke their gods from Ginen to help them take their liberty in defiance of the white man's god.

Chapter 6

The Battle of Savannah

Sue Peabody

In the summer of 1779, at least 545 and perhaps as many as 800 black and mulatto troops recruited from Saint-Domingue fought alongside white French colonial soldiers and American troops in an attempt to oust the British army from the fort in Savannah, Georgia. According to Haitian tradition, many of those serving in the siege of Savannah went on to leadership positions in the Haitian Revolution, including Jean-Baptiste Mars Belley, Louis Jacques Beauvais, Martin Besse, André Rigaud, and the future king of Haiti, Henri Christophe. Although the Franco-American troops were routed, the attitudes of many men of color toward the French crown, as well as their status in colonial society, were shaped by their military service at Savannah.

Until the end of the Seven Years' War in 1763, militias in Saint-Domingue were racially segregated, led by officers of the same race as their troops. One unit, known as the "Chasseurs Volontaires d'Amérique," composed of free men of color, was devoted to tracking and fighting fugitive slaves or maroons, and it caught the eye of the governor of the French Antilles of the time, Charles-Henri d'Estaing. When the militias were disbanded after the war, d'Estaing proposed reorganization of this unit under the command of white officers. He argued that the pride, frugality, and familial attachment of the free men of color would make them ideal soldiers.

In 1778, shortly after the United States declared independence from Britain, France allied with the United States to support the nascent republic in the Revolutionary War. In March, 1779, the Chasseurs Volontaires were reorganized in Saint-Domingue for the purpose of serving d'Estaing, now General and Vice-Admiral of France, to assist the former colonies. The Chasseurs were recruited by the commanding officer, LeNoir de Rouvray, who celebrated their zeal and enthusiasm and expected their outstanding military service to counteract the racial prejudice of those who believed free people of color were inferior to whites. Individual companies were put under the command of white officers, who had led the free militias since 1769.

D'Estaing's fleet of 25 ships of the line, 15 frigates, and supply ships put in at Cap-Français, Saint-Domingue on July 31, 1779, following its successful conquest of British Saint Vincent and Grenada, and en route to support the American rebels. There the French navy was joined by 941 volunteers who were free men of color. The motives of these volunteers varied. Some no doubt responded to the patriotic call to serve their country, some responded loyally to the orders of their white officers; as with all army recruits, some no doubt sought adventure and escape. However, threats also played a part: the governor of Cap-Français threatened to demote quadroons to mulatto companies, and mulattoes to free black regiments, if they failed to volunteer, and the most resistant were subject to three months' assignment to a rural constabulary, a most unpopular posting. Though a large portion of these volunteers deserted before the fleet set sail on August 16th, the 545 Chasseurs Volontaires on board outnumbered their white counterparts in the 156 Volunteer Grenadiers by more than three to one.

After making inquiries at the American stronghold in Charleston, d'Estaing determined to test British-occupied Savannah, which according to intelligence was lightly defended. D'Estaing, however, did not count on Scottish Lieutenant Colonel John Maitland's 800 Highlanders from Beaufort, South Carolina, who joined the Savannah garrison on the eve of the French attack.

British, American, and French accounts of the Battle of Savannah largely concur in their description of one of the bloodiest engagements of the American revolutionary war. French troops landed on September 8th, including—according to various accounts—between 750 and 800 free men of color in the Chasseurs Volontaires. (The previous number of 545 comes from an official French military report, whereas participant estimates were in the vicinity of 800 free men of color.) The cold, damp autumn nights must have been a difficult challenge to the Antillean recruits, as d'Estaing remarked:

> It is extraordinary that there were so few sick among the 3,000 men who came from the
> islands and Saint-Domingue, who were constantly at arms for nearly a month, most of them
> without tents, dressed only in linen, suffering from heat in the daytime and freezing to death
> at night.[1]

D'Estaing ordered that "the people of color...be treated at all times like the whites...they aspire to the same honor, they will exhibit the same bravery," but rather than elevating the status of the soldiers of color, they may have been forced to serve in the most laborious and dangerous positions.[2] An official list noted that both the Chasseurs and the Volunteer Grenadiers, having been "raised recently in Saint-Domingue...are not capable of being employed for more than trench work."[3]

Just over two weeks into the siege, on September 24th, the British discovered French trench construction within 300 yards of their position. They attacked the trenches, but Rouvray's forces beat them back with bayonets. However, Rouvray and his officers urged their forces on, in the face of cannon fire, in an attempt to take the British position. As a result, Rouvray's forces suffered heavy losses, including 40 deaths and more than 100 wounded. Thereafter, Rouvray complained of a "spirit of insubordination" among his troops, and Major General Fontages reorganized the units under new officers.

D'Estaing, impatient with the siege, determined to mount an all-out attack on October 9th. It is likely that free men of color were positioned both in the vanguard and reserve units, with those in the forward unit facing the most danger. Those under the command of Bethisy, including 500 Grenadiers and Chasseurs, penetrated to a British position defended by felled trees, which they "chopped through...with hatchets" but were knocked down by "a single volley of musketry and a round of cannon fire as they jumped into the ditch which lay before them and uselessly climbed up the side."[4] The forces following the vanguard suffered heavy casualties, with nearly 800 killed or wounded, including General d'Estaing, who was shot in his arm and leg. Less than an hour into the attack, d'Estaing ordered a retreat, which was orderly under the protection of the reserve troops.

After the Battle of Savannah, the Chasseurs Volontaires were dispersed to France, Charleston, and Grenada, and a few returned to Saint-Domingue. Many veterans of Savannah resented the extended term of duty, and those who returned home resisted the formation of a new conscripted (rather than voluntary) troop of free men of color to be called the "Chasseurs Royaux." The government hoped to address the manpower shortage in the French army by forcing free men of color into obligatory service. Savannah veterans, conscripted free men of color, and their white officers resisted the new draft and, after some confrontation, the idea of the Chasseurs Royaux was abandoned.

There is some disagreement among historians as to the participation of Haiti's future leaders in the Battle of Savannah.[5] Those who rely solely on written archival records cite the lack of contemporary evidence for involvement by Belley, Beauvais, Besse, Rigaud, or Henri Christophe. Yet the absence of such records does not in and of itself prove the lack of participation by these leaders. At a time when literacy was limited among whites and free people of color, when non-whites suffered enormous legal and social discrimination, and when oral traditions kept alive the stories that were forced into secrecy, it must be allowed that hundreds of free men of color fought in the Battle of Savannah on behalf of the new American republic.

Notes

1. Quoted in George P. Clark, "The Role of Volunteers at Savannah in 1779: An Attempt at an Objective View," *Phylon* 41:4 (1980) 356-366.

2. Quoted in John D. Garrigus, "Catalyst or Catastrophe? Saint-Domingue's Free Men of Color and the Battle of Savannah, 1779-1782," *Revista/Review Interamericana* 199-222 (1-2):109-125.

3. Ibid.

4. Quoted in Clark, p. 364.

5. Claude Adrien, "The Forgotten Heroes of Savannah, " *Américas* (Organization of American States) 30 (11-12):55-57; Gérard M. Laurent, "Les volontaires de St-Domingue," *Conjonction: Revue Franco-Haïtienne*, 131 (December 1973):39-56; Leara Rhodes, "Haitian Contributions to American History: A Journalistic Record," *Slavery in the Francophone World: Distant Voices, Forgotten Acts, Forged Identities*, ed. Doris Y. Kadish. (Athens: University of Georgia Press, 2000) 75-79.

Chapter 7

Unknown Maroon Announcing the Uprising

Valérie Loichot

For Martinican writer Edouard Glissant, "the Maroon is the only true Caribbean popular hero. The atrocious tortures to which his capture led give the measure of his courage and determination. He is an undisputable example of systematic opposition, of total refusal."[1,2] Whereas in the "lesser" Antilles, acts of maroonage were often isolated gestures that did not lead to political emancipation, runaway slaves in Haiti became organized, created a society of their own, and played an essential role in the revolution and in the foundation of a new state.[3]

Jean-Pierre's "Unknown Maroon Announcing the Uprising (1791)" is a performance of historical memory. The maroon's individual name does not matter. His anonymity is even necessary, because it allows François Makandal, Boukman, and all the other named and unnamed heroes of the Haitian Revolution to converge in his body or to use Glissant's words, let "the 'We' become the site of the generative system, and the true subject."[4]

The term maroon, which originated from the Spanish word cimarron, referring to wild horses living near mountain tops (cimas), was later applied to the runaway slaves who took refuge in the hills and forests to escape slavery and the oppressive plantation world. Like most names used by Europeans to classify the enslaved or the colonized, maroon, drawn from the vocabulary of agriculture, makes the other less than human. However, the insulting nature of the name is transcended by its reappropriation in history and historiography. Maroon becomes a term of pride, not only for the Haitian collective, but also for the transnational consciousness—whether Jamaican, Martinican, or African American—of the African Diaspora.

August, 1791 marks the maroon and slave uprising of Saint-Domingue, which led to the death of an estimated 10,000 blacks and 2,000 whites. Even though the rebellion failed, it prepared the ground for the Haitian revolution.

In the painting, "Unknown Maroon Announcing the Uprising," the landscape is inherently part of the man as the man is part of it. In Caribbean aesthetics, Glissant claims, "My landscapes change in me; it is probable that they change with me."[5] As in Césaire's *Cahier d'un retour au pays natal*, the land and its inhabitants are kin: "Land red, sanguineous, consanguineous land."[6] Shared blood indicates not only a harmonious flow, but also recalls the violence and suffering of the enslaved who bled there. The body is marked by the same chthonian transformations as the earth. It is a mountainous body. As Jacques Roumain writes, "Those who are from a land, born on a land, inborn-native, as it were, well, have it in their eyes, their skin, their hands, with its trees' hair, its earth's flesh, its stones' bones, its rivers' blood."[7] The landscape is an integral part of the making of history. The maroon is an integral part of the landscape.

As Glissant observes, "The painted symbol is contemporary to the oral sign. It is the tightly woven fabric of orality that introduces (and is pertinent to) Haitian painting."[8] In his left arm the unknown maroon carries a *corne de lambi*. The conch shell has multiple political, sacred, and religious functions in Haiti. It is used to announce birth and death, and to communicate with the ancestors and *lwa*. It is also the tool of communication—along with the drum—that alerts maroons across the hills during the revolt. Its spiritual and political uses are inseparable because Vodou was actively used in strategies of rebellion. The conch shell, also used to mark the beginning of a story-telling session, here announces the demise of the European plantation system and the birth of a Haitian nation. The unknown maroon is not simply a black Gabriel or Sebastian (even though his loincloth and defined muscles misleadingly recall the Italian Renaissance). Another imagination has seized this aesthetic, has renamed it and reclaimed it. In Haitian cosmogony, gods are not in the sky but in the earth.

Notes

1. Le Nègre marron est le seul vrai héros populaire des Antilles, dont les effroyables supplices qui marquaient sa capture donnent la mesure du courage et de la détermination. Il y a là un exemple incontestable d'opposition systématique, de refus total." *Discours antillais* (Paris: Seuil, 1981) 104.

2. All translations of the French are my own unless otherwise indicated.

3. For an exhaustive historical analysis on marronnage in Haiti, see Jean Fouchard's seminal work, *The Haitian Maroons: Liberty or Death* (New York: Blyden Press, 1981).

4. "Le Nous devient le lieu du système génératif, et le vrai sujet." *Discours antillais*, 258.

5. "[M]es paysages changent en moi. C'est probablement qu'ils changent avec moi" *Discours antillais*, 255.

6. Aimé Césaire, *Notebook of a Return to the Native Land*, trans. Clayton Eshleman and Annette Smith (Middletown, CT: Wesleyan U P, 2001) 16.

7. "Si l'on est d'un pays, si l'on y est né, comme qui dirait: natif-natal, eh bien, on l'a dans les yeux, la peau, les mains, avec la chevelure de ses arbres, la chair de sa terre, les os de ses pierres, le sang de ses rivières." *Gouverneurs de la rosée* (Fort-de-France: Désormeaux, 1979) 36.

8. "Le signe peint est contemporain de l'oral. C'est la trame serrée de l'oralité qui introduit (et est pertinente) à la peinture haïtienne." *Discours antillais*, 269.

Chapter 8

Makandal's Rebellion
Charles Siler

History is selective in its definition of heroes, and the black hero in Western history has often been an anomaly, allowing for the selection of those most favorable to the dominant culture. The African-centered perspective gives the contemporary reader an alternative view, however. Though not well known in history outside of the academic community, one of the most important rebel figures in colonial Saint-Domingue was François Makandal.[1] This former slave led a revolt that lasted from 1751 to 1758, causing the deaths of thousands of whites on the island, and he became a model for resistance and an inspiration for the generations that followed.

Resistance always accompanied colonization and enslavement in the "New World." This resistance was not, as some historians prefer to argue, born of some natural inclination toward savagery. It was a resistance to the cruel (and not unusual) treatment and harshness of life imposed on enslaved Africans by those who would keep them in bondage. Because the first concern was profit, ill-fed Africans were worked 18 to 20 hours a day to produce the sugar cane, tobacco, coffee, indigo, and other goods that contributed to the wealth of France. As Carolyn Fick noted, "Despite all of the preparatory measures taken by the planters, or for that matter because of those inadequately taken, from one-third to one-half of the newly arrived slaves…died off during the first few years."[2] Yves J. Jérôme wrote that 7,000,000 Africans arrived on the island of Hispaniola between 1645 and 1789, and each of these could expect, on average, a 3- to 7-year life span.[3] Meanwhile, Saint-Domingue was the most productive single colony in the Western Hemisphere—the "Pearl of the Antilles." The atrocious acts of cruelty used to maintain the institution of slavery provide us with a glossary of abuses that make the skin crawl. However, instead of frightening the enslaved into submission, these acts only served to harden the resolve of those who understood that the only options were "liberty or death"—and that liberty required the oppressor to be completely overthrown.

It was against this background of suffering and resistance that Makandal, a maroon, emerged to lead an insurrection that struck fear into the hearts of white men throughout the colony. The story begins with Makandal leaving the plantation of Le Normand de Mézy in the northern region of Haiti (an area over which he would, one day, hold considerable influence). According to some, the loss of his hand while working the night shift in the sugar mill was the catalyst for his departure. Another story tells of a dispute with his master over a beautiful young woman. In the latter story, he escaped to avoid 50 lashes with the whip.

Intelligent and (for that time) educated, Makandal would symbolize everything that the grand blancs, or white colonists, feared. He was also despised by the petit blancs, mulattos, and free people of color who were slaveholders. But it must be further noted, and this is illustrated in the case of Jean Baptiste Cap decades later, that some free men of color did aid and participate in rebellions against the Europeans.

The belief systems that existed and coalesced on the island also produced those who would become its revolutionary leaders. In this instance, houngans and manbos became the leaders of the resistance. François Makandal was a houngan, and his gifts as a healer had elevated him to a leadership position in the community. His oratorical gifts, coupled with a messianic charisma, attracted followers to his campaign against the planters. He has been given credit for other powers, consistent with African legend. Of particular interest is his reputation as a shape-shifter and the belief that he actually defied death by changing into a bird or mosquito. To the maroons, Makandal himself was a gift.

From all indications, Makandal was a budding genius before being captured as a prisoner of war in Africa and sold into enslavement. Fick writes, "He was brought up in the Moslem religion and had an excellent command of Arabic."[4] He was also skilled in the arts, and displayed a level of creativity that indicated great talent at an early age. Makandal was versed in tropical medicine as a result of his training prior to his capture and enslavement, and this knowledge would later serve (perhaps as an impetus to) his revolutionary activity.

For nearly two decades after joining the maroons, Makandal led his own band and organized an island-spanning network of followers who were for the total abolition of enslavement practices. Over the years that he was a leader of his community, Makandal led numerous forays from his stronghold. The planters' response to the scope and spirit of Makandal's resistance was to become increasingly paranoid, and, as their fear increased, they behaved with greater cruelty toward the enslaved. The Europeans' arrogance underscored the feeling of hopelessness among the slaves, and inspired them to more violent responses.

The key to Makandal's resistance was that he carefully organized his followers, including many free people and those among the vendors (or *pacottilleurs*) who traveled about selling items needed by those who lived on the plantations, free and enslaved. His people infiltrated the system, doing their damage from within the plantation itself. His most ambitious plot involved an attempt to poison all the whites on the island simultaneously by contaminating their water. The plan ultimately failed due to treachery and Makandal himself was murdered by the whites in retaliation, but his followers continued the struggle.

There are a number of stories of Makandal's capture, and there is the classic tale of his death by burning at the stake. Many of his followers, however, believed that he transformed himself into a fly, bird, or some other winged creature and flew to the mountains to await the coming revolution. His influence was so strong that talismans called "makandals" created after his death were outlawed by the colonial government, along with the casting of evil spells. New laws that included mulattos and free blacks in their sweep were even more strictly enforced, but increasingly harsh treatment of the slaves simply did not work to subdue them. But indeed, would any technique have worked?

Makandal's revolution, though not considered successful by the whites, instilled a deep fear in them that did not abate even with his death. His self-proclaimed immortality and the widespread belief in his supernatural abilities made his followers continue to believe that he would be reincarnated. The white and mulatto slave owners did not take heed of the message that Makandal's revolution delivered, and one can only wonder about the impact of Makandal on the 13 year-old boy named Toussaint who must have heard the stories of the *prophète* told among the people in the slave quarters.

Notes

1. There are several important works on the Haitian Revolution and Haitian heroes, including Makandal. For more information see C.L.R. James, *A History of Negro Revolts* (Chicago: Research Associates School Time Publications, 1994) and *The Black Jacobins: Toussaint L'Ouverture and the San Domingo Revolution*, 2nd edition (New York: Vintage, 1963); Carolyn Fick, *The Making of Haiti: The Saint Domingue Revolution from Below* (Knoxville: U of Tennessee P, 1990); Robert Corbett, *The Haitian Revolution of 1791-1803: An Historical Essay in Four Parts* <(http://wwww.webster.edu/corbetre/haiti/history/revolution/revolution1.htm>, 2002; Cali Ruchala, "Sonthonax and the Haitian Revolution: Flypaper Messiah," *Degenerate Magazine Online*, 2002. <http://www.diacritica.com/degenerate7/sonthonaz10.html>.

2. Fick, 27.

3. Yves J. Jérôme, *Toussaint L'Ouverture* (New York: Vantage Press, 1978).

4. Fick, 60.

Chapter 9

The Franco-African Peoples of Haiti and Louisiana
Population, Language, Culture, Religion, and Revolution
Gwendolyn Midlo Hall

There are important similarities and differences between the creative, vibrant, and indomitable peoples who created the cultures of Saint-Domingue/Haiti and Louisiana. Both places were colonized by France. Some of the colonizers of both places were pirates. Although Saint-Domingue/Haiti remained a French colony until it achieved its independence in 1804, Spain took effective control of Louisiana by 1770 and the United States by 1804. Despite these changes in administration, Louisiana's population remained almost entirely French, Cajun and Creole speakers.[1] These languages survived widely in rural areas until the mid-twentieth century and are still spoken today in some places in southwest Louisiana.

The colonizing population of Saint-Domingue/Haiti and Louisiana was both similar and different. Saint-Domingue's Native American population, the Arawak, had developed an extraordinarily just, productive, spiritual, and artistic civilization. The first Africans were introduced in 1502 by the Spanish. During the first few decades of Spanish colonization, the Arawak and enslaved Africans, first Ladinos who were African-born or socialized in Spain, and then mainly Africans of the Wolof ethnicity brought directly from Senegal, cooperated in revolts against Spanish rule. The Ladinos and then the Wolof taught the Arawak how to revolt effectively against the Spanish and the Arawak helped the Africans escape to the mountains and create runaway slave communities.[2] But before French rule began in Saint-Domingue/Haiti, the Arawak population had been utterly destroyed as corporate groups by the Spanish conquerors and colonizers.

In sharp contrast, in Louisiana, the first slaves were Native Americans. Several of these nations, including Alabama, Attakapas, Choctaw, Chickasaw, Creek, Mobile, Natchez, Natchitoches, and Tunica remained powerful throughout the eighteenth century. While some colonizers of Louisiana were born in France, many were Canadian *coureurs de bois* who lived among and merged with Native Americans both biologically and culturally. Africans often allied and merged with Native Americans as well. Following the same patterns as in early Saint-Domingue, Africans taught Native Americans how to combat Spanish and French methods of warfare, and Native Americans helped Africans escape to the forests and swamps and create runaway slave communities.[3] (Whites with deep roots in Louisiana often have ancestors who were African slaves as well as Native Americans, but they were rarely acknowledged after a few generations, especially the Africans.) Thus, Louisiana was a frontier society where peoples of various racial designations and cultures mingled freely.[4] In contrast, in Saint-Domingue, the vast majority of the population were enslaved Africans and their descendants, slave and free, black and mixed blood. Both Saint-Domingue and Louisiana had a very competent, wealthy mulatto or mixed blood free Creole elite.[5]

Both Saint-Domingue and Louisiana had slave systems, but large scale commercial agriculture geared toward the export of crops developed much earlier in Saint-Domingue/Haiti than in Louisiana.[6]. Two distinctive Franco-African Creole languages were created in Haiti and in Louisiana. Louisiana Creole developed within the first decade of the arrival of the first transatlantic slave trade ships in 1719.[7] Two-thirds of these Africans were brought from Senegambia. As a result, the Louisiana Creole language is closest to the Creole of Mauritius Island in the Indian Ocean, where Senegambians were also the formative African population. Folktales and proverbs in Louisiana Creole, most notably the Bouki/Lapin stories, are mainly Wolof in origin. But terms for religious amulets, for example gris-gris and zinzin, derive from Mande languages, which were the lingua franca in Senegambia throughout the Atlantic slave trade.[8]

Both Haiti and Louisiana were deeply influenced by massive imports of new Africans, but their ethnic origins and the timing of their arrival varied. Senegambians were feared in the Caribbean because of their rebelliousness. But they were preferred in colonies which became part of the United States, especially in Louisiana and South Carolina, where rice and indigo were widely cultivated and slaves were barely a majority and therefore less feared. It was a matter of technology transfer from Africa to America. Africans taught Europeans how to cultivate and process rice and indigo; crops which had been domesticated, grown, and produced in Greater Senegambia for many centuries before the transatlantic slave trade began.[9]

The religious influence of Africans living near the coasts of the Bight of Benin, especially the Dahomeans, was strong in both Saint-Domingue and Louisiana. These Gbe language-group speakers were usually recorded as Arada in documents in Saint-Domingue and as Fon(d), Aja,

Arada, or Mina in Louisiana, but sometimes in Saint-Domingue as well. The Vodou gods of both Haiti and Louisiana derive from Dahomean gods. There were six recorded transatlantic slave trade voyages from the Bight of Benin that arrived in French Louisiana, the last in 1728. Africans from this coast came to be prized in the parishes upriver from New Orleans and were sought out by Louisiana slaveowners during the active transshipment trade to Louisiana from the Caribbean Islands.[10] Slaves from the Bight of Benin were brought directly from Africa to Saint-Domingue in large numbers before 1750. After 1750, the transatlantic slave trade to Saint-Domingue tilted heavily toward West Central Africa. Almost all West Central Africans were listed as Congo and they were clustered in coffee-growing regions.[11] The Congo began to arrive in Louisiana in large numbers much later, after 1780. They were concentrated in and near New Orleans, especially after sugar became a major crop in Louisiana.[12.]

There is little evidence that significant numbers of Saint-Domingue slaves or free people of color were brought to Louisiana during the eighteenth century. Export of slaves from the French Caribbean Islands was first discouraged and then outlawed in 1763, because they were considered dangerous poisoners; no doubt a reaction to the Makandal conspiracy of 1758 aimed at abolishing slavery.[13] After the great slave revolt erupted in Saint-Domingue in 1791, serious efforts were made to keep slaves from this colony out of Louisiana. These included outlawing the foreign slave trade and at times allowing only new Africans to be brought in.[14] No doubt, some slaves from Saint-Domingue were brought in illegally. But there is no evidence in the extensive surviving testimony of slaves involved in conspiracies and revolts against slavery that any slaves or free people of color from Saint-Domingue participated in any of them. The resistance of Louisiana slaves to slavery, while inspired at times by the Haitian Revolution, was never led by Haitians. During the Age of Revolutions, they were led almost entirely by Louisiana Creole slaves, along with some enslaved Africans brought to Louisiana directly from Africa.[15]

The long, bloody slave revolution of Haiti produced many refugees. They went in waves to various places in the Americas. The main contingent of these refugees to Louisiana arrived very late. During 1809 and 1810, shiploads of refugees from the Haitian Revolution entered the port of New Orleans. They totaled about 10,000 people. About one-third of them were white elite, another one-third free colored elite, and the other one-third slaves who were the property of either elite group. A special law was passed by the Congress of the United States allowing these refugees and their slaves to enter Louisiana because their slaves were considered very loyal to their masters and not a danger to Louisiana's slave system.[16]

Who were these Haitian refugees? The free colored elite left Saint-Domingue after they had been defeated by the slaves revolting against slavery led by Toussaint Louverture . Almost all of them had gone to nearby Santiago on the extreme eastern end of the island of Cuba before Haitian independence triumphed. These refugees brought the coffee industry to Cuba and were very knowl-edgeable about sugar production. Although they had made a great contribution to the Cuban econ-omy, they were expelled from Cuba after France invaded Spain in 1809 and anti-French sentiment boiled over. Louisiana was especially attractive to them because the Louisiana Creole language had been created by African slaves who arrived in Louisiana almost a century earlier. Louisiana Creole is close enough to Haitian Creole (now often spelled "Kreyòl") that speakers of these two languages could understand each other. French was the language of the elites of both Haiti and Louisiana, although they were also speakers of the Creole languages. The climate was warm, humid, and familiar. Both Saint-Domingue and Louisiana had prosperous slave plantation systems growing some of the same crops: sugar, cotton, and indigo. When the Haitian refugees expelled from Santiago de Cuba arrived in Louisiana during 1809 and 1810, their slaves remained almost entire-ly in New Orleans. They were mostly young, female domestics.

There was much unrest among Louisiana slaves, even before the slave revolt in Haiti. In July 1791, a month before the slaves revolted in Haiti, there was a conspiracy among Mina slaves in Pointe Coupée Parish, Louisiana, to rise up and abolish slavery.[17] Throughout the Haitian Revolution, there were conspiracies against slavery as well as mass runaways among Louisiana slaves. Louisiana slaves were very well aware that the slaves in Saint-Domingue were fighting against their masters to abolish slavery. The 1795 slave conspiracy in Pointe Coupée was inspired by the slave revolt in Saint-Domingue/Haiti as well as by the slaves' knowledge that the French National Assembly had abolished slavery in all French colonies in 1794. Joseph Bouavel, a Walloon (Franco-Belgian) teacher-tailor in Pointe Coupée, read to the slaves from the Declaration of the Rights of Man.[18]

In 1811, the biggest revolt in the history of slavery in the United States took place on the German Coast in the parishes along the Mississippi River north of New Orleans. Historians have long tried to portray Louisiana slaves as incompetent, content, and passive, attributing all unrest among them to "outside influences." Charles Gayarrée, a white Creole historian of the nineteenth century, claimed that Charles Deslondes, the main leader of the 1811 Revolt, was a free man of color from Haiti. But he was actually a mulatto Louisiana Creole slave. On October 15, 1795, he was list-ed as a Creole mulatto, aged 18, inventoried among the slaves of his deceased master Deslondes. He was listed as a slave of the widow of Jacques Deslondes in a document dated January 13, 1811, which listed slaves involved in this revolt. There was a free man of color named Charles involved in the 1811 revolt who was also a mulatto, but he too was a Louisiana Creole.

Nevertheless, misinformation about Charles Deslondes' status and origin has been passed down through the generations, misidentifying him as a free man of color from Haiti. This is an example of racist historiography which assumes that Louisiana slaves were happy with slavery, and/or too incompetent to resist it without "outside agitators" to instigate and lead them. While the antislavery movements among Louisiana slaves during the Age of Revolutions were partially inspired by the successes of the Haitian Revolution and the instability of the times, there is no evidence of direct involvement by Haitians in any Louisiana conspiracies and revolts against slavery.[19]

The presence of Haitian refugees in Louisiana doubled the free colored population of New Orleans. They certainly influenced Louisiana's evolving Creole culture, especially among Louisiana's mixed-blood elite. There was intermarriage between members of the Louisiana and Haitian free colored elite refugees. Many of their descendants trace at least some of their ancestors to Haiti. But the cultural influence of these Haitian refugees in Louisiana has been exaggerated. They arrived long after the Louisiana Creole language, folklore, cuisine, and music had been created by enslaved peoples brought directly to Louisiana from Africa and by their Louisiana Creole descendants. Many of the slaves brought in by these Haitian refugees were born in Cuba, not in Haiti. Many of them were young, with little or no memory of Haiti. As mentioned, the slaves brought in by Haitian refugees remained almost entirely in New Orleans.[20] Their direct impact on unrest among Louisiana slaves was not likely to be great, especially in rural areas. The unrest among Louisiana slaves during the Age of Revolutions stemmed mainly from their competence, their courage, and their love of freedom.

The Haitian Revolution was an extraordinary achievement. It was the only successful slave revolt in the Western Hemisphere. It was the second successful independence movement in the Western Hemisphere. After achieving its own independence, Haiti helped and inspired the Latin American independence wars that began in 1810. President Pétion of Haiti gave refuge and support to Simón Bolívar and his followers after their movement suffered reverses in South America, in exchange for Bolívar's promise to abolish slavery when Latin America became independent. The entire world owes much to the Haitian Revolution. It is one of very few instances of the triumph of a movement for freedom among slaves anywhere at any time. It was a vanguard of independence throughout the Americas. Our debt to Haiti, the Haitian Revolution, and the Haitian people has not yet been recognized.

Notes

1. The language of the Acadian refugees who arrived in Louisiana during the eighteenth century.

2. Franklin J. Franco, *Negros, mulatos y la nación dominicana* (Santo Domingo: Editora Nacional, 1969) 5-61; Gwendolyn Midlo Hall, *African Ethnicities in the Americas: Restoring the Links* (Chapel Hill: U of North Carolina P, 2005) 82, 83, 85.

3. Gwendolyn Midlo Hall, *Africans in Colonial Louisiana: the Development of Afro-Creole Culture in the Eighteenth Century* (Baton Rouge: Louisiana State U P, 1992) 13, 14, 15, 97, 100-106, 115-18, 238.

4. Gwendolyn Midlo Hall, "Historical Memory, Consciousness and Conscience in the New Millennium," Plenary address at symposium on the 300th anniversary of French colonization of Louisiana. Concluding chapter in *Greater French Colonial Louisiana: Atlantic World Perspectives*, ed. Bradley Bond (Baton Rouge: Louisiana State U P, 2005) 291-309.

5. Gwendolyn Midlo Hall, "Saint-Domingue," in *Neither Slave Nor Free: The Freedmen of African Descent in the Slave Societies of the New World*, ed. David W. Cohen and Jack P. Greene (Baltimore: The Johns Hopkins U P, 1972) 172-192. For Louisiana, see Hall, *Africans in Colonial Louisiana*, 100, 129, 130, 173, 174, 237-74, 370-372; and Hall, "Historical Memory, Consciousness and Conscience in the New Millennium," Plenary address at symposium on the 300th anniversary of French colonization of Louisiana.

6. Gwendolyn Midlo Hall, *Social Control in Slave Plantation Societies: A Comparison of St. Domingue and Cuba* (Baltimore: Johns Hopkins U P, 1971).

7. Hall, *Africans in Colonial Louisiana*, 187-95.

8. For coastal origins of slaves brought to Louisiana during the French Atlantic slave trade, see Hall, *Africans in Colonial Louisiana*, Table 2, 60 and Appendix A, 381-397. For gris-gris and zinzin see Hall, *Africans in Colonial Louisiana*, 38, 63, 163, 235n; for preponderance of Mande languages and their use as lingua franca in Senegambia throughout the transatlantic slave trade, see Hall, *African Ethnicities in the Americas*.

9. Gwendolyn Midlo Hall, *African Ethnicities in the Americas,* 66-68; 92-93.

10. For a detailed discussion of the meanings and evolution of these ethnic terms, see Hall, *African Ethnicities in the Americas*, especially Ch. 2, "Making Invisible Africans Visible: Coasts, Ports, Regions, and Ethnicities," 22-54.

11. David Geggus, "Sugar and Coffee Cultivation in Saint-Domingue and the Shaping of the Slave Labor Force," *Cultivation and Culture: Work Process and the Shaping of Afro-American Culture in the Americas*, ed. Ira Berlin and Philip Morgan (Charlottesville, VA: U of Virginia P, 1993) 73-98; Geggus, "The French Slave Trade: An Overview," *William and Mary Quarterly*, 3rd ser., 58, no. 1 (Jan 2001): 119-38; Geggus, "Sex Ratio, Age and Ethnicity in the Atlantic Slave Trade: Data from French Shipping and Plantation Records," *Journal of African History*, Vol. 30 (1989): 23-44.

12. See Hall, *Slavery and African Ethnicities in the Americas*, Figure 3.2, 75, and Figure 7.1, 161.

13. Gwendolyn Midlo Hall, "Myths About Creole Culture in Louisiana: Slaves, Africans, Blacks, Mixed Bloods, and Caribbeans," *Cultural Vistas*, Vol. 12, no. 2 (Summer 2001): 78-89.

14. Paul LaChance. "The Politics of Fear: French Louisianians and the Slave Trade, 1786-1809," *Plantation Societies in America*, I (1979): 162-97.

15. Calculations made from Gwendolyn Midlo Hall, Louisiana Slave Database 1719-1820. Slaves who testified in trials involving these conspiracies identified their own origins and ethnicities. None of them were born in Saint-Domingue/Haiti. See "Miscellaneous Searches, Conspiracies and Revolts" at <www.ibiblio.org/laslave>. For slaves born in Saint-Domingue, click on the search engine and choose "Saint-Domingue" as the birthplace. For more complex calculations, the entire database may be downloaded..

16. Carl A. Brasseaux and Glenn R. Conrad, *The Road to Louisiana : The Saint-Domingue Refugees, 1792-1809*, with translations by David Cheramie (Lafayette, LA: Center for Louisiana Studies, U of Southwestern Louisiana, 1992).

17. Hall, *Africans in Colonial Louisiana*, 316-42.

18. Ibid., 343-74.

19. Charles Deslondes' identity as a mulatto Louisiana Creole slave was first reported to me by Robert Paquette, and confirmed by my consultation of the following documents: 15 October 1795, St. Jean the Baptist Parish Courthouse, Estate of Deslondes, which lists Charles Mulatto Creole, age 18. He was listed as a slave of Deslondes in documents relating to the 1811 slave revolt in the St. Charles Parish Courthouse, 13 January 1811.

20. Calculations made from Gwendolyn Midlo Hall, Louisiana Slave Database 1719-1820.

Chapter 10

The Battle of Vertières
John T. O'Connor

Soon after Napoleon became First Consul of the French Republic in 1800, the privileged position of Toussaint Louverture, governor of Saint-Domingue, became a matter of increasing concern. Toussaint gave every indication of enjoying his autocratic position to the hilt. By 1801 he conquered the territory of Santo Domingo and declared the abolition of slavery. Later that year he wrote a new constitution for Saint-Domingue, assuming the governorship for life with the right to appoint his successor. That was not the way colonial administrators were expected to act; indeed, he seemed close to announcing independence from France. Determined to restore white authority in Saint-Domingue, Napoleon sent his brother-in-law, General Leclerc, with about 10,000 troops to the colony; they arrived in February, 1802, and within two months the number of troops in Saint-Domingue had doubled. The initial plan was to calm the suspicions of black officers before disarming their soldiers and deporting the officers themselves. Slavery would return to Santo Domingo; plantations restored to white planters in Saint-Domingue, and with the colony under control, many of the troops would go to Louisiana and rendezvous with thousands of French soldiers sent from the French-controlled Netherlands. That joint force would in turn ensure a strong military position in the Louisiana territory, intended to be an essential part of France's overseas empire.[1]

Developments in 1802 changed all of Napoleon's plans. Initial skirmishes with Toussaint and other black generals concluded with the willingness of black leaders to cooperate with France upon assurances of keeping their military ranks. Napoleon's real intention became clear when Toussaint was lured into discussions with Leclerc, captured, and sent off to a French prison in the Jura Mountains, near the Swiss border. Even before he entered prison, the scene in Saint-Domingue totally changed upon news that the governor in Guadeloupe had announced the restoration of slavery. Black generals such as Dessalines and Christophe deserted the French and a battle to the death ensued. By the time General Leclerc died of yellow fever in November, 1802, about 25,000 French soldiers were already dead, and 8,000 were in hospitals: the campaign in Saint-Domingue was mired in quicksand. Momentum shifted to the insurgents, who were motivated by hatred of slavery and hatred of those who sought to restore slavery in the colony. If events had unfolded according to Napoleon's original schedule, the return of slavery to Saint-Domingue would already have been assured and thousands of troops under Leclerc would be strengthening France's control of Louisiana. Those expectations were dashed by the bravery of the insurgents and by the lethal diseases that cut down thousands of French soldiers.

General Rochambeau, who succeeded Leclerc as commander of the French army in Saint-Domingue, proved to be both a competent military man and a sadistic maniac. His extermination policies for the insurgents included a series of atrocities that in turn led to wholesale reprisals against French troops. Mass hangings and drownings, victims burned at the stake, ambushes and massacres—such episodes became common occurrences. Meanwhile, in 1803 hostilities between England and France resumed. The English soon blockaded the principal ports in Saint-Domingue and sold supplies and munitions to General Dessalines, who led the struggle against the French. In June, 1803, Rochambeau was ordered to transfer his headquarters from Port-au-Prince to Cap-Français. As the end game approached, Dessalines relentlessly besieged one town after another. Cayes and Jacmel were taken, followed by Léogâne and Jérémie. Saint Marc was occupied on September 2nd; the French commander in Port-au-Prince capitulated on October 3rd, setting the stage for the assault on Cap-Français.

Referred to as "The Paris of the West Indies," Le Cap had been the principal French naval base in the Caribbean. It could once boast of more ship traffic in and out of its harbor than Marseilles, the leading port in France. About two-thirds of Le Cap went up in flames in June, 1793 during the rebellion of 10,000 slaves in the city. Ten years later, French presence in the colony had dwindled until only their hold on Le Cap remained. Rochambeau personally led the defense of the city with about 5,000 troops. Blockhouses, or forts, were set up at strategic points: Forts Vertières, Bréda, Champain, and, at the highest elevation, Pierre-Michel. Each fort had artillery and many well-armed soldiers. Fort Vertières was pivotal because it controlled the road from Port-au-Prince into Le Cap. Naturally, the defenders used the terrain effectively, with forts positioned over a ravine if possible so as to expose assailants to a maximum of murderous fire.

Commanding about 15,000 soldiers, Desssalines ordered one unit after another into the battle that raged from dawn through late afternoon on November 18, 1803—a legendary day celebrated by Haitians and extolled by her leading poets. Before the insurgents could break through the line of defense, they had to seize control of the hill Butte Charrier, which overlooked Vertières and from which the fort could be bombarded by artillery. Getting up the hill while hauling the needed artillery under withering French fire was the first task. Dessalines chose the most intrepid of his generals, François Capois, to lead the initial attack. He and his men first had to cross a bridge over a ravine. Against extraordinary odds, they charged into a hailstorm of bullets, shrapnel, and artillery shells. Bodies of the dead and dying piled up, many horses collapsed, the smoke became thicker by the minute, and yet the place of each man who fell was quickly filled by someone else dashing in from the rear.

Ulrick Jean-Pierre's paintings of the Battle of Vertières marvelously capture the élan and raw courage of officers and men on attack, with bodies under foot, horses falling, and plumes of smoke everywhere. The most cited and extraordinary episode on this historic day concerned the ardor and incredible luck of General Capois in the heat of battle. At one point, Capois had his horse shot out from under him. He leapt ahead, sword in the air, urging his men forward. Then his hat was shot off his head and still he kept plunging ahead, with two-thirds of his men already dead or wounded. From the French side came shouts of "Bravo! Bravo!" Drums rolled. All of a sudden the French ceased firing and a cavalryman galloped out to deliver a public message: "Captain General Rochambeau sends his admiring compliments to the officer who has just overed himself with so much glory."[2] Then the messenger returned to his line and the battle resumed. Recounting this surreal moment in his book *The Black Jacobins*, C.L.R. James remarked, "The struggle had been such a nightmare that by now all in San Domingo were a little mad, both white and black."[3]

Dessalines pulled back Capois and what remained of his unit and ordered another unit under General Gabart into the struggle. Attacks were launched against all blockhouses at the same time so as to make it impossible for the French to concentrate their fire on any one target. After an hour of hand-to-hand combat, Gabart and his men secured the hill position, ringed it with mounds of earth to absorb the bullets, and proceeded to fire artillery shells into Fort Vertières until the French were forced to retreat back toward Le Cap. By the end of the afternoon, a haze of smoke and gunpowder fumes practically obscured all vision. Suddenly a violent thunderstorm drenched the field strewn with the dead and dying men and horses. Night fell. The French withdrew to their base in the city. The insurgents had triumphed; their casualties included 1,200 dead and 2,000 wounded.

Late that night, Rochambeau proposed an armistice in a dispatch to Dessalines. Dessalines flatly refused and demanded capitulation. In effect, Rochambeau had no choice but to accept the demand. Withdrawal was to take place within nine days to ensure an orderly French departure from the colony. However, the English blockade resulted in the French surrendering to the English. In less than a month, on January 1, 1804 at Gonaïves, Dessalines proclaimed the independence of Saint-Domingue and gave the new state the name it had been given by Arawak inhabitants of the island before the arrival of Columbus: Ayiti, or Haiti, meaning "Land of Mountains." The Battle of

Vertières clinched the success of the independence movement. November 18th has since been celebrated as Armed Forces Day in Haiti.

In January 1803, when Napoleon learned of Leclerc's death and the huge loss of French soldiers in Saint-Domingue, he must have glimpsed the need for a radical change of plans for Louisiana. Napoleon intended to send the thousands of French troops stationed in the Netherlands to Louisiana, but icy weather conditions kept the ships in port. Before they could set out, the English blockaded the port. On May 18th, Great Britain declared war on France, ending the brief lull created by the Peace of Amiens in 1801. This stage of the war continued until Napoleon fell from power in 1814. The drain of men and resources in the colony, together with the resumption of the war against England, forced Napoleon to scuttle his plans for Louisiana. The dominance of English sea power, the loss of the naval base at Le Cap, and the absence of a strong army to defend Louisiana all persuaded the First Consul to sell the territory to the United States rather than have it seized by England. President Jefferson was wary of a strong French military presence in the Caribbean and Louisiana. But as a slave owner, he loathed the prospect of an independent black republic. Indeed, after Haiti won its independence, Jefferson arranged for an embargo against the new state. His contemporary and rival, Alexander Hamilton, who staunchly opposed slavery, fully appreciated the close link between the revolution in Saint-Domingue and the purchase of Louisiana:

> To the deadly climate of St. Domingo, and to the courage and obstinate resistance made by its black inhabitants are we indebted for the obstacles which delayed the [continued French] colonization of Louisiana, till the auspicious moment, when a rupture between England and France gave a new turn to the projects of the latter, and destroyed at once all her schemes as to this favorite object of her ambition.[4]

Notes

1. This brief summary of the war of independence in the colony owes much to David Patrick Geggus's superb overview ,"The Haitian Revolution," in *Haitian Revolutionary Studies* (Bloomington: Indiana U P, 2002) 5-29.

2. C.L.R. James, *The Black Jacobins: Toussaint L'Ouverture and the San Domingo Revolution*, 2nd ed. (New York: Vintage, 1963) 367-368.

3. Ibid., 368.

4. Cited by Robert L. Paquette, "Revolutionary Saint-Domingue in the Making of Territorial Louisiana,"in *A Turbulent Time: The French Revolution and the Greater Caribbean*, ed. David Barry Gaspar and David Patrick Geggus (Bloomington: Indiana U P, 1997) 211.

Chapter 11

Jean-Jacques Dessalines

Cécile Accilien

Jean-Jacques Dessalines served under Toussaint Louverture as his lieutenant and, while no one can argue that their styles differed greatly, it is clear that both men were driven by their desire to have all Haitians live as free people in a free country. "La Dessalinienne," the song that is still a symbol of Haitian pride, is attributed to Dessalines. And yet, Dessalines often remains in the shadow of Toussaint or is not mentioned at all. Novels and plays have been written about Toussaint, and most critical texts that deal with the history of the Caribbean or slavery or revolution at least mention Toussaint and often go into detail about him, but Dessalines is sometimes mentioned only in passing. In discussions among Haitians, I have often heard the argument that Dessalines was cruel and harsh compared to Toussaint, Christophe, or Pétion. Some have called him a savage. An illiterate ex-slave, he was meticulous in his battle plans and in his "street smart" ways of outdoing the French. He never hid his hatred for the French, under whom he had suffered decades of humiliation and indignity. He worked well with Pétion, the mulatto who joined him when he could no longer tolerate Leclerc's politics toward the mulattoes. The two men shared the goal of a free and independent country. Moreover, Dessalines trained many great leaders, such as Capois, Christophe, and Geffrard. His methods were bloody, to say the least, if only out of fear that the French might someday try to return to rule Haiti. As Louis Mercier, a Haitian educator, notes, "Whatever the means he employed to accomplish his ends, Dessalines remains the most powerful spirit in our history….One cannot be a real Haitian unless one is a Dessalinian."[1]

Dessalines was commander of the army that won the decisive battle in Vertières on November 18, 1803. The French surrendered at Butte Charrier, and later, on December 4th, they also surrendered Môle Saint Nicolas. Although these defeats were key events leading to the Louisiana Purchase, Dessalines's role in them is rarely recalled. Dessalines, sensing that independence was near, also created the Haitian flag exactly six months before in Arcahaie, on May 18, 1803.

The creation of the flag is one of the most important events in Haitian history for it symbolizes the fulfillment and belief that Haiti could and should be an independent country. The flag also concretely represents Dessalines's commitment to "Liberté ou la mort" [Liberty or death], a pact that was made decades earlier during the ceremony of Bois Caïman. There are various versions of the creation of the Haitian flag and the symbolic nature of the colors blue/red and black/red and the connection between the French flag and the Haitian flag. Max Beauvoir has rightly stated that it was unlikely that Dessalines would have modeled the Haitian flag on the French flag. Instead, Beauvoir makes a link between the Haitian flag and the spirit of Ogou Feray, who is regarded as a warrior and the god of iron because of his strength.[2]

Dessalines had already proven to be a strong leader when, in 1802, Toussaint put him in charge of defending the fort known as La Crête-à-Pierrot. On March 11, 1802, when he noticed the French army approaching the fort, Dessalines told the soldiers: " Nous serons attaqués ce matin....Je ne veux garder avec moi que des braves. Que ceux qui veulent redevenir esclaves des Français sortent du fort. Que ceux au contraire qui veulent mourir en hommes libres se rangent autour de moi." [We will be attacked this morning....I only want brave men to stay with me. Those who want to become slaves once again should get out of the fort. However, those who want to die as free men (should) gather around me.]

The whole garrison cried, "Nous mourrons tous pour la Liberté." [We will all die for liberty.] Dessalines declared: "Je vous fais tous sauter si les Français pénètrent dans ce fort." [I will blow up all of you if the French enter this fort].[3] Although the fort was eventually abandoned by Dessalines's soldiers, the French lost 700 soldiers and General Leclerc was injured during this battle.

On December 31, 1803, the eve of the day that Haiti officially recognizes as Independence Day, Dessalines and the other generals came together in a ceremony to officially proclaim Haiti's independence. During this ceremony, which took place in present-day Gonaïves (known as the City of Independence), Boisrond Tonnerre, secretary of the revolutionary army, was chosen by Dessalines to draft the act of independence: "Pour rédiger cet Acte...il nous faut la peau d'un blanc pour parchemin, son crâne pour écritoire, son sang pour encre et une baïonnette pour plume" [In order to draft this Act...we need the skin of a white man for parchment, his skull for a writing desk, his blood for ink, and a bayonet for a pen.][4]

The following day, January 1, 1804, Dessalines' officers gathered at the governmental palace and declared him "Gouverneur Général à vie" with the right to make laws, declare war, and name his successor. Dessalines declared himself emperor on September 22, 1804, and by 1805 had drafted a new constitution that gave him supreme powers of governance. On October 17, 1806, he was assassinated.

There are very few biographies on Dessalines, perhaps because he is such a controversial and misunderstood figure. But whether we consider him a tyrant, a bloody lieutenant, or a liberator, the fact remains that he is the man who ultimately led Haiti to independence.

Notes

1. Selden Rodman, *Haiti: The Black Republic* (Old Greenwich, CT: Devin-Adair Co., 1973) 15.

2. For more information on connections between the Haitian flag and Vodou, see the informative article "The Colors of the Flags in Haiti" by Max G. Beauvoir, Ati-Houngan, at <http://www.vodou.org/colors_of_the_flags.htm>.

3. See *Histoire d'Haïti* (Haiti: Henri Deschamps, 1942) 94-95. My translation.

4. Ibid., 115. My translation.

Chapter 12

President Alexandre Pétion

Philippe Zacaïr

The president of the Republic of Haiti, Alexandre Pétion, received a letter on February 17, 1816 from Venezuelan native Simón Bolívar, who was then established in the Haitian town of Les Cayes.[1] Bolívar was a leading protagonist of an armed struggle for independence of major proportions and complexity that had been undermining the foundations of Spanish rule in South America since 1812. The Venezuelan leader arrived in Haiti on December 24, 1815 after suffering terrible setbacks in his fight against Spanish and pro-royalist forces and subsequently forced into exile. Pétion's government guaranteed Bolívar not only safety but also critical political and military support for the continuation of his struggle.[2] At the time he wrote to Pétion, Bolívar was about to launch an expedition from Les Cayes to Venezuela with the aim of driving out the adversaries of independence. In his letter, Bolívar praised Pétion for his magnanimity and tolerance, and wished to express his gratitude to him personally. He insisted on his commitment to the abolition of slavery in the territories soon to be liberated from Spanish domination. Lastly, he expressed his desire to publicly acknowledge the Haitian president as the liberator of Venezuela and New Granada.

Pétion's response followed the next day.[3] He wished Bolívar complete success in his struggle for liberty and the end of slavery in South America, but demanded that his name not to be mentioned. Nevertheless, the remarkable role played by Pétion in Bolívar's triumph remains to this day a famous episode in the history of the Caribbean, as well as compelling evidence of the impact of the Haitian revolution on the Americas.

Nineteenth-century Caribbean nationalists such as Puerto Rican Ramón Emeterio Betances and Eugenio María de Hostos cited the name of Pétion in reference to their struggles for liberty and unity in the Caribbean.[4] A major figure of Haitian independence, Pétion is closely associated with the history of the struggle for liberty in the Caribbean basin.

Pétion was born in Saint-Domingue on April 2, 1770, the son of a free woman of color and a white colonist known as Pascal Sabès.[5] In Saint-Domingue, as in other American colonial establishments founded on African slavery, race was the determining factor of social, economic and political status. A free man, but devoid of political rights because of his African ancestry, Pétion was trained as a silversmith before joining the militia in 1788.[6] The colonial militias provided *gens de couleur* one of the few avenues of social advancement in the slave society.[7] In 1789, however, the advent of the French revolution brought about dramatic transformations in the French colony.

The proclamation of the principles of liberty and equality in August, 1789 posed a formidable challenge to colonial order. Indeed, the gens de couleur took action in Saint-Domingue as well as in Paris for recognition by France of their right to full equality with the whites. The failed revolt led by Vincent Ogé in Saint-Domingue in 1790 exemplified impatience with the unwillingness of revolutionary France to extend the principles of equality to the colonies. Ogé's rebellion unleashed brutal repression that demonstrated that white colonists were determined to keep their racial, social, and political privileges intact. However, in the wake of Ogé's brutal execution, revolutionary France extended political rights by a decree on May 15, 1791 to gens de couleur born of free parents.[8] The continuous resistance shown by the white colonists to this decree nurtured the increasing radicalization of the gens de couleur and their decision to resort once more to armed struggle. Pétion participated in the rebellion of the gens de couleur under the leadership of Louis-Jacques Beauvais.[9] He distinguished himself in battle not only by his military skills but also by his moderation and acts of humanity toward prisoners.

While the gens de couleur and the whites attempted to settle their differences, slaves rebelled in the northern province in August 1791. "From the night it began," wrote historian David Geggus, "the uprising was the largest and bloodiest yet seen in an American slave society."[10] The face of Saint-Domingue was to be changed forever.

By 1798, the armed conflict had taken new and dramatic dimensions. Blacks and gens de couleur were now competing for power. Toussaint Louverture, a black who had risen to undisputed political and military prominence and controlled most of the colony, ordered an invasion of the southern province, a stronghold of the gens de couleur. Pétion sided with their leader, André Rigaud, against the blacks and played a significant role in battle by directing the defense of the town of Jacmel, which was being besieged by Jean-Jacques Dessalines, Louverture's ablest lieutenant. However, Louverture's military success forced many gens de couleur to leave the colony. Pétion sought exile in France, where he remained until 1802 when he returned to Saint-Domingue with the expedition of French general Leclerc, whose official goal was the restoration of French rule over the once-prosperous colony. Louverture was arrested by Leclerc in June, 1802 and sent to France, where he died in prison.

The situation once more changed dramatically when the people of Saint-Domingue, blacks and gens de couleur alike, understood that Leclerc's campaign was leading to the restoration of the old regime based on slavery and racial inequality. The alliance between Pétion and Dessalines in October, 1802 sealed the union of the former adversaries and led to the beginning of the war of independence against the French. Their victory paved the way for the birth of Haiti on January 1, 1804, with Dessalines as first head of state.

The assassination of Dessalines in October, 1806 was an unmistakable sign that the struggle for power had resumed. This led to the partition of Haiti into two distinct states. In the north, the black general Henri Christophe established the kingdom of Haiti and ruled under the name of Henri I until 1820. In the south, Pétion became the first president of the Republic of Haiti and was reelected twice, in 1811 and 1815. He launched a large-scale program of land redistribution that transformed Haiti into a country of small peasantry. According to historian Dantès Bellegarde, Pétion "saw in such a measure the application of a principle of social justice."[11] Other historians, however, are more critical of Pétion's land redistribution policy. As Michel-Rolph Trouillot points out, Pétion "surrendered land in order to win control of the state. Thus Pétion initiated a land distribution program which, although it in fact turned the best properties over to members of the elites nonetheless had a tremendous ideological impact on the peasant masses."[12] During his administration, Pétion also took much interest in the development of male and female education, with the building of the first lycée in Port-au-Prince and the Pensionat National des Demoiselles. When he died due to illness in March, 1818, his people referred to Pétion as "Papa bon kè," or "father of good heart."

Notes

1. The wording of Bolívar's letter is: "A son Excellence M. le Président d'Haiti. Monsieur le Président. Je suis accablé du poids de vos bienfaits. M. Villaret est retourné on ne peut pas bien dépêché par votre excellence. En tout vous êtes magnanime et indulgent. Nos affaires sont presque arrangées et sans doute, dans une quinzaine de jours, nous serons en état de partir. Je n'attends que vos dernières faveurs, et s'il est possible, j'irai moi-même vous exprimer l'étendue de ma reconnaissance. Par M. Inginac, votre digne secrétaire, j'ose vous faire de nouvelles prières. Dans ma proclamation aux habitants de Vénézuéla, et dans les décrets que je dois expédier pour la liberté des esclaves, je ne sais pas s'il me sera permis de témoigner des sentiments de mon coeur envers votre Excellence, et de laisser à la postérité un monument irrécusable de votre philanthropie. Je ne sais, dis-je, si je devrai vous nommer comme l'auteur de notre liberté. Je prie votre Excellence

de m'exprimer sa volonté à cet égard. Le lieutenant colonel Valdès vous adresse une pétition que je me permets de recommander à votre générosité. Agréez, Monsieur le Président, les respectueux hommages de la haute considération avec laquelle j'ai l'honneur d'être de votre Excellence, le très humble et obéissant serviteur. Cayes le 8 février 1816." Quoted in François Dalencour, *Alexandre Pétion devant l'humanité* (En vente chez l'Auteur: Port-au-Prince, 1928) 112-113.

2. On Simón Bolívar's Haitian exile, see Paul Verna and Robert Sutherland, *Un amigo de Bolívar en Haiti* (Caracas: Fundación John Boulton, 1966); and Paul Verna, *Petion y Bolívar. Cuarenta años (1790-1830)* de relaciones Haitiano Venezolanas y su aporte a la emancipacion de Hispanoamérica (Caracas, 1969); François Dalencour, *Alexandre Pétion devant l'humanité*...; Carlos Gómez, "Alejandro Petion, Robert Sutherland y Luis Brion. Tres artesanos de Nuestra Independencia," *Boletín de Historia y Antigüedades* 87 : 811 (2000): 959-987; Ignacio de Guzmán Noguera, "La República de Haití y la Independencia de las colonias españolas en América," *Boletín de Historia y Antigüedades* 81: 786 (1994): 563-575; David Geggus, "Epilogue," *The Impact of the Haitian Revolution in the Atlantic World*, ed. David Geggus (Columbia: U of South Carolina P, 2001) 250.

3. The wording of Pétion's letter is: "Alexandre Pétion, Président d'Haïti, à son Excellence le Général Bolívar, etc. J'ai reçu hier, Général, votre estimable lettre du 8 de ce mois. J'écris au général Marion au sujet de l'objet que vous m'avez fait demander, et je vous réfère à lui à ce sujet. Vous connaissez, Général, mes sentiments pour ce que vous avez à cour de défendre, et pour vous personnellement, vous devez être donc pénétré combien je désire voir sortir du joug de l'esclavage ceux qui y gémissent, mais des motifs qui se rapportent aux ménagements que je dois à une nation qui ne s'est pas encore prononcée contre la République d'une manière offensive, m'obligent à vous prier de ne rien proclamer, dans l'étendue de la République, ni de nommer mon nom dans aucun de vos actes, et je compte, à cet égard, sur les sentiments qui vous caractérisent. J'ai bien reçu la supplique du lieutenant-colonel Juan Valdès et j'y ai fait droit. Le général Marion est chargé de lui faire donner l'objet de sa demande. Je fais des voeux pour le bonheur de votre Excellence, et la prie de me croire avec la plus parfaite considération. Port-au-Prince, le 18 février 1816, an 13e de l'Indépendance." Quoted in François Dalencour, Alexandre Pétion, 113.

4. Eugenio María de Hostos, "Quién Era Maceo," *Maceo en Santo Domingo*, ed. Emilio Rodriguez Demorizi (Barcelona: Gráficas M. Pareja, 1978) 187; Ramón Emeterio Betances, "Ensayo Sobre Alejandro Petión," *Revista del Instituto de Cultura Puertorriqueña* 13:49 (1970): 49-57.

5. Dantès Bellegarde, "President Alexandre Petion," *Phylon* 2:3 (1941): 205.

6. Ibid., 206.

7. Carolyn Fick, *The Making of Haiti: The Saint-Domingue Revolution from Below* (Knoxville: U of Tennessee P, 1990) 118-134.

8. Ibid., 85.

9. Ibid., 120.

10. David Geggus, "The Haitian Revolution," in *The Modern Caribbean*, ed. Knight Franklin and Colin Palmer (Chapel Hill: U of North Carolina P, 1989) 29.

11. Dantès Bellegarde, "President Alexandre Pétion," 211.

12. Michel-Rolph Trouillot, *Haiti, State Against Nation: The Origins and Legacy of Duvalierism* (New York: Monthly Review Press, 1990) 46-48.

Chapter 13

King Henri Christophe

Sue Peabody

Henri Christophe, a general under Toussaint Louverture and Jean-Jacques Dessalines, proclaimed himself king of Haiti in 1811 and ruled until his death in 1820. According to his Almanach Royal, Christophe was born on Grenada on October 6, 1767, four years after the island had passed from French to British control.[1] Historians are unsure whether he was born slave or free, and his parentage is also obscure. As a youth, he served as a cabin boy on a French frigate and later trained as a cook at the inn La Couronne in Cap-Français, Saint-Domingue. In 1780, at the age of 12, he accompanied the Comte d'Estaing's regiment of free people of color to Georgia to help the American colonists, and participated in the siege of Savannah. By 1788, at age 20, he was effectively managing the Hôtel de la Couronne in Cap-Français.

Christophe did not participate in the slave uprising of 1791 or fight in the Spanish army when this initial insurgency broke out. Instead, he remained in Le Cap and, after the fire of 1793, which destroyed La Couronne and precipitated the massive white exodus, became an infantry captain and later commander of a corsair. Around this time he married Marie-Louise Coidavid, the daughter of a free black liquor-shop proprietor. In 1794, their first child, François-Ferdinand, was born, and Toussaint Louverture promoted Christophe to major, along with Dessalines, Clervaux, Maurepas, and Moyse.

During the revolutionary period, in addition to leading his troops in battle and training others, Christophe was entrusted with several key missions. Toussaint appointed Christophe to intervene in the mulatto coup against Lavaux in 1796. Later, along with the French engineer Colonel

Vincent, Christophe devised the legal *codes rurales* that required former slaves to return to agricultural work; as a result, sugar production increased tenfold in the 18 months between 1798 and 1799.

By the time Napoleon's General Leclerc arrived in 1802 with secret orders to arrest Toussaint and restore slavery to Saint-Domingue, Christophe had emerged as a powerful and impressive figure in his own right, though still impeccably loyal to Toussaint. One French officer described Christophe as "handsome, chilly, and urbane...of unimpeachable morals."[2] After Leclerc trapped Toussaint, several subordinate officers, including Clervaux, Pétion, and Petit-Noël, and their troops rose in revolt, followed soon by Dessalines. Christophe did not abandon Leclerc immediately, despite his increasing distrust of Napoleon. But when Leclerc ordered black soldiers and their families massacred on board ships in Le Cap harbor, Christophe joined the others to oppose French rule. With Toussaint gone, the remaining officers fought over who would lead the opposition forces. During this period, Christophe ambushed and killed the African-born rebel Sans Souci, who would not submit to the Creole general.[3]

Christophe joined the rebel forces under Dessalines, and Haiti declared independence from France on January 1, 1804. Dessalines first appointed Christophe as General of the Northern Province and then, upon declaring himself emperor, named Christophe Commander-in-Chief of the Haitian army, his likely heir apparent. After Pétion's forces assassinated Dessalines, a military council recognized Christophe as President of Haiti, but Pétion's constitutional committee made the president a figurehead, with the real power in Pétion's position as President of the Assembly. Christophe rejected Pétion's arrangement and attacked Port-au-Prince, the seat of the Haitian assembly, beginning a civil war that would last for the rest of his life.

Christophe's power was centered in the northern province. which was the State of Haiti, while Pétion ruled the south and west as the Republic of Haiti. After four years, Pétion was reelected president and on March 28, 1811, Christophe declared Haiti a kingdom and himself King Henry I. At his coronation celebration, Henry proposed a toast to "My dear brother George [III of England]! May his life be preserved by the Great Ruler of the Universe, and may he oppose an invincible obstacle to the unbridled ambition of Napoleon and remain always the constant friend of Haiti."[4] Christophe likely anglicized his name to underscore his affinity with Britain and his rejection of Napoleonic designs on Haiti. While both Henry and Pétion sought foreign recognition as the true government of Haiti, hoping for economic and political connections to the wider Atlantic, Christophe especially sought to ally with Britain.

Christophe's rule of Haiti stands out for his ritual display of power as well as for the resources required to create and maintain his status. He invented an aristocracy modeled on the European with titles (dukes, counts, etc.) and adopted royal garb and military uniforms similar to those of England's George III. Foreign visitors often commented on the fine clothing and manners of the royal family and the Haitian aristocracy, although such observations may reflect their own lowered expectations for blacks as much as Christophe's stylistic flair.

The most monumental and enduring symbol of Christophe's power is the Citadelle Henry, with the neighboring palace of Sans-Souci below, two of seven chateaux built during his reign. The Citadelle towers above a 2,800-foot mountain, once accessible only by foot or donkey. Haitian soldiers and peasants labored for more than a decade to produce the imposing stone structure with 130-foot walls, the largest fortress in the Western Hemisphere. With batteries holding about 200 cannons captured from the Spanish, French, and English during the war of independence, Christophe's architect, probably Etienne Barré, wanted to create an impregnable stronghold, invulnerable to French attack.

Yet Christophe's reign was not exclusively built on militarism and pomp. An ardent anglophile, Christophe recruited English and American teachers to establish schools for elite Haitian children. Through dictation, Christophe corresponded frequently with the English abolitionists William Wilberforce and Thomas Clarkson, and even with Czar Alexander of Russia.

Henry Christophe's power depended on the forced labor of the Haitian people. A series of personal tragedies weakened the tyrannical ruler in his later years, presaging his downfall. On August 25, 1818, lightning struck the powder stores of Citadelle Henry, killing 159 men including Henry's son, and destroyed the troops quarters and royal apartment. Then, on August 15, 1820, Christophe suffered a stroke while attending church. Finally, troops of the eighth regiment revolted in Saint-Marc and joining the forces of Boyer, the new president of the Haitian republic, they sought to overthrow Henry Christophe. Deserted by his personal guard, Christophe committed suicide on October 8, 1820. Haiti was reunified under Boyer as the Republic of Haiti.

Notes

1. There are several important works that address the life and legacy of Henry Christophe. Hubert Cole's *Christophe: King of Haiti* (New York: Viking, 1967) is the most detailed biography in English. David Nicholls, *From Dessalines to Duvalier: Race, Colour and National Independence in Haiti* (Cambridge: Cambridge U P, 1979) and Ralph-Michel Trouillot's chapter "The Three Faces of Sans-Souci" in his *Silencing the Past: Power and the Production of History* (Boston: Beacon Press, 1995) provide useful insight into the complicated legacy of Henry Christophe. Karen Racine, traces the oft-overlooked English influence on King Henry's reign in "Britannia's Bold Brother: British Cultural Influence in Haiti During the Reign of Henry Christophe," *Journal of Caribbean History* 33:1-2 (1999): 125-145. Aimé' Césaire's dramatic rendition of King Henry's court is a powerful portrayal of the monarch's manipulation of the symbolic realm: *The Tragedy of King Christophe*, trans. Ralph Manheim (New York: Grove Press, 1969).

2. Cole, 81.

3. Carolyn E. Fick, *The Making of Haiti: The Saint-Domingue Revolution from Below* (Knoxville: U of Tennessee P, 1990) 231.

4. Racine, 127.

Chapter 14

Charlemagne Péralte and the Cacos

Emile Césaire

Translated by Jessica Adams and Cécile Accilien

Haiti has always nurtured brave men who rebelled against slavery, against exploitation, against occupation. Thus, from Boukman, Toussaint, and Dessalines to Charlemagne Péralte, a single refrain has echoed: Freedom or death. Yet while many historians have focused on the heroes of the Revolution, few have been interested in the contributions of Péralte, a main figure in the resistance against the American Occupation (1915-1934). Here, I want to recall this often-forgotten moment in history when the poor were primary actors in the theater of war.

U.S. troops invaded the sovereign nation of Haiti in 1915 in a self-interested attempt to quell economic and political strife. Between December 1908 and July 1915, Haiti had seven presidents. Cincinnatus Leconte, who was president from August 14, 1911 to August 8, 1912, unfortunately was killed on August 8, 1912 when the National Palace exploded. Under his government, there seemed to have been some stability. Five men took over the leadership of Haiti within the next five years. When President Vilbrun Guillaume Sam was assassinated on July 28, 1915 in a popular uprising following his order to execute 167 political prisoners, the United States saw an opportunity to "help" Haiti. The effects of this occupation on Haitian society were profound. As Mary Renda writes in *Taking Haiti*,

> The marines installed a puppet president, dissolved the legislature at gunpoint, denied freedom of speech, and forced a new Constitution on the Caribbean nation—one more favor-

able to foreign investment. With the help of the marines, U.S. officials seized the customs houses, took control of Haitian finances and imposed their own standards of efficiency on the administration of Haitian debt.[1]

The marines also "reorganized and strengthened the Haitian military" and rebaptized it as La Gendarmerie. This force was "officered by marines and molded in the image of the Marine Corps."[2] The occupiers also reinstituted the corvée, the system of forced labor akin to a return to slavery.

Resistance to the occupation came first from the peasants, in the form of the Caco movement led by Charlemagne Massena Péralte.[3] Caco resistance begun toward the end of the Haitian Revolution when former slaves mounted guerilla resistance in support of Christophe and Dessalines against the French. Later, they participated in the overthrow of a series of Haitian presidents whom they felt had failed to govern effectively.[4] The Cacos of the early twentieth century who massed against the American Occupation were revolutionaries primarily from the north. Péralte himself began his career in public administration and later became an army officer. According to historian Roger Gaillard, author of *Charlemagne Péralte, le caco*, Péralte had worked with men of state including Cincinnatus Leconte, Tancrède Auguste, and Vilbrun Guillaume Sam. He demonstrated a precocious maturity in handling public affairs.[5]

Beginning in 1917, while an officer in the army, Péralte played his most important role in Haiti's history as the leader of the popular resistance to the American Occupation and indeed as a martyr to the cause of resistance. Along with others who were charged with instigating rebellion, he was arrested and sentenced to five years of forced labor. But after 11 months, on September 13, 1917, he escaped from prison in the company of the guard who had been assigned to watch him. During the night of October 15, 1918, at the head of a group of peasants, Péralte organized an attack on the town of Hinche. Located in the northern part of Haiti's Central Plateau, Péralte's native region, Hinche was one of the towns where the corvée had been reinstated.

The Marines mounted a bloody campaign against the Cacos. As Army officer Frederick Spear testified before the U.S. Senate in 1921, "All Cacos were to be killed."[6] Péralte was murdered when two marines, Herman Hanneken and William R. Button, officers in the Gendarmerie who had learned to speak Kreyòl, blackened their entire bodies with cork and led a force of 17 other officers also posing as Cacos into the rebel leader's camp.[7] Péralte had been betrayed by his own lieutenant, Jean Conzé, who had sworn allegiance to the Americans to such an extent that he declared he would put a stop to the Caco war even if it meant killing his own father. Conzé remains infamous in Haiti today; interestingly, those unsympathetic to Jean-Bertrand Aristide have referred to him as a "new Conzé."

After Duvalier fell from power in 1986, Péralte was hailed anew in Haiti as a hero, because for many the end of the Duvalier régime was considered a new independence filled with hopes and new nationalist ideologies. His image was imprinted on coins and stamps, and he was favorably compared to Dessalines.[8] His gravestone in Cap-Haïtien bears this inscription:

> Dead at thirty three years of age, betrayed like Christ,
> Exposed nude under his flag, crucified;
> As one day he had dared to promise it to us,
> And for our Nation he sacrificed himself.
> Confronting the American, and alone to shout: "Halt":
> Let's bare our heads before Charlemagne Péralte![9]

Notes

1. Mary Renda, *Taking Haiti: Military Occupation and the Culture of U.S. Imperialism, 1915-1940* (Chapel Hill: U of North Carolina P, 2001) 10.

2. Ibid., 10.

3. The Cacos were a Haitian rebel army made up primarily of peasants who fought against the U.S. occupation between 1915 and 1919. The term "Caco" refers to a native bird. They are considered by many Haitians to be a group of nationalists who resisted U.S. control and mulatto domination, although they have also been described in Haitian oral history and elsewhere as bandits.

4. Renda, 140.

5. See Roger Gaillard, *Charlemagne Péralte, le caco* (Port-au-Prince: Imprimerie le Natal, 1982) 11.

6. Quoted in Renda, 138.

7. See Renda, 171-73.

8. See George Michel, *Charlemagne Péralte and the First American Occupation of Haiti*, trans. Douglas Henry Daniels (Dubuque, IA: Kendall and Hunt Publishing, Co., 1996).

9. Composed by Christian Werleigh, quoted in *Charlemagne Péralte and the First American Occupation of Haiti*.

SECTION III

Forgotten Women of Haitian Liberty

Se yo ki manman nou, se yo ki sè nou

Pouki sa-n pa bay fanm Ayisyèn yo vale yo merite....

Fanm Ayisyèn yo, se pou-n onore yo

Fanm Ayisyèn yo, se pou-n apresye yo

They are our mothers, they are our sisters

Why don't we value Haitian women as they deserve to be valued....

Haitian women must be honored

Haitian women must be respected

—Bossa Combo

Around the world, women's participation in making history has been obliterated or forgotten all too often. Haiti is no different. For the most part, Haiti's history has been written by men and for men, and in consequence Haitian women's contributions have not been fully understood or appreciated. But Jean-Pierre consciously reclaims and pays homage to the memory and the achievements of great women in Haiti.

Anacaona, the queen who ruled the last Indian kingdom, Xaragua, is among the first women to have been historically documented as taking part in Haiti's fight for independence. However, many historians focused more on her beauty than on her strength as a leader—a leader who, although she was betrayed in the end, did much to protect her kingdom and her people. Her social, economic, and political contributions have for the most part gone unexamined. We need a new history that challenges the current representations of Haitian women as merely incidental in the evolution of Haiti as a nation. To see Anacaona represented as a major figure in Haiti's history as she is here in these paintings is to reaffirm women's role in this history—a role they have played since the moment of Columbus's invasion.

In Haiti's history there has been one woman president, Ertha P. Trouillot, who governed from March 10, 1990 to February 7, 1991. As a lawyer, she has raised the awareness of the status of women in Haitian law through her writings. In a country where education is accessible only to a privileged few, women with formal education are even fewer than men. It is thus impossible to think about the place of women in Haitian history without thinking about the intersections of gender, race, class, and language. While the majority of Haitian women today do not have the luxury of talking about feminism because they are focused on trying to survive, they live feminism in their daily struggles.

A Haitian proverb states *"fanm gen nef so pou li pran avan ke pou li leve atè a"* [women have to fall nine times before they can get up off the floor], meaning that women must get up and move on simply because they have no choice.

The marginalization of Haitian women is evident in the realm of literature, where the focus is still very much on the few "canonical" Haitian writers such as Jacques Stephen Alexis and Jacques Roumain. Writers such as Edwidge Danticat are the exception to the rule, and this is partly because Danticat writes in English and is therefore accessible to a larger audience. Reading anthologies of Francophone literature from the 19th and 20th centuries, one would think that there are hardly any Haitian women writers. Their absence is due to a combination of the lack of translation of their texts into English, the fact that their book are out of print, and the political climate.

Haitian women are politically active in organizations whose objectives are to protect the rights of women. Although historically women have not been prominent in the political realm, they have been at the forefront of the revolutions. The recent violence that has permeated Haiti has directly affected women, and they have been raped, tortured, and murdered. Yet Haitian women today are the backbone of the Haitian economy, both in Haiti where the marketplace serves as a site of both resistance and livelihood, and in the diaspora, where they work to support families remaining in Haiti.

Chapter 15

Anacaona, the Golden Flower
Cécile Accilien

I'm not surprised to get over 3,000 hits when I enter "Anacaona" into an internet search engine. After all, Queen Anacaona's great courage, grace, beauty, and charm have been recognized by the people of Haiti and the Caribbean for centuries. What seems sad and unfortunate is that as I search through the various traditional print reference guides to Haiti and the Caribbean, I find very little about this heroic queen. This discrepancy dramatizes the fact that, even as Anacaona has been acclaimed in popular culture throughout the Caribbean, official history has a marked tendency to forget her.

Anacaona was queen of the Arawak over five centuries ago. She is believed to have been born in Yaguana, the area that is known today as Léogâne. Yaguana was then the capital of Xaragua, the most populated and prosperous kingdom of Hispaniola, located in the part of the island that is now Haiti. She led Xaragua during the early days of European attempts to colonize the region. Anacaona, whose name translates as "golden flower," continues to be a source of inspiration for many people in Haiti and the Haitian diaspora, even those who do not know exactly who she was.[1]

The Haitian poet Jean Métellus pays her homage in his play *Anacaona,* describing her as: "Fleur d'Or incarne avec magnificence l'âme des Indiens de la Caraïbe, submergés puis exterminés par l'irruption sans merci des troupes de Christophe Colomb.... Anacaona laisse un message toujours actuel:

> Je suis poète plus que reine
> Car je ne désespère pas."

[The Golden Flower embodies with splendor the soul of the Caraïbe Indians, a people overcome, then exterminated, by the merciless eruption of Columbus's troops....Anacaona leaves us with a message that is still relevant today:

> I am more of a poet than a queen
> For I do not despair.][2]

The well-known Haitian singer Carole Demesmin also pays tribute to the queen in her famous song "Anacaona." There is an internet site "Ask Anacaona Anything," which is sponsored by the Caribbean Amerindian Centrelink Chatroom.[3] Here Anacaona, given voice by the site editors, answers questions regarding the aboriginal cultures and societies of Haiti and the Caribbean.

It is therefore not surprising that Ulrick Jean-Pierre has painted her as an important historical figure of the Indian period in Haiti. Even Las Casas called her "la grande dame d'Ayti."[4] Other writers, such as Emile Marcelin, describe her as extraordinary, generous, and the most beautiful woman on the island.[5] Another critic writes, "C'était une femme d'un génie beaucoup au-dessus de son sexe et de sa nation." [She was a woman of genius who transcended her gender and nation.][6] These words of praise are also critical because they describe her intelligence in a derogatory manner. Europeans were fascinated by her beauty, as is evident from the various references to her in the letters of Columbus.[7] In *Hommage à la femme noire*, Simone Schwarz-Bart recounts her physical attributes: "Une chevelure noire, plus parfumée que la nuit des tropiques encadre un visage que nul ne peut contempler sans en demeurer à jamais émerveillé.... Les proportions de son corps sont si justes et nobles que l'oeil le plus rustre ne peut se lasser d'en admirer les courbes gracieuses." [Dark hair, more perfumed than a tropical evening, frames a face that none can gaze upon without falling into a profound amazement..... Her proportions are so perfect and noble that even the most jaded eye cannot fail to admire them.][8]

Anacaona was a woman of many talents, the spiritual ancestor of great Haitian women such as Marie-Jeanne Lamartinierre, Défilée, Cécile Fatima, and Catherine Flon. She was considered a very gifted samba, or poet. In *Histoire et littérature haïtiennes: Langue et littérature des aborigènes d'Ayti*, Jean Fouchard writes:

> La reine Anacaona n'était pas seulement le premier poète de l'île; elle en formait
> encore la poésie la plus suave. Sa personne, sa vie, ses conceptions tenaient de l'en-
> chantement. Elle était inspiratrice avant d'être inspirée. On lui devait des ballades
> et des ballets; des poésies parlées et chantées, enrichies de pas chorégraphiques,
> rehaussés d'une pantomime savante. Le crédit littéraire d'Anacaona rendait
> nationaux les areytos de son invention; et tous les souverains de l'île se trouvaient

tributaires de sa chorégraphie. Reine de la langue, du cérémonial, des jeux et des plaisirs, elle avait fait adopter l'étiquette de sa Cour, mis à la mode ses parures, ses meubles, ses fleurs préférées. Son palais regorgeait d'ustensiles élégants, de coquettes frivolités, d'instruments fragiles, petits chefs-d'oeuvres de l'art indigène.

[Queen Anacaona was not only the first poet of the island; she was creating the most accomplished poetry. Everything about her, her life, her ideas and ways of doing things, are magical. She was an inspirer before she became inspired. To her we owe a number of ballads and ballets, poetry both spoken and sung, rich with movement and dance, uplifted by a learned theatricality. Anacaona's literary strengths have made her areytos [dances] national treasures. All the island's sovereigns have found themselves in tribute to her dances. Queen of language, of ceremony, of games and pleasures, she caused all to adopt the etiquette of her court, and set the fashion with her costumes, furniture, and favorite flowers. Her palace was full of elegant useful things, charming frivolities, fancy goods, and masterpieces of indigenous art.][9]

Queen Anacaona remains famous for her areytos (dances). Unfortunately no written copies exist. But it is said that there is an authentically Indian poem, known as the "Areyto of Anacaona," which is often sung by warriors to pay her homage:

Aia, bombaia, bombé
Lamma samana quana
Aia, bombaia, bombé
Lamma samana quana.[10]

We cannot be sure how old Anacaona was at the time of Columbus's arrival in Haiti. She was already married to Caonabo, the cacique of the kingdom of Magua and the most influential leader among the five caciques. Although it is commonly accepted that Anacaona was the wife of Caonabo, it is not clear whether she was his first wife, for it was common among caciques to have more than one wife. (For example Bohéchio, Anacaona's brother, is said to have had 30 wives.)

Anacaona had a daughter who became famous around 1498 because of her relationship with a Spanish officer, Fernand de Ghevara, who wished to marry her. The Spaniards did not approve of this union and the love affair eventually led to Ghevara's death. After the death of Caonabo, Anacaona ruled the Xaragua kingdom equally with Bohéchio and was considered queen. After he died, she ruled the kingdom of Xaragua alone until she was murdered by the Spanish in 1503.

Anacaona was a great leader, a graceful and peaceful person, and it was in part her love of peace that enabled the Spanish to deceive and eventually to kill her. Nicolas de Ovando, the governor of Hispaniola, meticulously planned his betrayal, first announcing that he would be making a friendly visit to her kingdom in Léogâne to pay homage. Although by 1503 and after years of war with the Spanish Anacaona did not trust him, because she deeply wanted peace she chose to give Ovando the benefit of the doubt. She welcomed him into her home, decorated the streets with flowers and palm trees, and invited dancers to honor him and his troops. The feast lasted for several days. At the conclusion of the visit, Ovando invited Anacaona to the territory he had captured in order to thank her and, he said, to sign a peace treaty. He asked her, furthermore, to bring all the other caciques to the gathering, a request with which she complied. They went together to Ovando's kingdom, dressed in royal attire. Ovando had a special room made ready for their party. But he had also prepared his troops for a surprise attack. He had arranged a signal with one of his captains, and when the captain touched his cross, one of the worst known massacres in Xaragua's history began. Not expecting violence, the Indians were unarmed, and most were killed. Xaragua was completely burned along with 84 other caciquats. Anacaona was imprisoned and taken to Santo Domingo where after a "trial," she was burned alive in the middle of the public square. With her death, the kingdom disintegrated.

Queen Anacaona's artistic spirit and the cultural tradition she engendered remain in the artistic expression and creativity of Haiti. The residents of Léogâne proudly claim her as their queen and inspirational leader. Her name stands as a symbol of beauty and as proof that women have always participated in Haiti's struggles of liberation.

Notes

1. For information on other writers inspired by Anacaona, see "Dit de la fleur d'or" in *Romancéro aux étoiles*, Jacques Stephen Alexis (Paris: Nathan, 1978); *La reine Anacaona*, Emile Marcelin (Port-au-Prince: A. Damour, 1980); *Anacaona, reine martyre: tragédie en 3 actes*, St. Arnaud Numa (Port-au-Prince: Editions Fardin, 1981); and *Anacaona y las tormentas*, Luis Dario Bernal (Mexico: Fondo de Cultural Economica, 1994), for example.

2. See Jean Métellus, *Anacaona* (Paris: Editions Hatier) 95, (Acte III, scène 2). My translation.

3. See <http://www.Centrelink.org> (c2005).

4. See Jean Fouchard, *Langue et littérature des aborigènes d'Ayiti* (Paris: Editions de l'Ecole, 1972) 131.

5. For more information, see Herman Corvington, *Deux caciques du Xaragua: Bohéchio et Anacaona* (Haiti: Librairie Samuel Devieux, 1954).

6. Fouchard, 138.

7. In *Hispaniola: Caribbean Chiefdoms in the Age of Columbus*, Samuel M. Wilson notes the following reference by Las Casas concerning the beauty of the Xaraguan women: "As for the young girls, they covered no part of their bodies, but wore their hair loose upon their shoulders and a narrow ribbon tied around the forehead. Their face, breasts, hands, and the entire body was quite naked, and of a somewhat brunette tint"(121).

8. See Simone Schwarz-Bart, *Hommage à la femme noire* (Paris: Editions Consulaires, 1989) 12.

9. Quoted in Fouchard 138-139. My translation.

10. Critics have speculated about the meaning of the song and its origin, but have been unable to draw definite conclusions. For more information see Fouchard, 140-141.

Chapter 16

Heroine Maroon Slave

Catherine A. Reinhardt

Resistance to slavery was a pervasive phenomenon in the world of Caribbean plantations. Fugitive slaves and maroons had existed since 1503, when the first black slaves brought to Hispaniola from Spain in 1499 began to revolt and were joined by the Indians.[1] The struggles of women and men against the institution of slavery were complementary.[2] However, since few women engaged in marronnage (running away from the plantation to join a maroon band in the forests), women's roles in resisting slavery have historically been marginalized. Women were often believed to have less desire for liberty or to prefer the protection of the master to the uncertainties of life in the forests.[3] But this point of view disregards the importance of other forms of resistance in destabilizing the plantation regime and fails to recognize the vital role women played in slave uprisings throughout the Caribbean.

Although the runaway slaves and maroon bands were the most subversive forms of slave resistance, some other frequent and effective acts of resistance were suicide, arson, poisoning, and large gatherings of slaves. Women were particularly notorious for using these forms of resistance to cause disorder on the plantations. They were far more troublesome than men and their insubordination frustrated the masters.[4] Women engaged more frequently in verbal or physical confrontations with whites.[5] African women were also more apt to commit suicide upon arrival on the plantation than men, believing they would return to their homeland after death.[6] Both women and men took revenge by poisoning the master and his family and farm animals, as well as fellow slaves on the plantation. Planters dreaded the ravages of arson and poisoning on their properties and the French king specifically legislated against such acts in December 1746.[7] Because women often worked as domestic slaves for their masters and mistresses, they were in a uniquely favorable position to poison the food and drink they served.[8]

Slave gatherings were especially threatening to plantation order because they were the focal point from which other forms of resistance, particularly marronnage, originated. During such gatherings slaves might conduct African ceremonies, plot poisonings, arson, or other revolts, or even plan to leave the plantation to found maroon communities. Women often played a fundamental role during such gatherings as leaders of ritual ceremonies. A well-known example is the legendary Vodou ceremony of Bois Caïman, held near Morne Rouge in Saint-Domingue on August 14, 1791, which sealed the slave conspiracy to revolt.[9] Although there is no clear historical evidence, it is believed that Cécile Fatima, a Vodou priestess or manbo, participated in the ceremony. She was a mulatto, daughter of an African woman and a Corsican prince.[10] Another legendary female was Cormantine Cubah, who played an important role as queen in the last African-led uprising in Jamaica in 1760.[11] Obeah priests and priestesses in general inspired slaves to engage in rebellions in Jamaica. They used magic, poison, and herbs in secret ways that were directly African in origin. Traditional African religious practice was fundamental to rebellion as it unified the slaves both spiritually and physically during gatherings.[12]

Marronnage took two common forms in the Caribbean. Fugitive or runaway slaves who fled from their plantations for a few days and remained close to their master's property, stealing food or exchanging fish, game and stolen objects for manioc and vegetables were said to engage in petit marronnage.[13] This type of marronnage did not concern the planters much and runaways had a good chance of being pardoned if they returned within two to four weeks.[14] They might return around the time of a big celebration, such as Christmas or the New Year, and enlist the help of a "protector"— the oldest woman in the master's family, the parish priest, or even a neighbor—to plead their cause. Generally they were not denied a pardon and received only mild punishment.[15] Far fewer women ran away than men, probably because their children rendered them much less mobile than their male counterparts.[16] Women who did run away individually generally left for the city. They sought the support of free black friends who hid them, hired them, or helped them find work.[17]

Grand marronnage, defined as "flight from the plantation with no intention of ever returning,"[18] led to the formation of maroon bands and even communities in the mountain regions of the islands. Female maroons represented approximately one-fifth of the maroon population.[19] Because it was difficult for women to flee from plantations with their children, many were kidnapped when maroons raided the plantations for food, farm animals, tools, and arms. However, women and their children did also joined maroon settlements.[20] This meant that the maroon communities could perpetuate themselves.[21] Through pillaging and regular raids on plantations, maroons were able to procure food as well as tools and arms for survival in the wilderness. Women were indispensable for the sustenance of maroon communities as they largely took over the cultivation of the land.[22]

Maroon bands were headed by a leader and rarely comprised more than 100 members. Groups communicated with one another across the distance using conch shells and African drums. The devastating effects maroon communities had on the smooth functioning of plantations throughout the Caribbean, and the magnetic attraction they had for other slaves made these bands a prime target of the mounted police, the militia, and even the army. Only a few groups were eventually captured and punished.[23] In the 1700s in Jamaica and Suriname, full-scale maroon wars forced colonial authorities to negotiate treaties with maroon bands demanding liberty for all their members and the right to continue as autonomous and independent communities. In return, they agreed to hunt down and turn in would-be maroons in exchange for payment or arms.[24] French authorities were almost driven to the same extremity in Saint-Domingue when the maroon community of Le Maniel, which had survived a century of pursuits, could not be dislodged from valuable territory the French wanted to settle.[25]

Women were vital to armed revolts by transporting weapons, ammunition, food, and supplies, and by carrying messages and taking care of the injured. Their chants spurred on the male fighters and kept spirits high.[26] The mûlatresse Solitude, a mixed-race slave woman, exemplified the women's courage by fighting against the reinstatement of slavery in Guadeloupe in 1802, even though she was pregnant. She was tortured to death after giving birth.[27] The most famous maroon heroine is the Jamaican obeah Nanny, whose name was given to two maroon settlements. The spiritual leader of Jamaica's First Maroon Wars in 1739, Nanny also had considerable political influence and was an important tactician during the signing of the treaty with the British that settled the wars.[28]

Historically marginalized, women were fundamental in the resistance against slavery and the preservation of African spiritual and cultural beliefs. Although less active than men in certain aspects of resistance, they evidenced their rejection of the slave regime and their desire for freedom in ways that made them vital to rebellion in general and maroon communities in particular. By depicting a maroon woman in the foreground of his painting, Ulrick Jean-Pierre draws attention to women's fundamental yet neglected roles as rebels. With her broken chains hanging from her wrists, a brandished machete in her left hand and a shotgun in her right, Jean-Pierre's fighting maroon woman speaks for all those whose voices have been obliterated during the past three centuries. As she takes the center stage in the painting, her cry for freedom resounds loudly through the tormented history of her people.

Notes

1. Jean Fouchard, *Les marrons de la liberté* (Paris: Editions de l'Ecole, 1972) 450-51.

2. Bernard Moitt, *Women and Slavery in the French Antilles, 1635-1848* (Bloomington: Indiana U P, 2001) 125.

3. Arlette Gautier, *Les soeurs de la Solitude: la condition féminine dans l'esclavage aux Antilles du XVIIe au XIXe siècle* (Paris: Editions Caribéennes, 1985) 232-238.

4. Barbara Bush, *Slave Women in Caribbean Society, 1650-1838* (Kingston: Ian Randle, 1990) 53-61.

5. Gautier, 223.

6. Ibid., 221-222.

7. "We prohibit…all slaves from either sex to make or distribute any remedy…and to undertake the healing of any illness, with the exception of snake bites. Offenders will be subject to corporal punishment and even the death sentence depending on the case" (Archives Nationales de France 27 AP 11, Dossier 3).

8. Moitt, 142-143.

9. Gautier, 241-242.

10. Carolyn E. Fick, *The Making of Haiti: The Saint-Domingue Revolution from Below* (Knoxville: U of Tennessee P, 1990) 94-95, 264-266.

11. Bush, 72-73.

12. Ibid., 74.

13. Gabriel Debien, "Marronage in the French Caribbean," in *Maroon Societies: Rebel Slave Communities in the Americas*, ed. Richard Price (Baltimore: Johns Hopkins U P, 1979) 111.

14. Yvan Debbash, "Le marronnage: Essai sur la désertion de l'esclavage antillais," *Année Sociologique* 3rd ser. (1961): 84.

15. Debien, "Marronage in the French Caribbean," 117-18.

16. Bush, 63; Gautier, 229; Moitt, 133.

17. Gautier, 230.

18. Debien, "Marronnage in the French Caribbean," 108.

19. Pierre Pluchon, *Histoire des Antilles et de la Guyane* (Paris: Privat, 1982) 156.

20. Bush, 71.

21. Gautier, 232-33.

22. Bush, 71.

23. Debien, "Marronage in the French Caribbean," 107-9.

24. Debbash, "Le marronnage" (1962) 188.

25. Debbash, "Le Maniel: Further Notes," in *Maroon Societies: Rebel Slave Communities in the Americas*, 145.

26. Moitt, 128.

27. Gautier, 251.

28. Bush, 67-70.

Chapter 17

Marie-Jeanne Lamartinierre

Margaret Mitchell Armand

In the silence of Ulrick Jean-Pierre's studio, I suddenly hear drumbeats accompanying songs of struggles and prayers to the Haitian gods.[1] Ulrick sits in a comfortable chair covered with red satin brocade and goes into a deep meditation. He fills his breath and soul with the messages of his ancestors. Only then, with a steady movement, does he pick up a brown sable brush, and with soft and precise strokes he writes Haitian history on canvas. He has chosen a palette of warm colors mixed with precision that brings life to his subjects. He paints stories of centuries of struggle and triumph in the life of Haitian people, stories that are ever present in the life of Haitian people, and stories of centuries of enslavement and murder of our Arawak and African ancestors. Ulrick Jean-Pierre is our own. His art speaks; our voice is no longer silenced. In this essay, I will recount a story of Marie-Jeanne Lamartinierre: May this be yet another testament to her tremendous struggle, a struggle that we continue today in our life, in her name.[2]

Marie-Jeanne is a woman fighting on the side of enslaved men in the fort of Crête-à-Pierrot, in the northwest part of Haiti. A fierce battle rages in the background and, armed with bayonets and other weapons, enslaved men are fighting desperately for their lives. A wounded man lying on the ground with an agonizing look seeks her help. She looks out at the enemy, trying to help him. She wears a long white floating dress with a white sash tightly wrapped around her waist. She is a mulatto woman fighting on the side of the enslaved to secure the independence of Haiti. That was 1802. This image emerges in my research:

In the midst of the inferno…a young mulatto wearing a red bonnet, saber at her side, her waist knotted with a scarf and rifle in her hand, circling fearlessly within range on the walls of the redoubt shouting encouragement to the besieged. She was Marie-Jeanne Lamartinierre, wife of Brigade Commander Lamartinierre.[3]

It is rumored that after the murder of your husband, Marie-Jeanne, you became the lover of General Dessalines, hero of Independence in 1804.[4] Perhaps your beauty, your strength, your courage and determination bewitched him.[5] However, the essence of your personal life remains unknown.

Who are you, Marie-Jeanne Lamartinierre? I humbly state that you were raised on a slave plantation owned by white French colonizers. You may have been born from the rape of an enslaved African woman by her white master, or from a union forged as a form of survival. Like some free women of color at that time, you may have had Taino blood.[6] You were privileged to receive some formal education. Passages in history have portrayed you as a nurse or a healer. You learned about African culture, religion, and worldview, the secret knowledge of the ancestors, from teachers of Vodou.[7] This knowledge would have armed you with courage and strength for the fearless fight at La Crête-à-Pierrot. And Ezili—the spirit of love, healing, and courage—perhaps she gave you her strength.

> Ezili
> You have always been there
> In the darkness of the night
> To give strength to my soul
> To give light to my thoughts
> My body trembles from the pain of life
> You wake me and I feel your love
> You travel from far yet you are near
> Africa, Ayiti, Ginen
> I am here You are there
> We are both here and there
> To reclaim what is lost
> I scream your name
> I feel your power
> Ezili, Mother of us all.[8]

Marie-Jeanne, that day at Crête-à-Pierrot, were you a manbo possessed by Ogou, the spirit of courage, strength, power, and defense? Your red scarf holds back your long black hair, your sword is in your hand. The soldier lying at your feet shouts:

Ogou, I am wounded, Ogou Papa
I am wounded, Ogou Papa
I cannot see, my blood is red
I am wounded, Papa Ogou.[9]

With the blood of Ogou and his spirit possessing your soul, you lift this man from the ground, carry him toward a safe place, and after you have healed his wounds, you give him your rifle to finish the battle.

Since these moments at Crête-à-Pierrot, we Haitians have known violence through poverty, constant persecution of the Vodou religion and traditional ways, alienation from the outside world and dehumanization in our own, and economic and class divisions. Our natural resources have enriched foreign countries and covered their cathedrals with gold. Our human resources have helped build foreign lands. We repeat the structural violence of our colonizer in our own political system and with each other. We have been subject to the Napoleonic Code, and to cultural and economic dependency on the United States.[10]

Haitian women were the personal property of their husbands until 1979. Some of us only obtained the right to vote in 1950. Common-law marriages left us with children and no economic advantages. Most devastating for us in Haiti was the miseducation of our children. Their formal education was taken over by those with an agenda that promoted their own economic power. Some of us, still blinded by oppression, admired the enslavement of our children's minds. This miseducation became a new instrument for perpetuating the legacy of slavery, colonization, hate, mistrust, division, and misunderstanding that continues to haunt Haitians.

Have we been blinded by the false hope of independence? Not all of us. You live again in many of us, Marie-Jeanne, and the spirit of Ogou is a constant reminder of your past and our present struggle. We have stayed vigilant.

Ogou
Horseman of the night
Companion of the day
Brandishing your sword
Looking for your children

They are hurt
They are drowned
They suffer silently
They are fooled
They have traveled to far away places
But you Ogou, slowly
You find them one by one
Give them the sword
Of Victory.[11]

Many of us continue to honor and respect the true message of independence through our national heritage, learned through the stories passed down from our ancestors. Your story, Marie-Jeanne Lamartinierre, has remained stronger than ever. It has survived.

Marie-Jeanne, heroine of Haiti, you represent the ongoing struggle of every Haitian woman. You crossed religious, class, color, and economic divides. You stood firm at the battle of La Crête-à-Pierrot, setting an example that men and women alike might follow. Haitians are working to regain control of our lives, traditions, resources, and homeland, the Republic of Haiti, "the Land that is ours."[12] This was your dream, Marie-Jeanne Lamartinierre, that bloody day at La Crête-à-Pierrot.

Notes

1. I had the honor of visiting the home of Ulrick Jean-Pierre in New Orleans, where we spent hours talking. I saw for myself the great passion he has for his work. I watched him paint, and learned much from him. He granted me permission to record some of that experience.

2. Much of the information that helped to shape this essay comes from my 2004 interview with Bayyinah Bello, founder of Fondation Claire Heureuse Félicité Bonheur.

3. This statement is found in a document located and published by the Fondation Claire Heureuse Félicité Bonheur located in Port-au-Prince, Haiti. In *The Black Jacobins: Toussaint L'Ouverture and the San Domingo Revolution, 2nd ed.* (New York: Vintage, 1963), C.L.R. James asserts that Marie-Jeanne Lamartinierre was married to the Haitian officer Lamartinierre (315). See also Thomas Madiou, *Histoire d'Haïti, Tome II (1979-1803)*, (Port-au-Prince: Editions Henry Deschamps, 1989) 273.

4. See *Haitian Women in History* (Paris: UNESCO, 1988).

5. This is according to Haitian oral history.

6. According to notarized documents from this period of Haitian history (late eighteenth and early nineteenth centuries), some free women of color were partly descended from pre-Columbian people.

7. Interview with Bayyinah Bello, founder of Fondation Claire Heureuse Félicité Bonheur (2004).

8. This poem, "Ezili," is by Margaret Mitchell Armand.

9. This version of the song of Ogou is from traditional Vodou songs of Haiti.

10. See, for example, Robert I. Rotberg with Christopher K. Clague, *Haiti: The Politics of Squalor* (Boston: Houghton Mifflin, 1971) and Mimi Sheller, *Democracy after Slavery: Black Publics and Peasant Radicalism in Haiti and Jamaica* (Gainesville: U P of Florida, 2000).

11. "Ogou" is by Margaret Mitchell Armand.

12. See Max Beauvoir, "Ayiti Toma or the name of The Republic of Haiti," <www.Vodou.org> (c2001).

Chapter 18

Catherine Flon and the Creation of the Haitian Flag

Elmide Méléance

Dessalines requested that Catherine Flon sew the first flag of the Haitian nation. As a result, Flon herself became a symbol of union for Haïti. Her birthplace of Arcahaie, where she made the flag, is considered a historic city; it is called "flag city" or "flag town." The flag was officially recognized on January 1, 1804, and the date on which Flon sewed the first flag, May 18, 1803, became a national holiday.

Haitian women continue to use Flon as a reference point. Today, an increasing number of events start at places named after, or statues of, Flon, including protests against abuses of women, demands by women for the rights of their children, and just simple gatherings. Haitian women's growing interest in Catherine Flon is also reflected in popular youth festivities. Young women dress as Flon and other Haitian heroines, as reminders of their contributions—and by extension, the importance of Haitian women to the health of the nation as a whole.

In 1805, after Dessalines became emperor, he replaced the blue in the flag with black. Dessalines did not arbitrarily choose the flag colors; as a houngan initiated by the manbo Gran' Guiton in Arcahaie, he was likely influenced by his knowledge of the spirit in doing something as important as selecting the colors to represent Haiti. After his death in October, 1806, the country was divided, and his successor as emperor, Henry Christophe, decided to keep the red and black flag in the north, while President Alexandre Pétion in the south reverted to the original colors of blue and red. The motto that Dessalines had chosen was quickly removed by Pétion and replaced with his new motto, "L'Union fait la Force" (In Unity there is Strength), in 1806. This inscription has remained, although the flag has changed.[1]

From 1806 to 1964, a blue and red flag was used with white in the center; this particular flag is described in the Constitution of 1843. In addition, a black and red flag was used in the northern area during the administration of Henri I, from 1811-1820; this flag was simultaneously used in the eastern area. A major change was made in the flag in the years 1964 to 1986. Under François Duvalier, the coat of arms of the Republic was placed in the center of the red and black flag. Like Dessalines, Duvalier wanted to acknowledge the roots of Haitian culture by "committing to the proposition that Haiti should wipe away its French veneer and proudly acknowledge its African origins."[2] He also adopted a different flag with red and black, two colors that are used by Vodou practioners for various purposes. Red is sometimes used to keep away evil spirits, and as previously referenced, it is also a representation of Ogu, a warrior. As for Duvalier, he may have used red and black both as an allegiance to Vodou and as an affirmation of his dislike for Western cultures. It was not until 1986 that Dessalines's original flag, sometimes called the "Flag of Independence," was reinstated.

In *Voodoo in Haiti*, Alfred Métraux emphasizes both the importance of flags in the Vodou religion and what the colors represent. Flags play a vital role in Vodou just as the cross does in the Catholic church. As Métraux describes the importance of color in Vodou, one can see the parallel that exists between the colors of the vodou flags and those of Haiti's national flag. He describes this aspect, stating that the flags are usually "made of silk or velvet fringed with gilt and covered with glittering spangles," and are identified with a specific *lwa*.[3] Some of the colors attributed to the *lwa* are also part of the history of the national flag. The color red symbolizes the *lwa* Ogu, a "warrior god"; Agwé and Damballah favor white; Guédé prefers black, while Loco embraces white and red.[4]

"La Dessalinienne," the national anthem, written by Justin Lhérisson with music by Nicolas Geffrard, is sung daily in Haitian schools as a reminder of Revolutionary battles, heroes, and heroines.[5] The fifth stanza describes Dessalines's belief that the new flag was crucial to national pride and unity:

Pour le Drapeau, pour la Patrie
Mourir est beau, mourir est beau
Notre passé nous crie:
Ayez l'âme aguerrie
Mourir est beau, mourir est beau

Pour le Drapeau, pour la Patrie

Mourir, mourir, mourir est beau

Pour le Drapeau, pour la Patrie

This can be translated as follows:

For flag on high

For Native land

'Tis fine to die.

Our traditions demand

Be ready, heart and hand,

'Tis fine to die, 'tis fine to die

For flag on high,

For Native land.[6]

Although history may reference blue, red, and white as representations of the colonizers and the people who became united, each of these colors also represents important symbols of each *lwa* in Vodou. The flag underwent changes by different administrations, and though each leader's choice of colors might have been subconscious, the association with the Vodou flags remains evident.

Flon, the woman who helped create the flag, is a symbol of Haiti's pride and fight for sovereignty, but she has just begun to receive proper recognition in Haiti. In 1988, the Haitian government released a 10-gourde note depicting Flon sewing the Haitian flag. On May 18, 2000, a group of women from the organization CONAP (Coordination Nationale de Plaidoyer pour les Droits des Femmes) created the "Place Catherine Flon" as part of the Place des Héros de l'Indépendance on the Champ-de-Mars in Port-au-Prince. This memorial was officially recognized by the Haitian government in May, 2004, thus making Catherine Flon the first woman in a formerly all-male canon of national heroes.

Notes

1. For more information on the history of the Haitian flag. see Henock Trouillot, "Le drapeau bleu et rouge, une mystification historique," *Revue Société Haïtienne d'Histoire et de Géographie* 30:104, janv.-avril 1958, 7-28. Trouillot argues that the original flag was black and red, symbolizing a bond between blacks and mulattos, instead of blue and red, with the white removed from the French tricolor.

2. Robert and Nancy Heinl describe the different ways Duvalier embraced the Vodou religion. See *Written In Blood: The Story of the Haitian People, 1492-1995, 2nd ed. rev.* (Lanham, MD: U P of America, 1996) 562.

3. Alfred Métraux accurately describes the type of materials used to make the Vodou flags. See *Voodoo in Haiti*, trans. Hugo Charteris (New York: Schocken Books, 1972) 160.

4. Métraux also describes the function of each *lwa* as well as the colors with which it is associated. See 92, 161. Additionally, in *The Vodou Quantum Leap: Alternate Realities, Power and Mysticism* (St. Paul, MN: Lewellyn Publications, 2000), Reginald Crosley points out the different uses of certain colors by Vodou practitioners. See 227.

5. For more information on "La Dessalinienne" and how it was chosen as the national anthem over another song,   "L'Artibonitienne," consult Haiti Reference at <http://www.haiti-reference.com/histoire/symboles/hymne.html>. See also Marc Péan, *Vingt-cinq ans de vie capoise: Tome III: La ville éclatée (Décembre 1902-Juillet 1915)* (Port-au-Prince: Imprimeur II, 1993) 18.

6.. This translated version of the national anthem can be found at the Embassy of the Republic of Haiti's website, <http://www.haiti.org/general_information/nationalanthem.htm.>.

SECTION IV

Legacies of Vodou

Se moun ki pran kou ki pare kou

Those who have been hurt remember to be on their guard

Nanpwen lapriyè ki pa gen "Amen"

There are no prayers that go unanswered

Moun ou konen lajounen, ou pa bezwen chandel pou rekonet li nan nuit

When you know someone in the daytime, you do not need a candle to recognize him or her at night

—Haitian proverbs

Most historians agree that the Haitian Revolution began on August 14, 1791, with a Vodou ceremony in a place known as Bois Caïman, near Cap-Haïtien. Here, a *mabi* tree (a common tree with thorns, sometimes used for medicinal purposes) grows, perhaps the one under which the slaves gathered in 1791. A plaque in Creole memorializes Boukman's famous words inspiring the slaves to take up arms against the colonizers. Every year, Vodou ceremonies take place here to commemorate what has come to be called the Ceremony of Bois Caïman. Although local people disagree as to whether this mabi tree is the same one under which the ceremony took place in 1791, most regard the area as sacred.

In *Haiti, History and the Gods*, Joan Dayan notes that historian David Geggus locates the first written account of the ceremony in white writer Antoine Dalmas' *Histoire de la Révolution de Saint-Domingue*, published in 1814. Dayan suggests that the event might actually have been imagined by Dalmas out of a desire to represent the origins of this revolution, and by extension the revolution itself, as a sensational, bloody, "primitive" scene. Ultimately, however, as Dayan herself points out, it is irrelevant whether the ceremony at Bois Caïman was an imagined or actual event; Dalmas' aspirations, if indeed they are at the root of the legend, were not fulfilled. Instead, generations of Haitians claim this ceremony as a crucial moment not of shame and degradation, but of pride and unification.

The Haitian government reached a crucial cultural and historical milestone when it announced on April 5, 2003 that Vodou would be officially recognized as a religion and that chiefs and temple officials have the same rights as Christian priests and ministers. For centuries, Vodou has been used to stigmatize many Haitians both at home and abroad, and thousands of Vodou practitioners have been killed and persecuted. Now, Haitians no longer have to choose between Vodou and Catholicism or Protestantism. In Louisiana, where Vodou practice was influenced by those fleeing the Haitian Revolution, it has also been frequently misunderstood, but as the following pages reveal, it has also been nurtured and celebrated as the life-affirming force that it is.

Chapter 19

The Ceremony of Bois Caïman

Marc A. Christophe

Ulrick Jean-Pierre is famous for his vivid vision of Haiti's historical past, as well as for the energy that emanates from his works. A realist painter whose art is wrapped in romantic fervor, Jean-Pierre has attempted to recreate for over 20 years the landmark moments in the history of his country. His suite of paintings of the heroes of the Haitian revolution of 1804 has consecrated him as a master of the historical genre and as an artist in touch with his national identity and his emotional self. In observing Jean-Pierre's tribute to Haiti's historical past, we can compare him to a time traveler, unafraid of diving into the abyss of history to establish connections between Haiti's past and its present.

Unfortunately, due to the violence that engulfed the French colony of Saint-Domingue in the eighteenth century, few illustrations, etchings, stamps, or lithographs from the period currently exist. Those artifacts that did survive are hidden away in colonial libraries in Spain, England, and France, and are not known to the general public. In that respect, Jean-Pierre's series of historical paintings of colonial Saint-Domingue and its war of independence plays an educational and informative role in bringing to the fore a visual representation of Haiti's struggle for independence.

Although constructed around what can be considered a realistic narrative of events, Jean-Pierre's painting "Cérémonie du Bois Caïman" is nevertheless filled with mysticism and a sense of grandeur not found in the works of other Haitian historical painters. What is most striking is the tension between the sacred violence that permeates the work and grants it energy, and its subtext of epiphanic vision, of intense communion with the *lwa* that crossed the Atlantic Ocean with the enslaved Africans on their fateful journey to the New World.

"Cérémonie du Bois Caïman I" is based on an important event in Haitian history.[1] On the night of August 14, 1791, the enslaved Africans who had toiled for years on the coffee, sugar cane, and tobacco plantations established by the French in the northern part of the French colony of Saint-Domingue met at a place called Bois Caïman. At that meeting, the assembled slaves took a blood oath and swore to revolt against the white planters and break the chains of slavery.

This was not the first time the enslaved Africans of Saint-Domingue had revolted. In 1757, the slave François Makandal had fired the imagination of his fellow slaves and promised to lead them to freedom. Unfortunately, after years of harassing the French, he was captured and burned at the stake in Cap-Haïtien. Makandal was a houngan, a Vodou priest, a man who could speak with the African spirits, as was Boukman Dutty, the leader of the meeting at Bois Caïman. At Bois Caïman, Boukman celebrated a Vodou ceremony during which he called on the *lwa* to come and join the rebelling slaves, to bless their cause, and to march with them in combat.

The night of August 14, 1791, was dark and tempestuous—the wind was wailing through the gigantic trees of Bois Caïman and heavy drops of rain were falling from a dark and cloudy sky on the ragged leaves of the trees, on the group of men dancing slowly to the sounds of Vodou drum beats, on Boukman in the center, dancing slowly in the rain with the African Gods. And then Boukman spoke. He spoke of the whites living in luxury in the big houses on the plantations; he spoke of the blacks tilling the soil day in and day out with no rest. He spoke of freedom, of Africa, of the land they had left behind, of how the Africans should rise up against the whites to regain their freedom. And as Boukman was speaking, it became evident to the slaves that Boukman the houngan was in communion with the *lwa*, that the *lwa* were speaking through him.

And now Boukman's voice was rising above the crowd around him, above the branches shaking in the rain. As the wind began to howl stronger during the night, Boukman's voice grew stronger than the wind, and they could hear his words crackling with emotion, as if each word were a brazier, a ball of fire setting the night sky ablaze. Said Boukman:

"God who made the sun that shines upon us, who causes the sea to rise, the thunder to roar, do you hear me, all of you? Hidden in the clouds, God witnesses the atrocities the whites commit against you. The God of the whites sanctions their crimes and does not care about us. But God, who is so good, orders us to avenge ourselves. He will direct our arms and stand beside us. Destroy the image of the white man's God who is thirsty for our tears, listen to the voice of freedom rising in your heart."[2]

By positing his concept of God against the one espoused by the whites, Boukman drew a dialectical opposition between two belief systems, one dominated by an omniscient and protective God who watched over the Africans, and another one ruled by the evil God of the whites who condoned their crimes. In so doing, the rebel chief wanted to affirm the slaves' resolve and strengthen their belief that the "good God" supported their cause.

The next morning, all the plantations in Haiti's northern plain were on fire. Enslaved Africans started the revolution that would eventually chase the French army from Haiti and lead to General Dessalines proclaiming the creation of the independent Republic of Haiti on January 1, 1804.

The Bois Caïman blood pact is considered by Haitian historians and researchers to be the most decisive and significant moment in the fight for Haiti's independence.[3] Over the years, this ceremony has taken on almost cosmic proportions in the collective memory of Haitians, who view it as the mythical moment of the beginning of their nation, when their ancestors declared their right to live as free people. In the ensuing years the ceremony at Bois Caïman has fired the imaginations of writers, poets, musicians, and painters, who have found in it the drama that often lies at the heart of great works of art.

Although Jean-Pierre follows a long line of artists attracted by the tropes of the event that took place at Bois Caïman, his interpretation of that historical moment is at once exceptional and innovative. What differentiates Jean-Pierre's interpretation of the Bois Caïman ceremony from, say, André Normil's and Dieudonné Cédor's paintings of the subject are the allegorical and metaphysical notations that Jean-Pierre has added to his painting, as well as the immanent presence that he has granted to the two central characters: Fatima, the manbo, and Boukman.

Boukman, with a machete in his left hand and the sacred rattle in his right hand, dances evocatively to the gods. Fatima has a dagger in her left hand and a torch in her right hand and appears as a glorious representation of Liberty, not unlike Athena, the Greek goddess of war. Thus by granting equal importance to the manbo, Jean-Pierre knowingly embraces new research in Haitian history. Indeed, after being downgraded to a supporting role, Fatima is being slowly exhumed from history's *oubliettes*. By visually rearranging the position and actions of the main characters at the ceremony, Jean-Pierre has also rearranged the narrative to grant a more participatory role to Fatima and, by extension, to all the women who participated equally with men in Haiti's war of independence.

But what is most striking in this image is that, in spite of the drum beating, the singing and the dancing Boukman, Fatima, the drummers, the lanbi (conch) player, and all the other conspirators have their eyes shut, or turned inward, as if gazing upon a vision. Even Fatima's eyes are closed as she advances gingerly, lost in a mystical contemplation. Boukman's eyes too are closed while dancing to the beat of the drums, and Jean-Pierre's imagination has caught him turned inward, in a state of trance.

Indeed, strong mystical vibrations radiate from the painting and to us it represents a moment when connection is established between the human and the divine, and the latter bestows on the former all grace and benediction. Jean-Pierre seems to tell us that he believes that such protection was granted to the Africans in Haiti in their struggle against colonial France, and legend has it that the African warriors were protected by their *lwa* in their fight against the French, and when in combat, some would laugh at the guns pointed at their chests, while others would try to catch the bullets fired at them with their handkerchiefs.[4]

As we contemplate the power emanating from the painting, we can hear the Vodou drums pulsating in the night and the mournful songs of the slaves imploring the African spirits to come and help them in combat. Their angry voices explode in the night sky and roll like a rising sea of anger about to engulf Saint-Domingue, France's richest colony. Our eyes closed, we relive this moment, and like Boukman and Fatima communing with the African spirits, we too commune and feel this celebration of life, war, and liberation.

Notes

1. There are several works on Haitian history that describe this important ceremony, among them Patrick Bellegarde-Smith, *Haiti, the Breached Citadel* (Boulder, CO: Westview Press, 1990) and C.L.R. James, *The Black Jacobins: Toussaint L'Ouverture and the San Domingo Revolution*, 2nd edition (New York: Vintage, 1963).

2. Victor Schoelcher, *Vie de Toussaint Louverture* (Paris: Editions Karthala, 1982) 84.

3. In *Ainsi parla l'oncle*, Jean Price Mars elaborated extensively on the seminal influence that Vodou played in the development of Haitian art, music and literature. See Jean Price Mars, *So Spoke the Uncle*, trans. and intro. Magdaline W. Shannon (Three Continents Press, Washington, DC, 1983) 179-183.

4. In his study of the life of Toussaint Louverture, Stephen Alexis documents the African maroon's fearlessness in battle. See *Black Liberator, The Life of Toussaint Louverture* (London: Ernest Benn Ltd., 1949) 27-28.

Chapter 20

Slavery, Boukman, and Independence

Max Beauvoir

It is freely admitted that the economic importance of the colony of Saint-Domingue for France in the eighteenth century was greater than what that country drew from all of its later African colonies. Of course, in the process of colonization, some Haitians certainly developed, consciously or unconsciously, a so-called slave mentality, the pressures of acculturation having been so enormous. This state of mind could have been seen then, and may still be observed today, in some of the behavior and demeanor of their progeny, who adopted what W.E.B. Du Bois termed a "fractured or split identity." Having largely converted to one of the many adapted European Christian faiths, a purely psychological instrument put together to support European civilization and economic greed, these Haitians keep repeating that Vodou is the great evil of the Haitian people, a source of the economic underdevelopment of the population, and a religion that needs to be actively fought against just as they were taught centuries ago by the missionaries who imported a little cooking oil and a few bags of wheat in order to conquer their souls.

However, the overwhelming majority of Haitians never accepted the condition of slavery. It may seem strange, but at the same time how tremendously wonderful, to realize that words such as "slave" and "slavery" are not found in any of the many Vodou songs and prayers. Nor are they encountered in tales, proverbs, maxims, dictums, adages, or charades.

The slave rebellion of 1791 succeeded in getting rid of the colonial slave system in Saint-Domingue once and for all. "Down with slavery—Liberty or Death—cut heads and burn down the houses. The day has finally arrived!" Such words were heard throughout the island in those days.

Launched on August 14th, the upheaval culminated a long, drawn-out understanding among the black leaders, generating finally what became a true and total war, the War of Independence.

Boukman Dutty directed the 201 valiant and heroic leaders, male and female, who sealed the pact of freedom at the Vodou ceremony that night in Bois Caïman (Alligator Woods). Boukman was a maroon of Herculean strength and appearance. Also a Vodou houngan or priest, he was accompanied by Georges Biassou, who later made Toussaint Louverture his aide; by Jean François, who subsequently commanded some of the armed forces; and by Jeannot, the most fearless of them all. One should also mention names such as Romaine la prophétesse, Marie Kenge, Halaou, Sans Souci, Petit Noel Prieur, Tellier, Cagnet, Va Malere, Cacapoul, and Lamour Derans. A week later, the uprising of their black followers was launched.

No matter what has been said to defame Vodou, it is the culture of the Haitians, their traditional religion, and their art of living; it is not, and has never been, a secret society. Vodou may have had its secrets, at times, in view of the social, economic, and political pressures exerted against Africans in Saint-Domingue and elsewhere in the world. Some ceremonies may indeed call for great discretion. The ceremony of Bois Caïman was definitely one of these.

The ceremony at Bois Caïman was magico-religious, concentrating mystical forces in collective cosmic, social, and individual dimensions that materialized to objects, the ultimate aim being the fabrication of a *pwen* or magic protection for the group. The essence of that ceremony resides in its unifying function. It united the different nations or "nanchons" from the Senegalese, Dahomean, and Guinean to Congolese, from the slaves to the maroons, from the Amerindians to the Africans, all those who constituted the presence of the disenfranchised people of Saint-Domingue.

The ceremony is often depicted with the image of a sacrificial pig. It seems very unlikely that a pig would have been used for such a ritual. Most probably a misunderstood metaphor, that term might have simply implied the sacrifice of a "cochon sans poils," meaning an individual who would have offered him- or herself voluntarily in order to save all the children of Africa. It would then have been with the warmth of his blood that the pact was sealed.

Standing erect while directing the ceremony, Boukman Dutty invokes the Spirits as the people behind him beat on the drums. Through the sounds of these drums, the assembly was summoning the Spirits of the Ancestors, and inviting them to join and add their force to those of the living in these crucial moments of destiny. The *asson* or ritual gourd that Boukman holds in his hand, along with a bell, symbolizes the power that he exerts over the many forces of the universe, and the left side of his body points forward indicating that they were all in the proper position to receive blessings.

The cross over Boukman's head, far from being the representation of Jesus Christ, symbolically signifies what was really in their minds at the time—that they were at a crossroads in their lives, bound for freedom or death. The blood of the pig will be collected in the wooden bowl that appears somewhat near the central fire, and it will be distributed later to all participants. A mixture of various spices and a few other ingredients, this concoction will be called Kiman. Like a communion, it will be ceremonially tasted by all those gathered here. The purpose of this ritual is to seal, as it should, the "blood pact" that took place.

There was likely no scribe to write down the invocation pronounced that night. Yet that original invocation has never been forgotten by the Vodouists of Haiti. In oral tradition, we have maintained it for more than 200 years. We recite it in full before every major ceremony under the name of "Prayer Djó," and it is recited all over the country in the Fon language. The Prayer Djó, for us, is "the breath that surrounds the universe" and that breath is believed to be the Holy See, the place where the 401 Forces create "universal gravitation," so to speak, where all the *lwa* assemble. Vodou forces, the *lwa* are understood to be any one and all of the 401 divine expressions of God (as seen in Vodou). Supremely powerful, their equilibrium sustains the universe. The power of the invocation can be grasped by these two summons to the *lwa*.

Prayer Djó
Djo nouwazon é, Ayizan dolé Vodoulè soudo do Sè miwa
Damballa do Sè do miwayé, Ayida do Sè do miwayé
Ayizan dolè Vodou lè soudo do Sè miwa, Djó.

[Spirits who surround the earth, the eve of the ceremony has arrived.
All the Forces of the earth come to us. We want to close permanently that sacrificial hole.
Damballa Wedo rush to us, Ayida Wedo hurry up join us,
It is the winding-sheet that awaits us; it is the burial garment that waits for us.
All the Spirits of the earth, join us quickly we want to close at last that sacrificial hole.]

Saba yehge amiwa sa(ba) yehge
De Ayida e a miwa Danou sewa yehge o, djevo de
De Ayida Wedo Bade miwa.

[Death is looking out for us, death in a sacrificial way!
Ayida Wedo, come on quickly, hurry up quickly!
We are being hurt badly. They are hurting us.
Forces of thunder come and help us quickly.
Death is looking out for us, death in a sacrificial way!]

The Prayer Djó continues for more than forty paragraphs. These words offer us a glimpse not only into Vodou today, but back through the centuries to how it must have felt to be present at the ceremony of Bois Caïman in August of 1791.

Notes

1. There are a variety of resources describing the importance of the ceremony of Bois Caïman in Haiti's history. For more information see the following: Beaubrun et Celigny Ardouin, *Etudes sur l'histoire d'Haïti, Tome I (1840)*, ed. François Dalencourt (Port-au-Prince, 1958); Antoine Dalmas, *Histoire de la révolution de Saint-Domingue*, Tome I (Paris: Mame Frères,1814); Civique de Gastines, *Histoire de la République d'Haïti* (Paris: Plancher, 1819); R.B. Dominique et al., *Investigations autour du site historique du Bois Caïman* (unpublished manuscript, Collection Haïti 2004); J.-C. Dorsainvil, *Manuel d'histoire d'Haïti, par le docteur J.-C. Dorsainvil, avec la collaboration des Frères de l'Instruction Chrétienne. Ouvrage approuvé par de l'Instruction Publique d'Haïti, le 29 mars 1924* (Port-au-Prince: Procure des Frères de l'Instruction Chrétienne, 1925); Carolyn Fick, *The Making of Haiti* (Knoxville: U of Tennessee P, 1990). For more information on Vodou in general, visit Max Beauvoir's website: "The Temple of Yehwe," <http://vodou.org>.

Chapter 21

New Orleans Voudou and Haitian Vodou

Carolyn Morrow Long

African traditional religions, combined with the spiritual hierarchy of God the Father, Jesus Christ, the Virgin Mary, and the saints of the Roman Catholic church, are the basis of major New World African-based religions such as Haitian Vodou, Cuban Santeria, and Brazilian Candomblé. Many traditional African religions recognized a supreme being who was neither good nor evil, male nor female, and was far removed from the affairs of human beings. The Fon and Yoruba people believed that below the supreme being there existed lesser deities, called vodu by the Fon and orisha by the Yoruba, which acted as intermediaries between humans and the supreme being. The vodu and the orisha manifested themselves as the spirits of plants, animals, stones, and natural phenomena such as rivers, oceans, lightning, and wind, and exercised dominion over human creativity, sexuality and reproduction, warfare, commerce, agriculture, disease, healing, and death. The divine trickster, ruler of the crossroads, controlled access to the spirit world and served as a messenger between human beings and the other deities; he also governed chance and could be persuaded to alter a person's fate. The deities could be benevolent or vengeful, depending on how well they were served; they offered advice, foretold the future, and healed sickness, but they also could cause disease and bad luck. The Kongo people also recognized a supreme being and believed the universe to be inhabited by spirits personified by objects called *minkisi* (the singular is *nkisi*).[1]

African religious and magical traditions arrived in Louisiana along with the first slaves. The French brought a small number of Fon and Yoruba from the Bight of Benin, and some Kongo people from Central Africa, but most of the captives were Wolofs, Bambaras, Foulbes, and Mandingas from the region between the Senegal and Gambia rivers (collectively referred to as Senegambians).[2] Antoine-Simon Le Page du Pratz's *Histoire de la Louisiane*, which described events of the early

1700s, told of gris-gris amulets worn by the Senegambians, and warned that on Sundays "the negroes assemble together...to the number of three or four hundred, and make a kind of Sabbath."[3] Court records from a slave case tried in 1773 also spoke of gris-gris.[4]

New Orleans Voudou is said by both scholars and popular-history writers to have emerged as an organized religion with the arrival of refugees fleeing the Haitian Revolution during the early years of the nineteenth century.[5] Two-thirds of these newcomers were Africans or people of African descent, and an undetermined number were devotees of Voudou (usually spelled Vodou when referring to the Haitian religion), an African-based belief system that combines Roman Catholicism with Fon, Yoruba, and Kongo elements.

In Haitian Vodou the supreme being is called the Good God—Bondyé in Kreyòl—and is comparable to the Judeo-Christian creator. A pantheon of lesser deities called loa or *lwa* (*lwa* is the preferred Haitian Kreyòl spelling) mediate between human beings and Bondyé and are usually identified with one or more of the Christian saints. The spirits of departed ancestors are also honored. Within the Vodou temple are altars dedicated to the *lwa*, on which are displayed statues and pictures of their corresponding saints, and offerings of flowers, fruit, cooked foods, liquor, candles, cigarettes and cigars, perfume, and other symbolic objects. The *lwa* communicate with the members of the Vodou société (society or congregation) through spirit possession, during which the deity "mounts" the body of a worshiper and speaks through the possessed serviteur (one who serves the spirits). The large ceremonies, in which the whole congregation participates, are presided over by an initiated houngan (priest) or manbo (priestess). This spiritual leader also gives consultations and performs healing ceremonies for individual clients in order to resolve difficulties with relationships, money, employment, or health. The goal of all Vodou worship is a balanced life characterized by harmony with the human community, the natural environment, the *lwa*, and the ancestral spirits.[6]

There are no authentic eyewitness reports of African-based religious and magical practices in New Orleans during the colonial period and the first decades of the American era. What has come to be accepted as the description of an early Voudou ceremony held in a swamp near New Orleans did not occur in Louisiana at all, but was lifted verbatim from a 1797 history of colonial Saint-Domingue by Medric Louis Moreau de Saint-Méry. Here Moreau described a ceremony for a snake deity presided over by a "king" and "queen." This would have been a service for Dambala, the wise and gentle rainbow serpent of Haitian Vodou, derived from Dan, the sacred python of the Fon people. The king and queen would have been the houngan and manbo. Like most subsequent writers, Moreau felt compelled to characterize the possession trance as a sexual orgy.[7]

In 1883 Moreau's description of this ceremony reappeared in a travel journal called *Souvenirs d'Amérique et de France par une Créole,* published anonymously in French by New

Orleanian Hélène d'Aquin Allain.[8] In 1886, an English translation of Moreau's narrative turned up in George Washington Cable's "Creole Slave Songs."[9] While Allain and Cable credited Moreau as the author of the Voudou description, later writers did not, and it has been endlessly paraphrased and repeated. What may have been Moreau de Saint-Méry's imaginative rendering of a second-hand account has come to be considered the classic New Orleans Voudou ritual, complete with queen, snake, gris-gris, bloody animal sacrifice, and sexual debauchery.[10]

In addition to the obvious influence of Haitian Vodou, nineteenth-century New Orleans Voudou also absorbed the beliefs of blacks brought into Louisiana from Maryland, Virginia, and the Carolinas by American slave traders. Unlike Louisiana's Creoles of color, whose ancestors came primarily from the upper west coast of Africa, these newcomers were descended from the Kongo of Central Africa. They were English-speaking, at least nominally Protestant, and practiced a heavily Kongo-influenced kind of "conjure" or "rootwork" that was incorporated into New Orleans Voudou. The religion that evolved during the early nineteenth century combined traditions introduced by the first enslaved Africans with Haitian Vodou, African American conjure, European magic, and folk Catholicism.

Newspaper reports of the 1820s through the 1880s, while greatly sensationalized, give some idea of nineteenth-century Voudou practice.[11] Voudou themes appear in two novels, George Washington Cable's *The Grandissimes* (1880), and Helen Pitkin's *An Angel by Brevet* (1904). Interviews with elderly black New Orleanians, conducted between 1936 and 1941 by employees of the federally funded Louisiana Writers' Project (LWP), provide valuable details on the religion as practiced in the later nineteenth century. Some of the LWP interviewees had frequented the home of New Orleans' most famous Voudou priestess, Marie Laveau, and described rooms filled with altars, candles, and images of the saints. They spoke of her weekly ceremonies, which featured chanting, dancing, and a communal meal; these meetings were called parterres or layouts, referring to the practice of "spreading a feast for the spirits" on a white cloth on the ground or on the floor. Some informants also attended the St. John's Eve ceremonies at Lake Pontchartrain. In addition, the LWP interviewees told of gris-gris provided by Marie Laveau for private clients.[12]

Nineteenth-century New Orleans Voudou differs in many ways from contemporary Haitian Vodou. Important components of the Haitian religion are missing from the published accounts and from the LWP interviews. The series of complex initiations by which one becomes a houngan or manbo in Haiti is never mentioned, and key elements of Haitian Vodou ritual are lacking, such as the procession of the flags and sword at the beginning of a ceremony, and the drawing of *vévé* (symbols drawn on the ground with cornmeal to summon the spirits).

We hear almost nothing of the Vodou deities—in fact the term *lwa* is never used. Instead, reference is made to the spirits. Some of the most beloved members of the Haitian Vodou pantheon, such as Ezili Freda (goddess of love), Ezili Danto (the protective mother), Ogou (the warrior), Agwe (master of the ocean), and Gede (lord of the cemetery), are conspicuously absent. It appears that only Dambala and Legba survived the trip to Louisiana. In the novels of Cable and Pitkin, and in the LWP interviews, we hear of Daniel Blanc, Blanc Dani, Danny, and Dambarra, all manifestations of the rainbow serpent Dambala. From the same sources we hear of the spirit variously called Papa Limba, La Bas, Lébat, or Liba, analogous with the Haitian Papa Legba, guardian of the crossroads and keeper of the gate to the spirit world. The song offered by one LWP interviewee, "St. Peter, St. Peter open the door," resembles the song for Legba by which all Vodou ceremonies are opened: "Atibo-Legba, l'uvri bayé pu mwé, agoé! Papa-Legba, l'uvri bayé pu mwé pu mwé pasé" [remove the barrier for me, so that I may pass through]. Other deities, unknown or less important in Haiti, are also cited in the LWP interviews and in the literary accounts of Cable and Pitkin. Vériquite might be Ayizan Velekete, mistress of the marketplace and patron of priestesses. Yon Sue and Vert Agoussou could be Agassu, known in Africa and Haiti as the founder of the Dahomean royal dynasty, the result of a union between a woman and a leopard. Onzancaire and Assonquer are probably the same entity, but this is not a name familiar in Haitian Vodou. Monsieur D'Embarras, Charlo, and Jean Macouloumba might be indigenous to Louisiana, or they may be the literary inventions of Cable and Pitkin.[13]

Nineteenth-century newspapers had much to say about a supposed Voudou snake deity called "Gran Zombi." There is no Haitian Vodou spirit of this name. While Zombi may refer to Nzambi Mpungu, the supreme deity of the Kongo people, the name first appeared in the *Picayune's Guide to New Orleans for 1900,* and one suspects that this gigantic snake was invented by journalists inspired by tales of Haiti's infamous living dead, combined with Moreau de Saint-Méry's endlessly repeated description of a snake-worshipping ceremony in colonial Saint-Domingue.[14]

Despite these differences, New Orleans Voudou was also strikingly similar to contemporary Haitian Vodou. Nineteenth-century written and oral descriptions of New Orleans Voudou indicate that worshipers chanted, danced, and became possessed by the spirits. Devotees wore white clothing as they do in Haiti. The ritual twirling of participants by the officiating priest or priestess resembles the salutations between priests and assistants during a Haitian ceremony. Several printed sources and LWP interviews describe the practice of sprinkling the congregation with rum or with liquor sprayed out of the mouth, a practice also seen in Haitian Vodou. Altars such as those observed in Marie Laveau's home are always found in Vodou temples, and the arrangement of offerings on a white cloth is also characteristic of Haitian ceremonies.[15]

There are also similarities between New Orleans gris-gris and the pwen of Haitian Vodou. Pwen, meaning a point of concentrated energy intended to control people and events, take the form of *pakèts kongo* (Kongo packets) for protection and healing; gad (bodyguard) for protection; and *wanga* to cause the downfall of an enemy.[16] In New Orleans, gris-gris became conflated with the mojo bags and "roots" of the English-speaking African Americans, European pre-Christian magical artifacts, and Christian sacred objects and rituals.

In comparing nineteenth-century New Orleans Voudou with modern Haitian Vodou, we are obviously working with incomplete data. Newspaper articles and other published accounts by outsiders are unreliable, and in the Louisiana Writers' Project narratives we have what the informants remembered, what they chose to tell their interviewers, and what the interviewers thought to ask them. We cannot assume that, because a deity or a ritual was not mentioned, it did not exist in nineteenth-century New Orleans Voudou.

It may be that the Haitian and New Orleanian versions of the religion are identical, or it may be that the religion documented in New Orleans represents a dilution and simplification of the Vodou brought to Louisiana by the Haitian refugees. On the other hand, the complex rituals and pantheon of deities now defined as Vodou may have evolved in post-revolutionary Haiti, after the departure of the refugees to Louisiana, and we may be seeking a connection that never existed. New Orleans Voudou was virtually eradicated by the end of the nineteenth century. The revival of the religion that occurred in the later twentieth century is more akin to Haitian Vodou than it is to earlier New Orleans practices. Contemporary priests and priestesses, some of them initiated in Haiti, have established temples that serve a middle-class, multiracial community of believers and endeavor to educate the public about Vodou through workshops, websites, and newsletters.[17]

Notes

1. For more on the Fon religion, see Melville Herskovits, *Dahomey: An Ancient West African Kingdom* (New York: J.J. Augustin, 1938) and Suzanne Preston Blier, "Vodun: West African Roots of Vodou," in *Sacred Arts of Haitian Vodou*, ed. Donald Cosentino (Los Angeles: U of California Fowler Museum of Cultural History, 1995). For the Yoruba religion, see Robert Farris Thompson, *Flash of the Spirit: African and Afro-American Art and Philosophy* (New York: Vintage, 1983). For the Kongo religion, see three works by Wyatt MacGaffey: *Religion and Society in Central Africa: The BaKongo of Lower Zaire* (Chicago: U of Chicago P, 1986); *Art and Healing of the BaKongo Commented by Themselves: Minkisi from the Laman Collection* (Stolkholm: Folkens Museum-Ethnografiska, 1991); and *"The Eyes of Understanding: Kongo Minkisi,"* in *Astonishment and Power: Kongo Minkisi and the Art of Reneé Stout*, intro. Sylvia H. Williams and David C. Driskell (Washington, DC: Smithsonian Institution, National Museum of African Art, 1993).

2. Gwendolyn Midlo Hall, *Africans in Colonial Louisiana: The Development of Afro-Creole Culture in the Eighteenth Century* (Baton Rouge: Louisiana State U P, 1992) 29-95. Especially see Figure 2, 35, "Slaves Landed in Louisiana by French Slave Trade: Numbers and Origins," and Table 2, "French Slave-Trade Ships from Africa to Louisiana."

3. Antoine-Simon Le Page du Pratz, *Histoire de la Louisiane (1758)*. The English translation is *The History of Luisiana or of The Western Parts of Virginia and Carolina, with an Account of the Settlements, Inhabitants, Soil, Climate, and Products* (London: Beckett, 1774). See 377, 387.

4. Laura Porteous, "The Gri-Gri Case, A Criminal Trial in Louisiana During the Spanish Regime, 1773," *Louisiana Historical Quarterly* 17, no. 1 (1934): 48-63.

5. Gwendolyn Midlo Hall, "The Formation of Afro-Creole Culture," *Creole New Orleans: Race and Americanization*, ed. Arnold R. Hirsch and Joseph Logsdon (Baton Rouge: Louisiana State U P, 1992) 85-86; Zora Neale Hurston, "Hoodoo in America," *Journal of American Folklore* 44, no. 174 (1931): 318; Herbert Asbury, *The French Quarter: An Informal History of the New Orleans Underworld* (New York: Garden City Publishing, 1938) 254; Robert Tallant, *Voodoo in New Orleans* (1946, reprint Gretna, LA.: Pelican Publishing Co., 1983) 12.

6. The literature on Haitian Vodou is vast, but a good understanding may be gained from Alfred Métraux, *Voodoo in Haiti* (New York: Schocken Books, 1972); Harold Courlander, *The Drum and the Hoe: Life and Lore of the Haitian People* (Berkeley: U of California P, 1960); Wade Davis, *Passage of Darkness: The Ethnobiology of the Haitian Zombie*, see the chapter "The Historical and Cultural Setting," 15-55 (Chapel Hill: U of North Carolina P, 1988); Karen McCarthy Brown, *Mama Lola: A Vodou Priestess in Brooklyn* (Berkeley and Los Angeles: U of California P, 1991); and Donald Cosentino, ed., *Sacred Arts of Haitian Vodou* (Los Angeles: U of California Fowler Museum of Cultural History, 1995).

7. Ivor D. Spencer, *A Civilization That Perished: The Last Years of White Colonial Rule in Haiti* (abridged translation of Moreau de Saint-Méry, *Description Topographique, Physique, Civile, Politique, et Historique de la Partie Francaise de l'Isle Saint-Domingue*, Lanham, MD: U P of America, 1985) 56 and 1-7. The description of a Vodou ceremony is found in Vol. 1, 45-51 of Moreau's original.

8. Hélène d'Aquin Allain, *Souvenirs d'Amérique et de France par une Créole* (Paris: Perisse Frères, 1883) 130.

9. George Washington Cable, "Creole Slave Songs," *Century Magazine* 31 (April 1886): 818-19.

10. Subsequent versions of Moreau's narrative appear in Henry Castellanos, *New Orleans As It Was* (1895, reprint Gretna, LA: Pelican Publishing Co.,1990) 91-96; Newbell Niles Puckett, *Folk Beliefs of the Southern Negro* (1926, reprint Montclair, NJ: Patterson Smith Reprint Series, 1968) 178-183; Doris Kent LeBlanc, "Beware These Closing Days of June," *Times-Picayune Sunday Magazine*, 26 June 1927: 2; Lyle Saxon, *Fabulous New Orleans* (1928, reprint Gretna, LA: Pelican Publishing Co.) 240-241; Marcus Christian, "A Black History of Louisiana/Voodooism and Mumbo-Jumbo" (unpublished manuscript, Marcus Christian

Papers, Archives and Manuscripts Division, Earl K. Long Library, U of New Orleans) 9-11; and Robert Tallant, *Voodoo in New Orleans*, 8. The source of this description was known by Louisiana Writers' Project workers, and was more recently noted by Violet Harrington Bryan in *The Myth of New Orleans in Literature: Dialogues of Race and Gender* (Knoxville: U of Tennessee P, 1993) 107, and by Stephan Palmié in "Conventionalization, Distortion, and Plagiarism in the Historiography of Afro-Caribbean Religion in New Orleans," *Creoles and Cajuns: French Louisiana–La Louisiane Française,* ed. Wolfgang Binder (Frankfurt: Peter Lang, 1998) 315-44.

11. All newspapers cited are published in New Orleans*: Bee*: "A Singular Assemblage,"29 June 1850: p. 1, c. 5. *Commercial Bulletin*: "Voodooism," 25 June 1869: p. 1, c. 7. *Daily Crescent*: "A Mystery of the Old Third," 29 June 1850: p. 3, c. 1; "Another Voudou Affair," 4 July 1850: p. 2, c. 1; "The Rites of Voudou," 31 July 1850: p. 3, c. 1. *Daily Delta*: "The Voudous vs Municipality No. Three," 14 July 1850: p. 2, c. 2. *Daily Picayune*: "Great Doings in the Third Municipality," 29 June 1850: p. 2, c. 6; "Voudouism," 24 July 1850: p. 1, c. 4; "Unlawful Assemblies," 31 July 1850: p. 2, c. 2; "More of the Voudous," 31 July 1850: p. 1, c. 6; "Superstitious," 12 July 1859: p. 1, c. 7; "Fetish Rites," 23 June 1870: p. 2, c. 5; "St. John's Eve–The Voudous," 24 June 1873: p. 4, c. 2; "Voudou Nonsense," 26 June 1874: p. 1, c. 5; "Fetish–Its Worship and Worshipers," 24 June 1875: p. 1, c. 4-5; "St. John's Eve–After the Voudous," 25 June 1875: p. 2, c. 1. *Daily States*: "A Voudou Entertainment," 29 May 1889: p. 2, c. 2. *Daily True Delta*: "A Motley Gathering–Superstition and Licentiousness, " 29 June 1850: p. 3, c. 1; "The Voudou Humbug," 25 July 1850: p. 3, c. 1. *Louisiana Courier*: "The Voudous in the First Municipality," 30 July 1850: p. 2, c. 5. *Louisiana Gazette*: "Idolatry and Quackery," 16 August 1820: p. 2, c. 3. *Republican*: "Fate and Mystery," 21 June 1874: p. 5, c. 1; "The Voudou Ceremonies," 25 June 1874: p. 3, c. 1. *Times*: "The Voudous' Day," 25 June 1870: p. 6, c. 2; "Voudouism Rampant in Louisiana," 17 July 1870: p. 3, c. 4-5; "Making a Night of It–A Search for the Vous Dous Queen," 26 June 1872: p. 2, c. 1-2; "The Vous Dous Incantation," 28 June 1872: p. 1, c. 6; "Voudou Vagaries–The Worshipers of Obeah Turned Loose," 26 June 1874: p. 2, c. 2-4; "Fetish Worship–St. John's Eve at Milneburg," 25 June 1875: p. 2, c. 1 and 2; "St. John's Eve Celebrations," 24 June 1887: p. 6, c. 4. *Times-Democrat*: "A Voudou Dance–Revival on the Lake Shore of Voudou Mysteries," 24 June 1884: p. 2, c. 3; "A Voudou Orgie–Sensational Disclosure in the Third District," 28 May 1889: p. 4, c. 3.

12. Louisiana Writers' Project, Northwestern State U, Natchitoches, Louisiana, Watson Memorial Library, Cammie G. Henry Research Center, Federal Writers' Collection. Some of these interviews are quoted in Chapter 3, Carolyn Morrow Long, *Spiritual Merchants: Religion, Magic, and Commerce* (Knoxville: U of Tennessee P, 2001). Altars and ceremonies in Marie Laveau's home: Marie Dédé, interview by Robert McKinney, n.d.; Charles Raphael, interview by Hazel Breaux and Jacques Villere, n.d.; Raymond Rivaros, interview by Hazel Breaux, n.d.; Oscar Felix, interview by Edmund Burke, 14 Mar 1940. St. John's Eve: Oscar Felix, Charles Raphael, "Pops," interview by Robert McKinney, n.d.; Joseph Alfred and Eugene Fritz, interview by Robert McKinney, n.d.; John Smith, interview by Hazel Breaux, n.d.; William Moore, interview by Edmund Burke, 1 Mar 1940. Gris-gris: Laura Hopkins, interview by Maude Wallace and Henriette Michinard, 9 Feb; 4 & 7 Mar; April 1940, LWP folder 43; Joe Landry, interview by Zoe Posey, 18 July 1939; John Slater, interview by Cecile Wright, n.d. Unless otherwise noted, the Marie Laveau interviews are in LWP folder 25.

13. George Washington Cable, *The Grandissimes: A Story of Creole Life* (1880, reprint New York: Penguin Classics, 1988) 55, 67, 216, 306, 308. Helen Pitkin, *An Angel by Brevet: A Story of Modern New Orleans* (Philadelphia: J.B. Lippincott, 1904) 179-212, 259-288. LWP informant Josephine McDuffy spoke of Papa Limba, interview by Henriette Michinard, 1940, LWP folder 25. The song "St. Peter, open the door" is from Mary Washington, who also mentioned Daniel Blanc, Yon Sue, and Onzancaire, interview by Robert McKinney, n.d., LWP folder 25. Song for Legba, Métraux, *Voodoo in Haiti*, 101.

14. *Picayune's Guide to New Orleans for 1900*, 66.

15. Music, dance, and white clothing: Marie B. Williams, "A Night with the Voudous," *Appleton's Journal* 27 March 1875: 403-404; Oscar Felix interview; Raymond Rivaros interview, James Santana, interview by Zoe Posey, 10 July 1939, LWP folder 25. Ritual twirling: "Fetish Worship–St. John's Eve at Milneburg," *Times* 25 June 1875; Charles Dudley Warner, "A Voudou Dance," *Harper's Weekly* 25 June 1887: 454-455; Pitkin, *An Angel by Brevet*, 201-02. Nathan Hobley, interview by Zoe Posey, 25 October 1940; Therese Kavanaugh, interview by Zoe Posey, n.d., LWP folder 25. Sprinkling or spraying with liquor: "Fetish Worship" *Times* 25 June 1875; Williams, "Night with the Voudous"; Pitkin, 200; Raymond Rivaros interview, LWP folder 25. Offerings on a white cloth: "Fetish Worship–St. John's Eve at Milneburg," *Times* 25 June 1875; "A Voudou Dance–Revival on the Lake Shore of Voudou Mysteries," *Times-Democrat*, 24 June 1884; Pitkin in *An Angel by Brevet*, 192; Charles Raphael interview, LWP folder 25.

16. For more on the pwen of Haitian Vodou, see Elizabeth McAlister, "A Sorcerer's Bottle: The Visual Art of Magic in Haiti," 305-315; Karen McCarthy Brown, "Serving the Spirits," 213, 221-220; Robert Farris Thompson, "From the Isle Beneath the Sea: Haiti's Africanizing Vodou Art," 111-118, all in *Sacred Arts of Haitian Vodou*.

17. The contemporary New Orleans Voudou scene is constantly changing, as priests and priestesses disappear from public view and others take their place. My personal observations from the middle 1990s until the present include the following: Ava Kay Jones, Voodoo Macumba (website no longer operational); Elmer Glover; Miriam Williams Chamani, Voodoo Spiritual Temple; www.voodoospiritualtemple; Sallie Ann Glassman, Société La Source Ancienne, www.feyvodou.com/services; Houngan Aboudja (Mark Alexander Moellendorf) and Manbo Michelle Mehrtens, Société Flè d'Abome (website no longer operational); Sharon Caulder, Chez Vodou, www.africanvodun.com; Tribble (Don Glossop), New Orleans Mistic, www.neworleansmistic.com. All websites accessed 2005. Services are also held at the New Orleans Historic Voodoo Museum and Voodoo Authentica.

Chapter 22

Vodou in Louisiana

Sallie Ann Glassman

I came to New Orleans in 1977, seeking Vodou and jazz. Although I knew precious little about Vodou at the time, I knew somehow that New Orleans was the capital of Vodou in the United States. What I found at first was merely a marketed tourist show and not at all the beautiful religion, philosophy, and way of life that I had hoped to experience. But after many years of searching, the real thing began to reveal itself.

Soon after I had been initiated as a manbo, a Vodou priestess, in 1995, I had the opportunity to accompany a friend who was photographing the live oak trees at Evergreen Plantation in Edgard, Louisiana. Evergreen is one of the few plantations that still has its original slave quarters. As we walked up to the slave quarters that stand within the magnificent oak alleys, the atmosphere seemed to shift, change, and waver. I saw people standing on the porches, could hear children's voices, and heard songs being called. I poured libations, lit candles, and fed the spirits of the slaves—Vodou's early ancestors—in the slave quarters. It was clear that their spirits had moved out of these sparse cabins where so many had suffered and into the trees that line the alleys. I thought how appropriate it was that these trees had become containers of spirits. No one had bothered to record or document the lives of the slaves, but their spirits had grown into the convoluted root systems and twisting limbs of the live oaks, just as Vodou's presence, legacy, and history influenced and became encoded within Louisiana's culture.

The French kept clear and detailed accounts of the "cargo" carried on slave ships. They recorded how many slaves came from which African nation to Louisiana plantations. But there is little documentation of the development of the Vodou religion from its African roots in the colony.

Conditions in colonial Haiti or Saint-Domingue and colonial Louisiana were quite similar. It is possible to extrapolate what happened in Louisiana from Vodou's experience in Saint-Domingue. In the same way, the Creole language developed independently but simultaneously and similarly in Louisiana and Haiti. In Haiti, however, the development of Kreyòl may have been more politically oriented. Not only did Kreyòl allow slaves from different African nations to speak a common language, but it also provided a means of communication secret from the whites. Kreyòl became a form of coded language by which the slaves were able to organize the Haitian Revolution without detection from the French. Kreyòl remains the language of Vodou in Haiti, while French is the preferred language of the bourgeoisie.

Vodou in Colonial Louisiana

Life in French Louisiana was not strictly divided between the white European oppressor and subjugated but defiant slaves. Many of the colonists were nearly as poor as the slaves. The colonial life was largely a desperate effort at survival in a chaotic environment. American-born colonists and slaves both spoke Creole (the common spelling in Louisiana) and it is still spoken by Louisiana Creoles, though it is becoming an endangered language in Louisiana. The development of the language can be considered to parallel the development of Vodou in both countries, with Haitian Kreyòl and Vodou culture in general more political—"hotter"— than in Louisiana.

Combining information from a variety of sources, we can start to extract how Vodou took root in Louisiana. Vodou's similar development in Haiti offers many clues. The *lwa* (intermediary, ancestral deities) offer insights into these beginnings through ceremonies when they come down and express themselves through servitors. Remnant clues can be retrieved from song lyrics and other cultural footprints that track throughout Louisiana's history, and from the legacies left by the spirits of slave ancestors that are sprinkled throughout contemporary Louisiana cultural practices. Altogether, these combined sources may make up for the lack of documentation on Vodou.

Vodou arrived in French colonial Louisiana with the first slave ships in 1719. The French colony was not well organized, not populous, and not very healthy. Louisiana was for the most part a penal colony. Criminals and socially undesirable French citizens were shipped off to Louisiana, where they were left essentially to eke out an existence from the inhospitable swamps amid pestilence, famine, floods, and numerous dangers. Most of the soldiers and settlers were rejects from French society and unsuited to establishing a coherent social structure in the colony, and slaves from Africa provided the work force for the French.

According to Gwendolyn Midlo Hall's *Africans in Colonial Louisiana,* most of the slaves in French Louisiana came directly from Africa, and two-thirds of these were taken from Senegambia, the territory between what is now Senegal and the Gambia River.[1] Some people from that region were Muslim, but the majority of the slaves from Senegambia were Bambara. The Bambara held many beliefs recognizable as core to the Vodou religion as it developed in Louisiana. The Bambara also devised ways to maintain their culture after their empire dissolved in Africa. Although priests only had deep knowledge of religious beliefs, ceremonies and practices were in the hands of all people, so they were able to maintain those practices even when isolated from religious leaders on plantations in Louisiana.

The Bambara created amulets of power—zinzins and gris-gris—which are still used in New Orleans Vodou. Hunters carried a bag in which sacred power items were collected: animal horns, claws, teeth, and herbs. The Bambara had extensive knowledge of herbal remedies and recognized the sacred life force in all living things. In many ways, the Bambara were better suited to life in the colonies than were the French. They were certainly better adapted to the climate, more resistant to malaria, and more skilled at growing rice and other crops than the French.

Upon arrival in Louisiana, slaves were required by the French Code Noir to convert to Catholicism.[2] Conversion consisted mainly of showing slaves chromolithograph images of the saints. In these images slaves recognized symbols of their own spirits. Saint Patrick, for instance, was shown driving snakes out of Ireland and became associated with Danbala or Damballa, Vodou's creative, divine serpent. The saints were used as masks to hide the Vodou spirit who was actually being worshipped. Over time, Catholic iconography found its way onto altars and throughout Vodou's sacred arts. Catholicism in Louisiana was also touched by its encounter with African traditions and still reflects an almost Vodou-esque take on honoring the saints. Catholic saints are prayed to as intermediaries to the divine, for favors, guidance, protection, and empowerment—not unlike the *lwa*, who act as intermediaries between God and humans.[3]

Maroon and Revolutionary Influences

The Bambara slaves encountered Indians in Louisiana, the first people enslaved in North America by the French colonists. Many Indian slaves had already escaped into the swamps by the time the French started importing Africans, and many more escaped with runaway Bambara slaves and became known as maroons and formed communities in the swamps from which they plotted armed uprisings and forays against the French. The uprisings failed to effect liberation but did trouble the French settlers and added to the fears and dangers that plagued their lives. Marronnage in Louisiana allowed Indian and African bloodlines and cultures to mingle, infusing African traditions with Native American practices. It is not clear how much influence Native Americans had on Vodou traditions, but as Vodou formed, it absorbed the cultures encountered in the Americas.[4] For example, *vèvè*, the ritual drawings of Vodou, are thought to be Creolisations of Indian sand and cornmeal ritual drawings, and contemporary Mardi Gras Indian songs apparently contain words from African languages.[5]

Armed maroon incursions into French settlements combined with famine and drought made the colony more trouble than it was worth to the French. The Spanish took over governing Louisiana from 1769 until 1803, and re-Africanized it by bringing not only more Senegambians, but also Fon, Yoruba, and Congo slaves. The Congo nation was probably not as influential in Louisiana Vodou as was once thought, but did contribute the bamboula dance, and introduced wangas—magical amulets—into Louisiana Vodou. These can take many forms such as bags, packets, or bottles. These peoples from different nations did not speak the same language, but they learned to communicate through image, rhythm, dance, and ritual gesture. These became forms of language that encoded history and legacy. Vodou was the common bond that held together the assembled beliefs and practices of these peoples.

It was known in Louisiana that the revolution in Saint-Domingue was organized and incited through Vodou rites. Five years after the death of the hero Makandal, in 1758, Carondelet, Louisiana's Spanish governor, banned the importation of slaves from Saint-Domingue.[6] The colonists feared Vodou magic and slave poisonings. As Haiti's slave uprising developed into revolution, the Louisiana colony became increasingly nervous. In 1804, however, at the end of the Haitian revolution, the port of New Orleans was reopened to an influx of Haitians both black and white, free and slave. Many Haitians came to New Orleans by way of Cuba. However, when France declared war on Spain, Cuba retaliated by expelling the Haitians. Ten thousand refugees came into New Orleans, doubling the population. The Fon, Yoruba, and Congo cultural presence was reaffirmed, and the Vodou religion was clearly being practiced in Louisiana, if in a slightly watered-down form. Most contemporary practitioners of New Orleans Vodou speculate that Cuban orishas entered Louisiana's Vodou pantheon during the 1960s and 1970s, when African Americans were reclaiming an African heritage. However, knowing how quickly and readily Vodou incorporates elements of the cultures it encounters, it is possible that elements of orisha worship combined with Vodou practices during the refugees' stay in Cuba from 1804 to 1810.

It is equally possible that the orishas entered Louisiana Vodou during Spanish rule of the colony and orisha worship developed with Cuban Santería and Lucumí. Some of the orishas may have come "on the backs" of African slaves during the ceremonies performed in Louisiana. Gradually those spirits became part of Louisiana Vodou's unique pantheon. No doubt after the Cuban revolution, the orishas' presence was reaffirmed in American Vodou. However it came about, contemporary Louisiana Vodou maintains some of the Afro-Cuban spirits. The *lwa* and orisha are often served side by side. Yet, Vodou developed uniquely in each country where it took hold. Some spirits were brought from Africa, some developed in the New World. New spirits continue to develop, just as in Louisiana Marie Laveau's archetypal force may be developing into a *lwa*.

Effects of Revolution

The Spanish returned Louisiana to the French, who in turn sold it to the United States in 1803 when Napoleon was abandoning his New World colonies. The Americans were aghast at the lax behavior of the French colonists in Louisiana who had mingled with the slave population and often emancipated their interracial offspring along with their slave mothers. Quadroon balls and the French practice of *plaçage*, or keeping quadroon women as mistresses in relative comfort, were common. The Americans clamped down on slave freedom, but still allowed slaves to congregate on Sundays at Congo Square in New Orleans for dances. It is unclear whether these dances included Vodou ceremonies, but the dances preserved the meaningful essence of Vodou encoded in rhythm, song, and dance.

These rhythms also made their way into the music of Louisiana, particularly in the compositions of Louis Gottschalk (1829-1869), whom many jazz historians credit as the forefather of jazz. As a child he listened to the rhythms and sacred songs in Congo Square and later incorporated them into his music. One of his compositions is titled "Bamboula," for the Congo-inspired dance. But while Vodou's musical themes survived in American culture, Vodou in Louisiana did not survive as an established religion as it did in Haiti for several likely reasons. The slaves in Louisiana did not successfully revolt, but were forced to remain on the plantations. The Americans feared and frowned on Vodouism and did their best to suppress it. After the Civil War, northerners ridiculed Vodou and encouraged freed slaves to give up "superstitious, old ways." Most adherents were unable to maintain organized Vodou societies.

In contrast with Louisiana, a greater number of African slaves were imported into and absorbed by the Caribbean colonies. Although there was a high ratio of blacks to whites in Louisiana, there was a higher ratio of Africans to Europeans in Haiti, so it was easier to establish Vodou as a coherent religion. However, a few charismatic leaders in New Orleans, notably Marie Laveau (1804-1839) and Dr. John, who is believed to have been a little older than Marie Laveau, helped to keep Vodou alive in Louisiana. Dr. John was a notorious root doctor, drummer, and Vodou priest believed to have drummed at Marie Laveau's ceremonies, well attended by people from all levels of society. But after each of her events, newspaper articles published lurid and probably fabricated accounts of lascivious and orgiastic behavior at these ceremonies, discouraging participation in them.[7]

Marie Laveau was instrumental in combining Catholicism with Vodou in New Orleans and also introduced the commercialism prevalent in the "tourist voodoo" of New Orleans today. The real practice of Vodou was forced underground. It survives in its purest form probably in the Spiritual churches, such as the Black Hawk churches in Louisiana, where the spirit comes down upon participants in much the same way that the *lwa* come down in flesh and blood among Vodou servitors. (It is important to note, however, that some members of Spiritual churches would be uncomfortable with the idea that they were practicing a form of Vodou, due to the persistent association of Vodou with "black magic.")

Adaptations of Vodou

Some people claim that the Vodou *lwa* disappeared from the Louisiana servitors' awareness as the religion became hidden within Spiritual churches. After the Civil War, however, there is evidence of the presence of the *lwa* in the earliest blues and jazz songs. From the eighteenth to twentieth centuries, several bluesmen sang of selling their souls at the crossroads to Papa Labas, a version of Papa Legba, the Vodou gatekeeper and guardian of the crossroads. Mothers in New Orleans threaten their children that Papa Labas will get them if they don't behave. Papa Legba and Papa Labas are variations on the ancient African Alegba, who has been watching at the crossroads and guarding the gate from the beginning of time. Tourism and commercialism may have corrupted Vodou, but they also allowed Vodou to remain solvent and legal. It's ironic that Americans tried hard to suppress Vodou, but now it is one of the attractions for which New Orleans is known.

While the colonists subjugated their slaves, they also left the raising of their white children largely to domestic slaves, and later to nannies. African culture made its way into Louisiana's cooking, music, aesthetic, and worldview. Most people raised in New Orleans know a little something about dressing a candle, and what a chicken foot fetish or a gris-gris bag is for. It also seems there is a general movement among contemporary Vodou practitioners in New Orleans to return to and honor Vodou's religious traditions as opposed to tourist performances or Hoodoo spellcraft.

Vodou's story may not have been written down, but it has left its footprints all over Louisiana's culture: in song lyrics and rhythmic patterns, in graveyard displays, in gumbo recipes, in wrought iron vèvè on porches and gates, in the Mardi Gras Indians' sequined suits and dance steps. Vodou's presence is nearly as long and consistent in Louisiana as it is in Haiti. Those who claim that there is not and never was any real Vodou present in Louisiana insult the many manbo and houngan, root doctors and queens who have worked creatively within Vodou traditions, adapting and transforming them according to the changing needs of their environment. These critics do a great disservice to Vodou's early ancestors, whose resilience, creativity, and courage gave birth to a life-affirming religion of hope and healing that helped them endure the unendurable.

Slaves were isolated on individual plantations in Haiti and in Louisiana. They were not allowed to learn how to read and write. Vodou has no central church, no orthodoxy, and no canon.

Perhaps Vodou's ability to tolerate differing approaches and perspectives allowed it to adapt to the New World. Vodou developed as a religion of survival in both Louisiana and Haiti. Vodou allowed its followers to maintain connections with ancestral spirits and find a sense of coherence in nature. It helped its practitioners move from disempowerment to empowerment, from slavery to freedom, and from fear to faith. A doorway opens from contemporary Louisiana down under the waters of the Caribbean to Ginen, Vodou's spiritual home, the island under the sea.

Afterword

My Vodou society recently had the opportunity to perform a ceremony at Laurel Plantation near Vacherie, Louisiana. It was an extraordinary privilege to be able to serve the *lwa* openly without fear of persecution in the very place where early Vodou practitioners had suffered and died. We went to the slave cabins near the Mississippi River levee, offered food, lit candles, poured libations, and gave praise to the spirits of the ancestors. We all saw hundreds of spirits come up over the levee. They stood shoulder to shoulder among the trees and received our offerings and thanks. Everything had been taken from these people—their homes, families, identities, and dignity—but they kept the rhythms of their gods alive in their hearts. We owe them a great debt of gratitude.

Notes

1. Gwendolyn Midlo Hall, *Africans in Colonial Louisiana: The Development of Afro-Creole Culture in the Eighteenth Century* (Baton Rouge: Louisiana State U P, 1992).

2. According to the Society of American Archivists, the first Code Noir or Black Code was enacted in 1724 to restrict freedoms of Africans and African-descended people.

3. Saints are "worked with" almost on the level of spell casting. For instance, it is common practice to bury a statue of St. Joseph in the yard to encourage the sale of a house. St. Expedite candles are lit to hurry the outcome of any desired event.

4. Maya Deren, *Divine Horsemen: The Living Gods of Haiti* (New York: McPherson and Company, 1983).

5. For example see the song, "Jockomo," originally recorded in the 1950's by James Crawford but popularized more recently by New Orleans bands such as the Meters and The Neville Brothers. The lyrics include:
"Hey now
Hey now
Iko Iko un day
Jockomo feeno ah na nay
Jockomo Feena nay."

6. See Hall, cited above.

7. Martha Ward, *Voodoo Queen: The Spirited Lives of Marie Laveau* (Jackson: U P of Mississippi, 2004).

SECTION V

Behind the Mountains Are More Mountains

Ayisyen suiv kouran, kote dlo-a koule pi fre-a, se la li ye.
Haitians follow the direction of the current where the water
flows fresher–that's where they go.

Egzile miyò pase-l pran kout fizi [Pito ou ale manje mizè laba pase pou mouri].
To be exiled is better than to be shot.
–Haitian proverbs

If there is no struggle there is no progress. Those who profess to favor freedom, and yet depreciate
agitation, want crops without plowing the ground. They want rain without thunder and lightning.
They want the ocean without the awful roar of its many waters. This struggle may be a moral one; or it may
be a physical one; or it may be both moral and physical; but it must be a struggle.
Power concedes nothing without a demand. It never did and it never will.
–Frederick Douglass, U.S. Ambassador to Haiti, 1889-1891

As Thomas Jefferson's antipathy for the Haitian Revolution—which began just a few years after the American Revolution ended—makes clear, Haiti's very existence was a reminder that if freedom applied equally to all in the New World, society would be absolutely overturned. Haiti's radical place in the Atlantic world was also reflected in the Louisiana Purchase, over which Jefferson presided. The United States openly benefited from the Haitian victory over the French, as his defeat spurred Napoleon to sell his New World holdings, and the United States added more than 50 million acres to its territory.

When the United States finally recognized Haiti's independence in 1862, even then it did not act as a good neighbor. After Haiti gained its independence, people in the United States feared that the slaves' revolt would poison the minds of U.S. slaves. This was a main reason why it was not considered safe to have close ties with Haiti. Even so, the 10,000 or so Haitian refugees contributed significantly to the South's, and particularly to Louisiana's, economic growth through the sugar plantations that came with the Haitian migration during and after the revolution.

In other ways, Haiti has contributed to the culture and economy of the United States.[1] The famed naturalist John James Audubon (1785-1851) was born in Haiti, the son of a French officer and his Creole mistress, as was Jean-Baptiste Point du Sable. Point du Sable was a free black born in Haiti in 1745, the son of a wealthy Frenchman and an enslaved African woman. He was educated in France before traveling to New Orleans as a seaman. He left New Orleans in 1779 and established the first permanent trading post in what would become Chicago. In 1968, the State of Illinois officially recognized him as the city's founder.

The twentieth century brought renewed troubles for Haiti in the form of imperialism and genocide. During the American Occupation (1915-1934), Marines killed over 15,000 Haitians and destroyed the constitutional system in their attempt to exercise "Wilsonian idealism." Many Haitians were forced to flee Haiti and some went to the Dominican Republic, the neighbor with whom they shared a turbulent and complex past. In 1937, economic instability in the Dominican Republic was creating the conditions for a popular revolt. In response, President Rafael Trujillo (whose maternal grandmother was Haitian) promoted the common cause of racial nationalism to unite Dominicans, the objective of which was to expel Haitians in an attempt to "whiten" the country. This situation led to what is now referred to as "Haiti's holocaust." Over 20,000 Haitians, Dominicans, and Dominican-Haitians were killed by the Dominican government during this period.[2]

It is important to remember that after its independence at the beginning of the nineteenth century, in its desire to make sure neither Spain nor France returned to Hispaniola, Haiti occupied Spanish Santo Domingo (the present-day Dominican Republic), and slavery was abolished on the entire island. In 1844, after 22 years of Haitian rule, the Dominicans gained their independence from Haiti. Later, when Spain re-annexed Santo Domingo, Dominicans turned to Haiti to end Spanish domination. However, official Dominican history often omits this part of the story, and Independence Day for most Dominicans means freedom from the Haitians, not the Spanish.[3]

Relations between the two countries remain fragile. In some United States communities with large groups of Haitians and Dominicans, a common saying is that if you want to start a new war, call a Dominican a Haitian. For its part, the United States has enacted immigration laws that target Haitians and limit their opportunities for political asylum, yet those same immigration laws welcome Cubans. Jean-Pierre's "Crucified Liberty" is a testament to the Haitians' fight to survive in the face of ongoing adversity.

Notes

1. For more information on connections between Haiti and the United States, and especially between Haitians and African Americans, see Léon D. Pamphile, *Haitians and African Americans: A Heritage of Tragedy and Hope* (Gainesville: U P of Florida, 2001).

2. There is a large body of literature on this topic. For more information, see, for example, Fernando Valerio-Holguín, "Primitive Borders: Cultural Identity and Ethnic Cleansing in the Dominican Republic," trans. Scott Cooper, in *Primitivism and Identity in Latin America: Essays on Art, Literature and Culture*, ed. Erik Camayd-Freixas and José Eduardo González (Tucson: U P of Arizona, 2000).

3. Ibid., 76-77; 84-85.

Chapter 23

Haitian Immigrants in Philadelphia

Charles Blockson

Wendell Phillips, the fiery American abolitionist orator, said this of Toussaint Louverture in 1860:

> You think me a fanatic tonight, for you read history not with your eyes but your prejudices. But fifty years hence when truth get a hearing the muse of history will put Phocion for the Greek, and Brutus for the Romans, Hampden for England, Lafayette for France, choose Washington as the bright consummate flower of our earlier civilization and John Brown, the ripe flower of our noon-day, then dipping her pen in the sunlight, will write in clear blue above them all, the name of the soldier, the statesman, the martyr, Toussaint Louverture.[1]

Along with his fellow generals Jean-Jacques Dessalines, Henri Christophe, and Alexandre Pétion, Toussaint defeated the mighty forces of Napoleon, claimed independence, and established Haiti as the first black nation in the Western hemisphere. It is a historical coincidence that Haiti celebrated its 200th birthday at the same time that the U.S. government was spending millions of dollars to refurbish the Valley Forge encampment of General George Washington's Continental Army of 1777-1978.

A monument honoring black patriots of African descent sponsored by Delta Sigma Theta, an African American sorority, was erected not long ago in Pennsylvania's Valley Forge National Park. Yet the full story of participation by African American and Haitian military men in the fight for America's independence has seldom been told. Hundreds of Haitians fought on United States soil as Washington's forces rebelled against the British. Both free and enslaved Haitians fought for the liberation of a country that was not their own. The Haitians who participated in the war included members of the Volunteer Chasseurs and the Fontages Legion, named after its French commander.

Among the ranks of the all-black legion that fought in the Battle of Savannah was the 12- year-old Henri Christophe, future King of Haiti, who had volunteered as an infantryman.

Moreover, numbers of African Americans before and during the Civil War were spiritually and culturally connected to Haiti. They named many of their societies, clubs, and political organizations in honor of Toussaint Louverture and called various locations in their communities "Hayti." As early as 1824, Bishop Richard Allen, the founder of Mother Bethel African Methodist Episcopal Church in Philadelphia, and other prominent leaders assisted 200 people of African descent who were living in Philadelphia to leave for Samaná, now located in the Dominican Republic. A number of these immigrants disembarked in Haiti.[2]

During the early years of the Haitian Revolution, free people of color and French-speaking whites from Saint-Domingue were terrified by the black-led revolt and fled to the United States, taking their slaves with them. Many of these immigrants settled in Philadelphia, New York, Norfolk, Baltimore, Wilmington, and New Orleans, and a number of Haitians established themselves in these cities as caterers, restaurateurs, cabinetmakers, undertakers, coffin makers, dressmakers, and hairdressers.

Many of these Haitian immigrants, among them a man named Pierre Toussaint, became quite wealthy.[3] Born in Haiti in 1776, Toussaint conducted business in New York City and supported his former master's widow as well as several charities and organizations for the benefit of poor and oppressed citizens of the city. Theodore Duplessis, another Haitian immigrant, became known in New York for his exquisite ice cream. Other Haitians, such as Peter Augustine and St. John Appo, won national recognition as caterers and confectioners in Philadelphia; Appo's wife was famous for her ice cream.

Included among the prominent families of Haitian descent who arrived in Philadelphia in 1793 were the Abeles, Dutrieulles, Montiers, Cuyjets, Le Counts, Baptistes, and Rolands. Many other descendants of prominent Haitian families are still living in New Orleans, among them Dollies, Forrests, Trevignes and Savarys. An ancestor of the Savarys, Jean-Baptiste Savary, led a battalion of freemen of color and Haitian Creoles to defend New Orleans in the War of 1812.[4]

Stephen Girard is perhaps the most famous, or infamous, American of French descent who was connected to Haiti. Girard was reportedly the richest American of his day.[5] His father Pierre, a wealthy merchant and slave trader, settled in Saint-Domingue; Stephen was born in Bordeaux in 1750. In 1776, the younger Girard settled in Philadelphia and New Orleans. He later helped the government finance the War of 1812. In 1816, he bought three million dollars worth of stock in the Second Bank of the United States and became one of its directors. There is still some controversy surrounding Girard, specifically in terms of the source of his vast fortune. French scholar Gragon-Lacoste charges that he appropriated the funds. Interestingly enough, it appears that Girard left his money to Hannah, his brother's black mistress, because he himself had no descendants.

Girard was also implicated in other intriguing financial dealings. According to some accounts, Toussaint Louverture, who had accumulated a large amount of money as a general in charge of the army, entrusted Girard with the sum of two million francs in gold, perhaps because Toussaint believed that the banker would take care of his money wisely. And herein lies another possible explanation for Girard's wealth. A legal suit entered in the court of common pleas in Philadelphia in 1886 by counsel for Madame Rose de Laulanie of Paris, a descendant of Toussaint, claimed that before Napoleon brought Toussaint to France, Toussaint handed over the two million francs to Girard, who was in Saint-Domingue at the time. Under their supposed agreement, Girard would use this to enable Toussaint's escape in the event Napoleon attempted to arrest him. Laulanie claimed that Girard sailed to Philadelphia and kept the money, but because she could substantiate her accusation only through oral family history, her suit failed. Attorneys representing Girard's estate claimed that Girard never had any contact with Toussaint, nor was he present in Haiti at the time Toussaint was leading the Haitian Revolution. Some writers speculate that Girard sent one of his agents to Haiti to represent him and to receive the money. Although definitive evidence was not presented during the trial, the evidence that did come to light is sufficiently persuasive to invite further investigation.[6]

Girard died in 1831, and his will set aside a large portion of money to buy coal to heat the homes of poor whites. Girard also left a large sum of money for the establishment of Girard College in Philadelphia. In his will, he stipulated that the college was for "poor, white orphan boys only" and that a high wall should be built around it.[7] This will sparked one of the longest cases in Philadelphia's legal history, settled only when the U.S. Supreme Court decided against the will in the early 1960s. Today African American students attend the college in large numbers.

Notes

1. See Wendell Phillips, "Eulogy of Toussaint Louverture," *Negro History Bulletin* Vol. 4 (Jan 1941).

2. See Chapter 2 of Leon D. Pamphile's *Haitians and African Americans: A Heritage of Tragedy and Hope* (Gainesville: U P of Florida, 2001).

3. Ibid., 66.

4. Ibid., 14-16.

5. For more information on Stephen Girard, see Charles Blockson, *The Haitian Revolution: Celebrating the First Black Republic* (Virginia Beach, VA: The Donning Company Publishers, 2004) 36-37.

6. In the case concerning Toussaint Louverture and Stephen Girard, Girard's lawyers argued that Girard was not in Haiti and had no contact with Louverture. However, in *The Life and Times of Stephen Girard: Mariner and Merchant, Vol. 1* (Philadelphia: J.B. Lippincott, 1918), John B. McMaster claimed that Girard had given a letter to a man named Thibaux to give to Toussaint. He also discusses Girard's holdings in Haiti as of 1797.

7. Blockson, 36-37.

Chapter 24

Accounting for Flight
Refugees from Saint-Domingue in the United States

Ashli White

When slaves on the French Caribbean island of Saint-Domingue set fire to their masters' plantations in August 1791, U.S. newspapers carried gruesome reports about what, in their opinion, was a calamitous event. The calamitous event grew into a revolution that ravaged the wealthiest colony in the Americas for the next 13 years. Americans avidly followed the course of this revolution because it affected them in numerous ways. One of the most visible consequences of the Haitian Revolution was the arrival of thousands of colonial refugees to American cities. Between 1793 and 1809, at least 15,000 exiles—white, black, and free people of color—disembarked in seaports from New York to New Orleans.[1] As white residents took stock of the flight of the Saint-Dominguans, they interpreted events in a self-serving way, looking to neutralize the threatening implications of the Haitian Revolution for the future of slavery in the United States.

The influx of white refugees from Saint-Domingue sparked sympathy among Americans. The exiles' chilling tales of the revolution—characterized by loved ones killed and property lost at the hands of rebellious slaves—shocked local white citizens.

The ragged appearance of many refugees testified to their harrowing experiences in escaping the island and moved their white hosts to action. Communities soon organized relief campaigns for the exiles in order to ease their transition to life in the United States.

In a matter of days, thousands of dollars were raised to support what was seen as a needy and pitiable population.[2]

Yet many commentators also blamed the refugees, in part, for the insurrection. For decades Saint-Domingue had been seen as a place with barbarous master-slave relations. At the outset of the Haitian Revolution, white Americans argued that had white colonists been kinder masters, their property would not have taken up arms against them. With these views of Saint-Domingue slavery, American masters congratulated themselves on their supposedly benign version of the institution. They thought that because their slaves received (according to them) better treatment, they would have no reason to rebel. Slaveowners assured themselves that their own slave system was secure—as long as black and colored refugees from Saint-Domingue did not show up on American shores.

But thousands of black and colored refugees did come to the United States. Former slave owners forced many blacks into exile, but others wanted to leave the island. The conflagration in the colony was as frightening to many blacks and colored residents as it was to white colonists. As wealthy land and slaveowners in Saint-Domingue, many free people of color may have sought asylum for reasons similar to those of their white counterparts. For slaves, freedom was not necessarily guaranteed although the French Assembly declared emancipation throughout its colonies in 1794. Given the uncertain fate of the colony, many slaves from Saint-Domingue preferred to flee with their owners and remain slaves rather than stay on the war-torn island.

White Americans, however, assumed these immigrants were bent on bringing revolution to the doorstep of the United States. Although this supposition certainly sparked fear among white residents, the black and colored immigrants also provided white Americans with a convenient scapegoat. Signs of discontent among free and enslaved African Americans were blamed on the negative influence of black and colored immigrants. In the myopic view of these white Americans, only the introduction of a foreign element could "spoil" American slaves. According to defenders of American slavery, slavery in the South was benign and beneficent; slaves were content, and only the reckless meddling of outsiders—especially from Saint-Domingue—threatened southern slave society.

The Haitian Revolution represented what slaveowners as well as abolitionists wanted to avoid. The black militant challenge opposed not only slavery, but also the idea of a gradual process of emancipation, which most antislavery white Americans endorsed. The French decision in 1794 to abolish slavery immediately was foolish and dangerous, according to white Americans on both sides of the slavery debate. Their predictions of calamity seemed borne out—at least in their own eyes—when the proclamation yielded not peace, but an escalation of the war on the island. The intensification of war on the island following emancipation was unavoidable as former slaves battled, on the one hand, intractable French colonists who refused to honor the emancipation decree and, on the other, invading British forces. Most white observers ignored this reality, and so the continued militancy bolstered their claims about the detrimental effects of immediate emancipation.[3]

In light of white reaction to the Haitian Revolution, African Americans, both free and enslaved, were placed in a precarious position. Evidence is scarce about African American views of the revolution in Saint-Domingue. This silence does not represent lack of interest in the revolution, but the realization that outspoken support was risky. A fragment of one surviving letter shows how free African Americans tried to navigate these treacherous political waters. In the mid-1790s, a group who identified themselves only as "citizens of color of Philadelphia" drafted a letter to the French National Assembly. In it, they thanked the legislators for passing the "immortal decree" that ended slavery in the French colonies. Although the writers made no mention of the rebellion in Saint-Domingue, they referred to the slaves in the French possessions as "our brothers."[4] Clearly, citizens of color in Philadelphia knew what was happening in France and Saint-Domingue, and they saw their interests tied to those of French Caribbean slaves. But aware of the maelstrom of opinion surrounding the insurrection, the Philadelphia authors emphasized the emancipation decree and said little about the actions of slaves in the name of freedom.

Not until the 1820s were African Americans (and by this time, many white abolitionists as well) more forthright about their support for the Haitian Revolution. They still faced bitter opposition from proslavery camps, who held that the revolution proved that black and white people could not live side by side except through slavery. Supporters of Haiti and its revolution countered these claims with an outpouring of pro-Haiti literature. These works celebrated the struggle of the slaves, the prowess of their leaders, and the achievements of the young Haitian state. Reversing proslavery reasoning about the link between race war and emancipation, they contended that race war and revolution were the consequences not of emancipation, but of the failure to abolish slavery. Radical abolitionists warned that without emancipation, the American South would witness scenes similar to those in Saint-Domingue.[5]

In their assessments of the refugees' flight, white Americans devised interpretations that suited their practical and ideological needs. In this view, a unique brand of slavery—not the institution of slavery itself—provoked the slaves of Saint-Domingue to rebel and colonists to flee, and immediate emancipation perpetuated the revolution and the influx of immigrants. The first justification attempted to defuse the explosive implications of the Haitian Revolution for slaveowners in the United States, ascribing the revolution to a particular context. The second conclusion extrapolated a universal conclusion from a single decree as a way to hold off abolition. Both conclusions highlight the selectiveness of readings of the Haitian Revolution in the United States, a selectiveness that maintained the status quo in the face of an event that made clear the contradictions of America's own revolution.

<u>*Notes*</u>

1. Ashli White, *"A Flood of Impure Lava:" Saint Dominguan Refugees in the United States, 1791-1820* (unpublished Ph.D. dissertation, Columbia University, 2003), Ch.1.

2. Ibid, Ch. 2.

3. Ibid, Ch. 5.

4. Draft of a letter by "Les Citoyens de couleur de Philadelphie à L'Assemblée Nationale," 1793. Révolutions de Saint-Domingue Collection: John Carter Brown Library, Providence, RI. Although dated 1793, this letter, because of its reference to the abolition decree of February, 1795, must actually have been written later. There is no indication as to whether this letter was actually sent or who wrote it.

5. White, Ch. 5.

Chapter 25

The Haitian "Sibboleth"

Andrea Schwieger Hiepko

Perejil - pewegil - persil - pèsi!

In his paintings Ulrick Jean-Pierre tries to illustrate historical facts so that they will be communicated and transmitted to subsequent generations. The painting "Awareness of Exploitation" evokes on first sight a situation of suppression and exploitation that enables the beholder to associate it with a definite historical moment. This impression is reinforced by the title of the painting. Children with dark skin are cutting sugar cane in the field. It is a scene that could happen anywhere in the Caribbean. One's first conclusion is that the picture shows a tropical region of the New World in which the native population was exterminated and replaced by African slaves, for whom the abolition of slavery did not necessarily result in better living conditions. Children were required to work in the plantation system. "Tristes Tropiques" would be an adequate title. However, on second glance we recognize an element from another semiotic system: a banner that uses the old rules of heraldry to designate a national body. The unique combination of colors allows us to locate the scene within the borders of a nation state. In this scene it is the Dominican flag in the background that defines the context. Yet where do these children come from? What is the historical setting of the scene?

The territory is defined through a national symbol, the flag of the Dominican Republic. But the flag tells us more: in addition to indicating a specific nationality, the mere fact that there is one points to a necessity. The flag seems to be located in a space where it is useful to know exactly where you are. This is the case in border regions, especially where border crossings occur every day. The Dominican Republic has only one border, the border with Haiti. What is decoded are not racial but rather economic and social issues: the necessity to hire illegal workers from Haiti to work on Dominican sugar cane plantations and thus maintain the structures of the former slaveowning societies even after the official abolition of slavery.

From the year 1930, when Trujillo was elected President of the Dominican Republic by terrorizing the voting public, he consolidated his dictatorship by taking control of every aspect of Dominican society. In 1937, a shocking event took place on the borders of the so-called Massacre River.[1] About 15,000 Haitians, mainly children and youths living and working on the sugar cane fields and in their masters' households, were systematically tortured and executed by the troops of President Trujillo with the help of some Dominicans. The population of the Dominican Republic had been indoctrinated with the fear of an uncontrolled invasion of foreigners, metaphorically depicted as an illness or a weakness of the state.[2] The poverty and national identity of the people immigrating to work on the plantations were regarded as threatening to the wealth of the Dominican nation. Such confused thought is best described in Mario Vargas Llosa's *The Feast of the Goat*, in which he tries to reveal the state of mind of the people during the dictatorship of Trujillo (whom the Dominicans called "the Goat"). This perspective is revealed through the memories of Urania Cabral, the daughter of former Secretary of State Agustín Cabral, who fell into disgrace. Urania recalls her father's justification of the massacre:

> You can say what you like about the Chief. History, at least, will recognize that he has created a modern country and put the Haitians in their place. Great ills demand great remedies!....The Chief found a small country barbarized by wars among the caudillos, a country without law and order, impoverished, losing its identity, invaded by its starving, ferocious neighbors. They waded across the Massacre River and came to steal goods, animals, houses; they took the jobs of our agricultural workers, perverted our Catholic religion with their diabolical witchcraft, violated our women, ruined our Western, Hispanic culture, language, and customs, and imposed their African savagery on us.[3]

Yet this was the wrong answer to a false problem. To negate the mix of races and cultures that resulted from the coexistence of Dominicans and Haitians, especially in the border area, shows a fear of losing supremacy over the so-called uncivilized. Physiognomic differentiation between Haitians and Dominicans became impossible due to intermarriage, and skin color could not reliably indicate a person's origin. Cultural creolization, with its strategy of constant amalgamation, overran the border between Haiti and the Dominican Republic, even if more or less in one direction. It was only through language and speech that the other could be identified.

In the Old Testament, "shibboleth" was a password to prevent Ephraimites from intruding the Galaadite camp.[4] Mispronouncing it "sibboleth" meant immediate execution. This situation was similar to that on the border of Haiti and the Dominican Republic. If it is impossible to make a judgment just by sight, another vehicle for selection is necessary. Ephraimites, Gaaladites— if you look at them there is no difference, but if you ask them to pronounce "shibboleth," the difference becomes obvious.

In 1937, on the border of Haiti and the Dominican Republic, the way an individual pronounced the word parsley became decisive: pronouncing it as *perejil* or *pewegil* could mean life or death at that specific place and moment in time. Parsley grew everywhere in the area. People used it for cooking, for making tea, for bodily hygiene as well as for medical and ritual purposes; it was used for the first washing of a child's hair and the last ablutions of a dead body. Whether a person was from the Haitian or the Dominican side of the river was determined by forcing him or her to pronounce the name of the plant. Those who spoke the word with a French or Creole accent were sure to be murdered. To speak Spanish "correctly" saved one's life. In this example it becomes obvious how racial, social, or national belonging can function as a matter of language; that is, as a symbolic system. In this case appearance becomes irrelevant.[5]

Migration of Haitians into the Dominican Republic began in the 1930s, when the repressive years of the U.S. Occupation that began in 1915 coincided with the sugar industry's cross-border expansion.[6] For decades, Haitians migrated to the Dominican Republic for political reasons or for higher wages. Many were employed on sugar and coffee plantations or in construction, thus supporting and sometimes even facilitating the economic development of their ungrateful host country. As a result of "El Corte," as the massacre was euphemistically called, the Dominican Republic had to pay reparations to Haitian victims. In the agreement of 1939, the amount of $750,000 U.S. would be paid by the Dominicans to the Haitian government. Nonetheless, no proof is to be found for the distribution of the sum. At least three centers of agrarian production near the border zone were constructed with the help of Dominican money. The intention was to provide jobs for the Haitian people. However they couldn't stop the migration flow.

At the same time, Trujillo withdrew from the 1938 election but maintained power during the term of the puppet President Peynado.[7] But even upon Trujillo's death in 1961 the government, still defending the massacre as a necessary means to protect the border, followed the same policy: officially maintaining anti-Haitianism while simultaneously exploiting Haitian *braceros* (cane cutters) on sugar plantations.[8] This time however, the Haitian government under Jean Claude Duvalier was a major beneficiary of the situation. Duvalier organized what we can call a neo-slave trade, receiving vast sums as recruitment expenses by virtue of an agreement he signed with the Dominican state sugar council. The Haitians (*kongos*) were recruited by contractors (*buscones*) and lived in *bateyes*, or camps, on sugar plantations in the Dominican Republic. This history, which can be read as a constant movement from amalgamation to segregation and back again, was initiated by the colonial experience and has now become embedded in a typical constellation of neocolonialism in the postcolonial era.

Notes

1. The river does not derive its name from the incidents that occurred in 1937 but from an earlier clash between the Spanish and the French.

2. For a reference on the difficult relations between Dominicans and Haitians, see Michele Wucker, *Why the Cocks Fight: Dominicans, Haitians, and the Struggle for Hispaniola* (New York: Hill & Wang, 1999).

3. Mario Vargas Llosa, *The Feast of the Goat*, trans. Edith Grossman (New York: Farrar, Straus and Giroux, 2001). See Ch. 1, "Urania."

4. Judges 12:1-6.

5. Similar to the biblical story of the Shibboleth, in Haiti the word "parsley" became the "Shibboleth" of the Haitians and the Dominicans. It shows the same semantic switch expressed in this quote from Jacques Derrida: "The word did no longer designate a herb, but became a password for: partaking in an alliance or death. As with Shibboleth, the meaning of the word matters less than, let us say, its signifying form once it becomes a password, a mark of belonging, the manifestation of an alliance." Jacques Derrida, "Shibboleth: For Paul Celan," *Word Trace. Readings of Paul Celan*, ed. Aris Fioretos (Baltimore: Johns Hopkins U P, 1994) 21.

6. For a reference on the U.S. Occupation, the massacre in 1937, and the racist politics of Trujillo, see Brenda Gayle Plummer, *Haiti and the United States* (Athens: U of Georgia P, 1992).

7. For a reference on Trujillo's regime, see Eric Paul Roorda, "Genocide Next Door: the Good Neighbor Policy, the Trujillo Regime, and the Haitian Massacre of 1937," *Diplomatic History* 20:3 (Summer 1996): 301-320.

8. For a reference on the "braceros," see Arismendí Díaz Santana, "The Role of Haitian Braceros in Dominican Sugar Production," *Latin-American Perspectives* III (Winter 1976): 120-132.

Chapter 26

Temwayaj Kout Kouto, 1937
Eyewitnesses to the Genocide
Lauren Derby and Richard Turits

Despite the enormous scale and monstrous character of the 1937 Haitian massacre, with some 15,000 ethnic Haitians slaughtered by machete in the northwestern Dominican frontier, we will probably never know with any certainty what triggered this genocide ordered by the Dominican dictator Rafael Trujillo and carried out by his military. Yet we can shed light on the historical context within which this massacre occurred, the pre-1937 frontier world shared by ethnic Haitians and ethnic Dominicans. That world and the massacre itself have remained shrouded in myths stemming both from official nationalist discourses in the Dominican Republic and from widespread conflation by peasants of Haitian descent living in the pre-1937 northwestern Dominican frontier and Haitian migrant laborers in the very different world of Dominican sugar plantations, most located far from the region where the massacre occurred.[1] Moving the narration of the massacre and the pre-1937 frontier world from this mythical realm to a more historical one requires listening carefully to the voices of those who lived in the frontier and who witnessed this unspeakable and seemingly mad state violence.[2]

In 1987, together with Edouard Jean Baptiste (then working at the Centro Pastoral Haitiano of the Archbishopric in Santo Domingo), we collected some 40 hours of oral narratives from ethnic Haitian survivors of the massacre as part of a larger effort to comprehend this genocide, its historical context, as well as how such massive violence has been woven into the national imaginations of both countries. We conducted fieldwork in many Haitian towns, including the still-extant refugee communities established in Haiti by then-President Sténio Vincent (1930-1941) after the massacre. Interviewing dozens of survivors in Mont Organisé, Ouanaminthe, Dosmond, Grand Bassin, and Terrier Rouge in the north of Haiti and in Thiote and Savane Zonbi in the south, we explored the lives of ethnic Haitians on the Dominican frontier as well as their memories of the violence they suffered. Through these interviews, we learned that most of those who managed to escape the killings had been born and raised on Dominican territory, hence they were, according to the Dominican constitution and also to most local officials at the time, Dominican citizens. Indeed, ethnic Haitians in the pre-1937 Dominican frontier provinces constituted an old, well-integrated, and fairly successful agricultural population with local roots dating back to the late nineteenth century. And what defined being "Haitian" or "Dominican" was far from transparent or consistent—both legally and socially—in this milieu.[3] Thus demographic figures on the "Haitian" population are especially problematic, though it seems clear that people of Haitian descent were not a minority of the residents in much of the vast rural Dominican frontier.[4]

In Haiti, we interviewed many people who recalled living relatively prosperous lives in the Dominican borderlands producing coffee, farming food crops, and, in the frontier towns, working heavily in the skilled trades: tailoring, baking, shoemaking, and iron smelting—prestigious occupations at the time.[5] In parts of the southern frontier, there appears to have been more residential ethnic concentration and more Haitians working as farm laborers, but there too social and commercial integration were high.[6] In oral histories we conducted on the Dominican side of the border, elderly Dominicans similarly recalled the relative agricultural prominence of Haitian farmers, including their development of coffee in the central border mountains. The predominant image of Haiti itself among ethnic Dominicans in the frontier provinces had been one of more commercial and urban vitality than Dominican cities offered in the 1930s.[7] This, in turn, contributed to the image of ethnic Haitians in the frontier neither as poor, backward, nor outsiders, as today prevails in the Dominican Republic.

Certainly, Dominicans and Haitians were not free from everyday frictions, racist constructions of beauty, or prejudicial ethnic stereotypes and other forms of differentiation.[8] But a unified community formed across ethnic difference and even across the national border that was characterized by relatively respectful and intimate relations between Haitians and Dominicans.[9] Haitian-Dominican unions were commonplace; bilingualism (Spanish and Kreyòl) was the rule; and Haitian and Dominican families frequently included relatives and properties on both sides of the border.[10] Regional markets, patron-saint festivals, and networks of religious pilgrimage were also highly transnational. In contrast to state leaders and ardent nationalists in the island's urban centers, local residents treated the border as a political fiction that was largely irrelevant to daily life.[11] For instance, during the 1930s some ethnic Haitian children residing in Dajabón (Dominican Republic) attended the École des Frères primary school in Ouanaminthe (Haiti), which was considered superior to the local alternative and for which they crossed the border twice daily. When we visited Ouanaminthe in 1987, we found a grim entry in the school's log for October 1937, mourning the world destroyed on both sides of the border following the genocide:

The number of students with parents disappeared is now 176 [of 267 students]. The poor creatures are all in tears. In the evening one hears nothing but cries and wails from the houses of the whole town. The Dominicans, without doubt awaiting an immediate riposte, have evacuated the civilian population in Dajabón for eight days....Father Gallego of Dajabón has lost two-thirds of his population....In certain parishes, in Loma and Gourabe, 90 percent of the population has disappeared; instead of 150 to 160 baptisms a month, there is not even one. Some schools which had fifty students before now have no more than two or three. It's grievous and heartbreaking what has happened.[12]

The question of whether some local Dominican civilians were involved in the slaughter is a vexed one. The testimony we collected on both sides of the border indicate disparate Dominican roles. We heard stories of courageous resistance by ethnic Dominicans—themselves terrorized by "El Corte" (The Cutting)—who hid Haitian friends and loved ones in their homes, transported them across the border, or emigrated with them to Haiti. On the other hand, the military enlisted numerous local civilians to help identify and locate "Haitians." And a few Dominican civilians were recruited to participate in the killings. Some of these civilians were prisoners from other areas; others were local residents tied to the Trujillo regime and its informal repressive apparatus.[13]

The following excerpts provide a glimpse into the memories of those who witnessed and survived the genocide and a fragmentary window into a world that came to an abrupt halt on October 2, 1937. The printed word, of course, cannot convey the outpouring of emotion, anger, and sadness generated by their recollections, including those who watched as their families were killed by machete. In one particularly painful and animated interview presented below, Irélia Pierre recounted how as a young girl she survived the killings by playing dead as she lay bleeding underneath the bodies of her slaughtered brothers, sisters, and parents. Scars covering her neck and shoulders still recorded the machete swipes that thankfully missed their mark.

Our interviews in Haiti were conducted in Kreyòl, though many survivors switched occasionally into Spanish while recalling their lives in "Panyòl" or "Dominikani," Haitian terms for the Dominican Republic. Most informants gave us permission to use their names, but a few preferred to remain anonymous. What follows below are translated transcripts of two of the interviews.[14]

Anonymous Man in Ouanaminthe

When the massacre happened, I missed becoming a victim as a child. When the massacre started, I was at school; I went to a religious school. The brothers had a choir for all the children who sang; and they had a group of kids who knew how to sing, and I was always singing with the brothers. When the massacre started, the children were in school, and I was at choir. And October 7th, the day of the patron saint festival at Dajabón, the brothers took us over there, since the border was free to cross, and no one was afraid to cross the border at that time. So the brothers took us to go to mass there, so that we could sing in the choir at mass there. And while we were in the church, I saw a band of Dominican military who were milling about outside while we were in church. Since we were children, we didn't understand anything. What was happening was that the military wanted to kill people at that very time, right in daylight—to take people from the church and kill them. But what happened was the brothers were foreign, they were French, and I think because of them, they didn't do this. But when night came, around six, around that time, they started killing people. They started killing people at six o'clock, while people started crying out for help, people started running, they came wounded, they crossed the Massacre River, they all came wounded, they killed a lot of people.[15] A lot of people who were saved came here. And so, this is how I came to Dosmond colony. When people started arriving, the Vincent government rounded up people in the Dominican Republic. The war began with a lot of people dead, a lot of Haitians were taken when war came to the frontier. They finished killing people after one week, a week later. The Vincent government sent for the rest of the Haitians. Then Trujillo sent his men to gather and haul out the rest of the Haitians left behind. They brought war to the border. In Ouanaminthe, when you looked at the river, it was completely a sea of people and donkeys—it was completely full!—because many of the people—in fact most of the Haitians on the Dominican side—were afraid to live in the Dominican Republic any more. They were forced to leave although they didn't have a place to go to in Haiti since they had never lived there. When they arrived in Haiti, they were homeless refugees. So the government had to make colonies for them because Dosmond was a big savanna, a place where I knew everyone by name. My father had a beautiful garden in the savanna. It really was a savanna—there weren't any houses at all, nothing like it. The place was a desert. Before the massacre, in the frontier, although there were two sides, the people were one, united. All the tradesmen in Dajabón—all the cobblers and tailors—they were all Haitian. And even today there are Haitians all over Ouanaminthe, even though they still die today, there are still Haitian children there today, crossing the border daily. Haitian children, even if they were born in Dajabón, they still went to school in Haiti, every morning they would cross the border to go to school, every afternoon they would return. Their parents lived in Dajabón, but they came to school here. Haitians have always liked the French system of education, and the Catholic schools. Even the Dominicans love the French language, and the French language helps them a lot to speak Kreyòl.

Irélia Pierre, Dosmond/Ouanaminthe

I was born in the Dominican Republic. When the massacre broke out, I was very small. I remember that I had been in school a while. The day of my brother's marriage, after the ceremony was over, a Dominican arrived at the reception. The reception was the morning that the massacre broke out, and people started fleeing. That night we hid. The next morning when we woke up, some of the older people said "Be careful if you go out." So we stayed at home. Everyone came to my grandparents' house. They said they were going to Haiti because a revolution had broken out, and that they were killing Haitians. They all slept at my grandparents'. During the night, a woman said to me, "You come with me to my house." I said, "No, I'm going to stay with my mother—I can't leave her here." So we went out to the garden where my mother was working, and she cut some bananas and put them in her bag. I carried a tree branch.

Suddenly, I looked over and saw a lot of guardias [Dominican soldiers] getting off their horses, and I heard them say, "There's one over there in the garden." Then they entered the garden and killed the girl. When I saw that, I ran. It was night. While I was running, I saw an uncle of mine, who took me into his house to protect me. When I arrived at his house I was terrified. They didn't let me sleep; they took me to another place. That morning at four o'clock they all took their bags, and we started to march toward Haiti.

While we were walking, some Dominicans told us to be careful and not go through Dajabón, but to pass around it, since they were killing people there. When we arrived at the Dajabón savanna, we saw a guardia. When we saw him I said, "Mama, we're going to die, we're going to die!" She told me to be quiet. Then a guardia screamed *"Está preso, está preso!"* [You're under arrest, you're under arrest!]. After that they had us all stand in the sun in the savanna. When we said we were thirsty, they said they would give us water soon. While we watched, we saw one guardia on a horse who had a rope to tie people up. When he saw that if he tied up too many people they started to run, he began to kill them and throw them into a hole.

He killed everyone; I was the only one who was saved. They thought I was dead because they had given me a lot of machete blows. I was awash in blood—all the blood in my heart. After all these tribulations, it's thanks to God that I didn't die. They killed them all in front of me. They tied them up, and after they killed them, they threw them down. I was small when I lived through all of this, but I remember it all too clearly. I remember calling out after the guardia had left, "Mama!" but she was dead; "Papa!" but he was dead. They died one after another. I was left alone in the savanna without anything to eat or drink. There were a lot of small children who were thrown up in the air and stabbed with a bayonet, and then placed on top of their mothers. They killed my entire family, my mother, my father. We were 28—all were killed. I was the only one to survive that I knew of. After they finished cutting me up, it was a group of older men who had come from Haiti who found me on the ground in the sand along the banks of the Massacre River. They picked me up and returned with me to Haiti. They brought me to Ouanaminthe, but they didn't take me in—they said they couldn't take care of me, so they said they would send me to Cap-Haïtien; when I arrived there, there would be people there to take care of me. I spent a month in bed in the hospital, after which time they sent me to live in Ouanaminthe.[16] When I arrived here, I didn't have any family to receive me, so I went back to Cap again. I stayed under the auspices of the state. After about a year, they sent me back to Ouanaminthe again, at which time I lived there with some other foreigners.

God gave me the strength to survive. Now I am married and have four children, but my entire family died during the massacre. Both my mother and father were born in the Dominican Republic. We lived in Loma de Cabrera. My father worked in agriculture, growing manioc, peanuts, rice on his own land— land that he had bought. He had ten karo of land.[17] He also kept some cattle, pigs, chickens, and goats. We grew enough food to feed the family (we never bought food at market) but also to sell. I used to go to market with my mother where we sold everything—peas, rice, bananas, corn. I only spoke in Kreyòl since we lived among Haitians. I hardly spoke in Spanish at all. There were some Dominicans in the area where we lived, but not many; there were mostly Haitians. There were both marriages between Haitians and Dominicans, as well as concubinage. There were no problems that I remember between Haitians and Dominicans—for example, no jealousy for Haitian land.

Notes

1. Dominican sugar plantations located near the coast and primarily in the eastern part of the country began employing large numbers of Haitian immigrants in the 1910s. In earlier decades, immigrant workers from other parts of the Caribbean supplied most of the cane cutters.

2. This past has also been explored in fiction. See Edwidge Danticat, *The Farming of Bones* (New York: Soho Press, 1998).

3. See Richard Lee Turits, "A World Destroyed, A Nation Imposed: The 1937 Haitian Massacre in the Dominican Republic," *Hispanic American Historical Review* 82, no. 3 (Aug. 2002): 595n-599.

4. In the Dajabón parish comprising the area between Dajabón and Restauración, a Jesuit missionary estimated 30,000 residents of Haitian descent (raza haitiana) out of a total population of 35,000. José Luis Sáez, S.J., *Los Jesuitas en la República Dominicana, Volumen 1 (1936-1961)* (Santo Domingo: Museo Nacional de Historia y Geografía, 1988) 60, 71. The U.S. delegation in Santo Domingo reported a more conservative estimate of 17,000 Haitians (Atwood to Sec. of State, no. 39, 25 Oct 1937, National Archives and Records Administration, College Park, MD [NARA], RG84, 800-D). In 1937, a Dominican colonel offered a high estimate of 50,000 "Haitians" in Monte Cristi province (Manuel Emilio Castillo to Trujillo, 18 Oct 1937), Archivo General de la Nación, Santo Domingo, cited in Bernardo Vega, *Trujillo y Haití, Volumen II (1937-1938)* (Santo Domingo: Fundación Cultural Dominicana, 1995) 77. Cf. Julián Díaz Valdepares, "Alrededor de la cuestión haitiana," *Listín Diario*, 10 Dec. 1937. Census data did not provide information on the number of ethnic Haitians in the Dominican Republic, but only of documented Haitian migrants, a mere 3,816 out of a total population of 87,022 in Monte Cristi province in 1935 (Vega, *Trujillo y Haití, Volumen II*, 345).

5. See Lauren Derby, "Haitians, Magic, and Money: Raza and Society in the Haitian-Dominican Borderlands, 1900-1937," *Comparative Studies in Society and History* 36, no. 3 (1994); Freddy Prestol Castillo, *Paisajes y meditaciones de una frontera* (Ciudad Trujillo: Cosmopolita, 1943) 33-40; Michiel Baud, "Una frontera-refugio: dominicanos y haitianos contra el estado," *Estudios Sociales* 26, no. 92 (1993): 42.

6. See also Jesús María Ramírez, *Mis 43 años en la Descubierta*, ed. Gisela Ramírez de Perdomo (Santo Domingo: Ed. Centenario, 2000) 13-75, 77-80; Derby, "Haitians, Magic, and Money," 511.

7. See also Ramírez, *Mis 43 años*, 22-23.

8. See Derby, "Haitians, Magic, and Money."

9. See Turits, "A World Destroyed," 598.

10. See also Héctor Incháustegui Cabral, "La poesía de tema negro en Santo Domingo," *Eme Eme: Estudios Dominicanos* 1, no. 5 (1973) 16-19.

11. Dominican intellectuals represented the Haitian presence in the frontier as a "pacific invasion" endangering the Dominican nation. See, e.g., Joaquín Balaguer, "El imperialismo haitiano," *El Imparcial*, 13 Dec. 1927.

12. Log book, Oct 1937, L'École des Frères, Ouanaminthe. See also Sáez, *Los Jesuitas*, 71.

13. See Turits, "A World Destroyed"; interview with Miguel Otilio Savé (Guelo), Monte Cristi, 1988; testimony of Cime Jean, Ouanaminthe, 3 Oct1937, NARA, RG84, 800-D; Juan Manuel García, *La matanza de los haitianos: genocidio de Trujillo, 1937* (Santo Domingo: Alfa & Omega, 1983) 59, 67-71; José Israel Cuello, ed., *Documentos del conflicto domínico-haitiano de 1937* (Santo Domingo: Ed. Taller, 1985) 60-85; and Freddy Prestol Castillo, *El Masacre se pasa a pie* (Santo Domingo: Ed. Taller, 1973) 49.

14. To avoid interruption, we have omitted our questions to the interviewees from these transcripts.

15. The river was renamed the Massacre in the 1700s, purportedly after a bloody clash there between French colonists and Spanish forces.

16. Most of the massacre victims were sent to a hospital in Cap-Haïtien, where they were attended by the Catholic Church.

17. One karo (or carreau) equals 1.29 hectares of land.

Chapter 27

The Haitian Refugees
Camila

The painting "The Haitian Refugees I" by Ulrick Jean-Pierre is a stunning rendition of the tragedy of a group of refugees known to many as the "boat people." It depicts a scrambling and desperate humanity hanging onto a flimsy boat. Overhead, Mother Liberty appears to look upon them with the same indifference Americans tend to show upon hearing that a boatload of Haitian refugees has tried to land, or has successfully landed, on American soil. This indifference, which sometimes borders on resentment, is further cultivated by negative publicity connected with these refugees. As a result, the American public has become insensitive to the real motivation behind those attempts.

In the late 1950s, Haiti experienced one of the fluctuations typical to any nation on the brink of political conflict, in the form of another bout of restlessness, followed by a series of ephemeral governments. This uneasy period appeared to be over when a jubilant nation went to the polls to elect one of Haiti's favorite sons, François Duvalier, affectionately nicknamed "Papa Doc" because of the years he had devoted to treating the rural poor. However, Duvalier turned out to be a great curse heaped upon Haiti's head. His capacity for evil far exceeded anything to which the people had grown accustomed. His regime remains the worst dictatorship the country has experienced. The damage done by Duvalier's dynasty and the ruthless army of thugs he let loose on the people has yet to be accurately assessed.

From his first day in office, Duvalier was obsessed with consolidating his hold on the country. He knew from history that his administration would remain vulnerable to a coup d'état if he did not find a way to neutralize the army. To accomplish this, he formed his own militia by recruiting the poor and uneducated. The members of his protective force were picked up from the most remote parts of the country and bused daily to the capital, Port-au-Prince, where they were unceremoniously dumped into the streets. Officially, they were there to protect national security, but in reality they acted more like keepers of Duvalier's august person. In an attempt at levity, the people gave them many names, such as "Tontons Macoutes" and "Ma Tante Sac Paille" [thieving relatives], but the bearers displayed such brutality that they remain infamous in Haiti. Highly visible in their green outfits complemented by a French beret and dark glasses, the armed Macoutes and their female counterparts went everywhere and served as the eyes and ears of the president. Since the treasury had already been depleted by previous administrations, as payment for their services, Duvalier awarded them the right to pillage at will.

No institution was safe from interference from the Macoutes. Businesses unwilling to go along with the new order were forced to close through the disappearance or death of their owners. The judicial system was rendered completely ineffective as court personnel were so fearful of going against the Macoutes that justice became a thing of the past. The educational system was equally corrupted. In many instances, decisions concerning students were based on the whim of the Macoute in charge. As illiterate individuals often made these decisions, they often had the disastrous effect of discriminating against the brightest students.

The repression did not stop with Haitians living in Haiti. Government spies monitored Haitian nationals all over the world, especially those attending school abroad. When they completed their education and returned home, they were systematically taken into custody, jailed, tortured, and sometimes killed. Educated citizens became the primary target of Duvalier's purges.[1] People thought that by becoming invisible they could escape victimization. This tactic did not always work. When it became obvious that Duvalier intended to remain in power, especially after he proclaimed himself "Président à vie" in 1965, everyone who could get a visa and afford a ticket left. From 1961 through 1970, 90,834 legal Haitian immigrants entered the United States.[2] Countless others went to Africa, Europe, and Canada.

Until Duvalier forced Haitians to abandon their land, exchanges between Haiti and the United States had been few, except for tourists, students, and contact between intellectuals and artists mainly during the Harlem Renaissance. But once Haitian immigration started in the 1960s, it never really stopped. Those arriving in the 1960s met with little resistance, not because the American public had become more tolerant of immigrants, as evidenced by the fact that the McCarran Immigration Act of 1952, which barred "colored races from immigration in favor of North Europeans," replaced the 1882 Chinese Exclusion Act. Rather, their arrival coincided with a shortage of skilled workers in the United States. Therefore, the reason for the lack of resistance to Haitians had more to do with economic realities, as the new immigrants were skilled professionals who were a welcome addition to the workforce. Moreover, they were able to blend into the multi-cultural communities of cities such as Miami and New York.

Following the departure of those emigrants, Haiti experienced a short time when there seemed to be hope for a brighter future. On his deathbed, Duvalier transferred power to his son, Jean Claude, nicknamed "Baby Doc." At first, the people were reluctant to celebrate, fearing a pretext for one of Duvalier's periodic political purges. But as nothing happened to confirm that this was a ruse, they gave free voice to their delight, which proved to be short-lived because the elder Duvalier had made provision for the continuation of his reign of terror. Not wanting to leave decision making to a young man devoid of any sense of administration and far more interested in fast cars and fast women, Duvalier bequeathed the day-to-day running of the country to a triumvirate of like minds: his mother and his oldest sister and her husband.

Soon after Jean-Claude's inauguration, it became apparent to the people that they had traded one misery for another. Not only did they not gain political freedom, but they also had to contend with another problem: François Duvalier had been a very frugal man; Jean-Claude and his wife, Michelle Bennett, lived in luxury that was an insult to people who could not even feed or clothe their children. In addition, he inflicted another band of thugs on the country, called "Les Léopards," without disarming the Macoutes. Life under his government was unbearable, with two groups of armed bandits extorting the people. The exodus that started in 1960 stretched well into the 1980s. Between 1977 and 1981, 50,000-70,000 Haitian refugees arrived in southern Florida, this time in small boats, and were immediately labeled boat people.[3] Many more would arrive in the ensuing years, even though the small likelihood of receiving sanctuary had been further diminished.

Looking at what has happened to Haiti since the Duvaliers turned the country into one of the greatest "exporters of brains," it is understandable why Haitians are forced to undertake such a perilous journey.[4] Even without the dangers inherent in a nation that has been brought to the brink of despair, the departure of Haiti's most valuable citizens left it incapable of forming effective institutions. In a single year, the country lost the services of an entire medical-school class, educated at the country's expense.[5] Similar losses occurred in almost every other area of life, with the disastrous effect of depriving the country of much of its economic output and professional expertise. Haiti became unable to provide any credible level of education and training for the remaining population. With no viable industries, the few available resources were grabbed by corrupt political officials or by bandits. When the more affluent departed, the rest of the population, even if they could pay for a plane ticket, which often cost less than boat passage, could not expect to secure a visa from the American government.

Incidentally, the partnership between Haiti and the United States to keep Haitians from fleeing Haiti went hand-in-hand with keeping any effective opposition from overthrowing the Duvalier dynasty. Despite the administration's long list of documented human rights violations and atrocities, the Western powers never tried to impose sanctions or help its demise because it provided a buffer against communist Cuba. Therefore, anyone seeking to leave Haiti, once America's needs had been satisfied, had to resort to more basic means of escape.

It is unfortunate that the hard work put in by the Haitian immigrants of the early 1960s did not grant much favor to the subsequent refugees. Far from creating a climate in which they felt safe and welcome, opposition to their entry into American life has met each new attempt. Parenthetically, Canada appears to be the only country to have publicly acknowledged the Haitian contribution to its educational system. The average citizen sees no other way out of this predicament than that offered by the boat. No matter how repressive the atmosphere of the country becomes or how loudly the United States deplores the lack of political freedom there, Haitians are being denied asylum that is readily available to many others.

Numerous excuses have been proffered to justify the disproportionately harsh treatment that the boat people have received, some more outlandish than others, such as undocumented reports that they carry tuberculosis. In the 1980s, the media circulated rumors that AIDS had originated in Haiti.[6] Although clearly not a rational suggestion because it implied that the disease, like a hurricane, had singled out Haiti after miraculously avoiding the Dominican Republic and Cuba, these and similar allegations have had the effect of adding fuel to the opposition to Haitian immigration. The rumors have since been proven untrue, but not before they stigmatized an entire nation.

President Reagan signed the interdiction treaty in 1981 on the basis that Haitians are "economic and not political refugees," and it has been upheld.[7] Despite the outcry from African American activists and white liberals who view the treatment of Haitian refugees as racially motivated, the few attempts at adjusting this obvious disparity have not always worked in the refugees' favor. Those who have successfully made it to the United States have been imprisoned. Many have voluntarily elected to return to Haiti when their confinement has proven too unbearable. Since the extradition laws have been put into place, countless numbers of Haitians have been summarily returned to Haiti without being given a chance to prove that they have a credible fear of persecution.

The world community, and especially the U.S. government, continues to clamor about the lack of democracy in Haiti. However, few want to accept the correlation between this lack of political freedom and the need of Haitians to seek more secure surroundings.

Notes

1. Camila, *The Common Dream* (Philadelphia: Xlibris, 1997) 79.

2. "Haitian Identity in the United States / History of Haitian Migration to the United States," from <http://www.hamline.edu/cla/academics/international_studies/diaspora/haitians/paper.html > (12/30/02).

3. "Afro-Caribbean Migration to the United States/Historical Origins of Caribbean Migration to the United States," from <http://www.africana.com/articles/tt_426.htm> contributed by Ramón Grosfogue (12/30/02).

4. Camila, *The Common Dream*, 40.

5. Ibid.

6. "Afro-Caribbean Migration to the United States/Historical origins of Caribbean migration to the United States."

7. "No Port in a Storm: The Misguided Use of In-Country Refugee Processing in Haiti," *Americas Watch, National Coalition for Haitian Refugees and Jesuit Refugee Service/USA*, September 1993, Vol. 5, Issue 8.

Chapter 28

A History of Haitian Painting[1]
Michel-Philippe Lerebours

Translated by Jessica Adams and Cécile Accilien

The history of Haitian painting begins with Haiti's birth as a nation. It has strong roots in the society of colonial Saint-Domingue; contrary to a long-accepted myth, colonial society had a vibrant cultural life, and placed special importance on the arts, particularly literature, music, and painting. All social classes in the colony participated in this cultural life. Well-known French artists spent time in Cap-Français, Port-au-Prince, Saint-Marc, and Cayes, where they attracted a clientele eager to have themselves painted, or to celebrate the delights and happenings of colonial life. It is also worth noting that art galleries and private classes in drawing and painting flourished in the main cities in the colony, a fact that testifies to the colonists' passion for the visual arts.

Often trained in France but remaining close to the tastes and aspirations of their class, some free people of color made a name for themselves in the colonial art world, sometimes even becoming celebrities—for example Michel de Léogâne, a painter of portraits, landscapes, and historical scenes, was considered one of the best artists in Saint-Domingue. Shortly before the revolution, planters from La Plaine du Cul-de-Sac honored his talent by commissioning him to paint works to adorn the parish church in Croix-des-Bouquets.

Slaves were not completely cut off from the arts. Certainly, under the circumstances, they were unable to develop or even to preserve traditional African art forms. However, whether out of snobbery, vanity, or love of lucre, some slaveowners, if they thought they detected a glimmer of artistic or musical talent in their slaves, would allow them to develop it, to profit from a stay in Europe or the visit of an artist to Saint-Domingue. In colonial newspapers doesn't one often find notices of runaway slaves, or slaves for sale, noting that this or that black or mulatto, créole or bossal[2] knows how to draw or can paint a little?

Thus the artistic life of the young Haitian nation did not begin from nothing. As was the case all over Latin America, Haiti benefited from artistic traditions born elsewhere and transported by different social groups, with their own aesthetics and ideas about the world, which were grafted onto a pre-existing native heritage. One can thus understand the interest that Haiti's founders had in maintaining the arts and helping them to flourish.

After he had become king and established himself in Milot, in the palace of Sans-Souci, Henri Christophe surrounded himself with eight painters who were charged primarily with painting the portraits of the leading personages of his kingdom, and preserving for posterity the great acts of heroism that had marked the three years of struggle for liberty and independence, as well as depicting the main events of Christophe's rule. These were Frédéric Toucas, Baptiste, Chatel, Beaumy, Manuel, Bazile, Charles, and Revinchal. The last was named official painter of the king. Charles was given the leadership of the Academy of Drawing and Painting established at Sans-Souci. In 1816, Richard Evans, an English painter and a follower of Sir Thomas Lawrence, arrived in Haiti and was appointed professor at the Academy. His stay in the kingdom was unfortunately rather brief. In 1818, he returned to England, bringing with him a portrait of King Christophe that was exhibited that year in London.[3]

Like Sans-Souci in the Kingdom of Haiti, Pétion's villa in Volant-le-Tort, a few kilometers to the south of Port-au-Prince, served as the center of artistic activity in the Republic of Haiti until the fall of Boyer in 1843. The interest taken by the first Haitian president in developing the arts is evident, for example, in the law of June 30, 1817, which regulated the practice of the artistic profession and worked to protect local painters from foreign competition by painters either living in or passing through Haiti.

As had been true before 1804, artists came from France and the United States to put their skills at the service of the population, among them the American Charles Hardy and the Frenchman Barincou. During Barincou's last stay in Haiti, from 1816 to 1829, he enjoyed the greatest acclaim in Port-au-Prince and its environs. As for Charles Hardy, he taught courses in drawing and painting and attracted many disciples. It was from him that Pétion commissioned the portraits of the heroes of the War of Independence that decorated his villa in Volant-le-Tort and the Government Palace. At the same time, the national artists who had come out of Saint-Domingue society—portraitists, landscape painters, and painters of historical subjects—continued to work as much in the capital as they did in towns across the countryside. One young artist, Denis, began to gain a reputation during this time. After having painted the portraits of the "Grands Capitaines" that were destined for the villa at Volant, he helped Barincou finish his paintings of the heroes of Independence. However, like Numa Desroches and Thimoléon Déjoie, who were trained at the Academy of Drawing and Painting in Sans-Souci, Denis would only display the true measure of his talent under Boyer's regime.

Haitian Painting in the Eras of Boyer and Soulouque

Boyer's tenure began well, and, until about 1830, his solicitude for the arts was clearly apparent. Pursuing the political philosophy inaugurated by Pétion, and undoubtedly motivated by colonial tradition, Boyer took care to decorate the public buildings with portraits of revolutionary heroes and friends of the republic. In February of 1819, Denis presented him with portraits of Generals Lamothe Aigron, Bergerac-Trichet, Nicolas, and Frédérique, works that were intended to hang in the Government Palace. That same year, under a scholarship sponsored by the senate, Boyer asked Denis to paint a portrait of Abbé Grégoire, a French citizen who had been completely committed to the cause of the blacks during the revolution. A copy of this painting was bought by the Senate and placed in the main hall of the Government Palace.

Around 1821, Ardouin tells us, "a Haitian painter from Cap-Haïtien (Thimoléon Déjoie) painted Boyer arriving in town that we see in the Palace in Port-au-Prince. In the House of Representatives one finds an allegorical work depicting Liberty seated on the ruins of the colonial system." We could mention many similar examples of the support that this government gave to the arts and to artists.

Founded by Pétion, the Lycée National was developed by Boyer, who did not neglect to reserve a special place for the arts. Two teachers of drawing, of painting, and of lithography were appointed—a Haitian, Denis, and a Frenchman, Adolphe Duperly. Denis remained at the Lycée until about 1835, when the school fell victim to budgetary constraints and its operations were reduced to a bare minimum. Before this, however, courses in drawing and painting had been instituted in all Haitian private schools and, beginning in 1821 under the supervision of Denis, a course was also set up for state employees.

Encouraged by the public, many artists such as Denis, Duperly, Simonis, and Ramsey started teaching private classes in drawing and painting. In 1822, Duperly began publishing a series of works focusing on the principles of drawing. And interest in the arts was not confined to Port-au-Prince. If we are not well informed about what was happening in Cap-Haïtien, we do know that in Cayes, Mme. Albert Goldman, née Clara Petit, who immigrated from the United States in 1825, directed a program there in painting and music, and succeeded in educating many pupils. Portraitists, painters of historical and religious themes, and landscape painters had a large and diverse clientele. In his book *Brief Notice of Haïti* (1842), John Candler wrote, "In this country there are a certain number of artists who manage to earn their living by painting portraits. Paintings of this type are quite numerous, and they strike your eye in the most modest houses, where you would least expect to see them."

It is therefore mistaken to describe the era of Boyer as a dark period in the history of Haitian art. Certainly, one can hardly say that painting was equally a part of the life of every social class, but, in contrast to what would happen in 1944, it was supported by a national clientele whose tastes and desires, as well as problems and prejudices, it represented. Although it went through a period of uncertainty, and often fell victim to slavish imitation, this was only normal in a new society that was just getting acquainted with itself.

No empire has been as widely condemned as the second Haitian Empire, and no emperor has been the object of as much scorn as Faustin Soulouque, who has entered history as a symbol of ignorance and cruelty.[4] Yet no other Haitian head of state, with the exception, perhaps, of Christophe and Pétion, has been as close to artists, and as interested in fostering artistic production during the course of his administration. The splendors of empire, and the advent of a new aristocracy, are certainly factors that help us understand Soulouque's attitude, but they are not enough to explain it. He was motivated by much more than ambition and a taste for magnificent displays, for until the end of his reign he maintained close relationships with artists, received them into his intimate circle, and gave them noble titles and special privileges. The events organized to celebrate paintings were numerous during this period. Each time a portrait of the emperor had been completed, it was formally presented to him. The court, led by the empress, would parade multiple times through the streets of the capital with a religious painting by Colbert Lochard or Alcide Barreau before hanging it on the walls of the former Cathedral of Port-au-Prince.

Haitian Painting from 1860 to 1930

The fall of the Empire and the restoration of the Republic in January, 1859 did not adversely affect the nation's artistic life. The artists lost their noble titles but they remained on intimate terms with those in power, and the new government showed itself to be particularly interested in culture and the arts. Classes in drawing and painting continued to be part of school curricula. A. Sévère was named instructor of drawing at the Lycée Alexandre Pétion. In 1863, a school of painting and drawing opened under the direction of Colbert Lochard, who was assisted by professors Archibald Lochard (his son) and Saint-Hubert Emmanuel. As in the past, private art classes continued to be offered throughout the country. In Cap-Haïtien, for example, T. Daguilh taught a course that was open to anyone who wanted lessons in painting or drawing.

Supported by a clientele that commissioned landscapes, portraits, and ex-votos, many artists, both Haitian and foreign, were able to make a living from their art. In 1863, seven painters had their studios in Port-au-Prince: Colbert Lochard, Bernadotte Ulysse, Douglas, A. Sévère, Mathieu, Vergès, and Lacombe. More than ever, Haitian painting seemed assured of a bright future.

The years 1865-1870 marked an important turning point in the history of visual arts in Haiti. Artists were faced with a rather sudden decline in clientele, just as the political and economic situation in Haiti began to seriously deteriorate. Officials became too preoccupied with defending the government against the many insurrections that perpetually broke out all over the country to interest themselves in art. Artists no longer received government commissions. Salomon and Hyppolite did send a number of young people to study visual arts in France, but these were unusual cases. In the 1850s photography had appeared in Haiti, and it soon became a popular medium. In order to survive, many portrait painters, both Haitian and foreign, were now compelled to devote themselves to making pictures by this new means.

The 1860 Signature du Concordat gave authority to the foreign clergy and, in the name of "civilization," the clergy decided to impose upon the Haitian people the aesthetic ideals of the West, and attempted to stamp out any customs and traditions that had been inherited from Africa. They taught the people to prefer imported goods over local products. In place of traditional Haitian religious painting, which the clergy judged to be in bad taste, they supplied discordantly foreign images. Chromolithographs presenting alpine meadows, exotic still lifes, and illustrations of European proverbs replaced local still lifes and images of the Haitian countryside. Landscape painters and painters of religious history were thereby forced into unemployment. The pervasive sense of anxiety created by frequent military reviews, fires, and pillaging made the environment for art significantly worse. Constantly threatened with exile, the leading members of the aristocracy were hardly inclined to invest in works of art.

Nevertheless, until 1915, there was no lack of painters, and despite everything they managed to maintain their faith in the prospects of art in Haiti, Archibald Lochard most of all. Lochard, "the tender, patient artist, the wonderful man,"[5] devoted himself body and soul to nurturing the youngest students, creating art school after art school (the last in 1915, in collaboration with the sculptor Normil Charles) in an attempt to ensure that art would live in Haiti. He also worked to repair paintings that had been damaged in the fires and pillaging. A true leader, he was a powerful figure of the last half of the nineteenth century. His work is certainly not free of weaknesses (his drawing is sometimes awkward and unsure), but it is the product of an unusually refined mind. In his portraits one finds the anguish and the frustration that characterize the last years of the Haitian belle époque.

Despite being subjected to intense competition from foreign artists such as Vientéjol who had established themselves in Haiti, and despite that they often suffered from the indifference of the public, many Haitian artists—among them Rodolphe Thomas, Edouard Goldman, and Albert Rigaud—never allowed themselves to fall victim to despair. Even after the arrival of the Americans in 1915, they continued to work implacably, celebrating the past and the aristocratic leaders of Haiti. Those who would locate the beginning of Haitian painting in 1930, with the indigénistes, or even in 1944-46, fail to realize that, through their own prejudices, they deprive Haitian cultural heritage of the most accessible evidence that has been left to us of the nineteenth and early twentieth centuries.[6]

The Indigéniste Revolt

The indigéniste movement was born out of the reaction of Haitian youth against the American Occupation and the abuses that accompanied it. Indigénisme accused the traditional aristocracy of being responsible for Haiti's political, economic, and cultural failures, and proposed the rediscovery of beliefs and traditions that were the legacy of Africa. The movement took shape in 1927 around the publication Revue indigène. A year later, Jean Price-Mars' novel *Ainsi parla l'oncle* [So Spoke the Uncle] appeared, which both developed possibilities for action and gave the movement a clear theoretical framework.

The indigéniste movement necessarily influenced Haitian painting, especially because it developed at a moment when Haitian painting was practically dead. Like Haitian literature, which was striving to get at the most profound realities of Haitian existence, Haitian painting tried to mirror peasant life, indeed making this almost its sole source of inspiration. After having eradicated nineteenth-century artistic conventions with the stroke of a pen, the new generation of Haitian painters proclaimed the principles of la nouvelle peinture: 1) To be inspired only by the realities of everyday life in Haiti (landscapes, peasants, rural life, local flowers and fruit); and 2) to begin with the most advanced techniques in Western art, and to adapt them to the particular needs of Haitian art.

In their hope that through their ardor and good faith they would make Haitian art acceptable and even praiseworthy again, the indigénistes faced an uphill battle, as we shall see. Artists during this period include Maurice Borno, Edouard Dupoux, Lucien Price, Jean Pariscot, and Anton Jeagerhuber, and they showed great energy and enthusiasm. But the public remained indifferent to their efforts, and sometimes did not even bother to hide their hostility to this type of painting—which, even though it received no response from the general public, shocked the elite with its stance on social and racial issues.

Despite some successes outside of Haiti (in 1938, Pétion Savain received first prize for his painting "Marché sur la colline" in a California competition sponsored by IBM; the following year, Georges Ramponneau brought back second prize for "Marchande de Cocos"), discouragement quickly came to the indigénistes. As of 1940, the same moment at which the so-called anti-superstition campaign was being unleashed, leading to the disappearance of the real treasures of popular art, the artists, feeling completely unsettled and uprooted, thought of either leaving the country never to return, or of abandoning painting completely.

The history of Haitian painting might thus have begun in 1944. But the 1940s cannot be explained without 1933-35, without the Pont St. Géraud group, without the courage of Pétion Savain, Georges Ramponneau, Edouard Preston, Jean Parisot, Antoine Derenoncourt, and Andrée Malbranche. The indigéniste movement is clearly mistaken in its claim that it gave birth to Haitian painting; but it certainly marks a rupture, and a new beginning in its history. The movement at first faltered, often forgetting, in its ideological poses, that art itself comes before theories and always refuses to follow them—that art is always interested only in serving the cause of art. The efforts of the indigénistes are commendable nonetheless. Rejecting an artistic legacy that they judged to be insufficiently theoretical, the indigénistes wanted to connect Haitian painting to the major currents within contemporary art. The opening to "modernity" was no longer viewed as a form of alienation for Haitian art because it was accompanied by a uniquely Haitian quest, by uniquely Haitian goals. This move for connection was not experienced as a dilemma, a mutilation, or an effort at some sort of impossible synthesis, but rather as a challenge to be met. Despite the reluctance, the indifference, and even the hostility of the Haitian elite, the indigénistes maintained an incredible level of enthusiasm. But what new movement is immediately acclaimed by the public? What new movement does not, for a time, have to confront confusion? Demanding that Haitian painting be updated and renewed, that it join with the major trends of modern painting, and reclaim subjects that were profoundly Haitian, drawn first and foremost from rural life, the indigénistes cleared the way for a double development of sophisticated painting and of popular painting. The indigéniste movement did not lead directly to primitivism. However, it did prepare the way for people to accept that art was not purely the exercise of technique, nor simply a game that could be played by dilettantes, but instead the direct and immediate expression of the soul of a people and the articulation of a unique vision of the world.

Le Centre d'Art

Le Centre d'Art came about at a time when indigéniste painters, having been rejected by their society, were questioning their chances for survival. The Centre was, in a sense, born out of this terrible questioning, and since its beginning has emphasized its close ties with indigénisme. On May 14, 1944, at the first exhibition, the Centre paid homage to Savain, who, despite his absence from Haiti, was not considered less important to the indigéniste movement. Taking the ideas of the indigénistes as his own, in his address to Haitian President Elie Lescot, Dewitt Peters, the Centre's new director stated: "The Centre d'Art, which is open to all without distinction as to class, aims to form a Haitian School of Painting, a style of painting that expresses Haiti, drawing partly from folklore, from the national past, and from our natural riches, and for all this without excluding or repressing the artist's personality."

It was therefore not a coincidence that the first event put on by this new institution was an exhibit of the work of Haitian and foreign artists living in Haiti who shared Haitian artists' preoccupations. This in itself was a way to recognize and assume the mantle of the past. Although from the school's earliest days, foreigners were invited to teach there (among them Jason Seley, Paul England, William Calfee, Robel Paris, and Paul Keene), the permanent faculty, with the exception of Dewitt Peters, were all Haitian: Georges Remponneau, Albert Mangonès, Andrée Malbranche, and later Lucien Price and Maurice Borno, among others.

And yet the Centre d'Art did not pretend that it was forging a style of Haitian painting per se. Peters himself, to whom words cannot do justice, recognized this. In an article published in the American magazine *Harper's Bazaar* in January, 1947 entitled "Haïtian Primitive Painters," he wrote: "I ask myself why, in a country of such fascinating beauty, with a climate as luminous as that of Italy and a people who enjoy so many pastimes, is the art of painting almost dead?" Peters' intentions were simple and realistic. He recognized "the urgent necessity of breaking Haiti's isolation and allowing the nation to enter into relationships with other countries in the western hemisphere," as he declared to Morisseau Leroy, then director general of instruction. Additionally, as he mentioned to President Lescot, he aimed "to organize talents, to stimulate them, to create, through energy and enthusiasm, a collegial atmosphere that will allow talent to ripen and to produce work." Above all, it was important to give artists a space in which they could exhibit their work and meet to discuss their ideas, and to establish a school of art.

Because, since its beginnings, the Centre d'Art was a school where all who came were accepted, the idea that it would suddenly produce something called "primitivism" never entered anyone's mind. Peters would have been quite surprised if, in 1944-1945, someone had told him that in the near future he would be proclaimed the father of primitive painting, for the simple reason that he had not yet heard of Le Douanier Rousseau, of Séraphine, or of Grandma Moses, and indeed a piece by Hector Hyppolite or Castera Bazile would have met with his disapproval. When Philomé Obin sent him a painting from his studio in Cap Haïtien, the painting was abandoned in a warehouse because it was judged as lacking in interest. Peters' sincere and touching confession was reported by Philippe Thoby-Marcelin in *Panorama de la peinture haïtienne*:

> But it was later, in Port-au-Prince, that I had my second revelation, when José Gómez Sicre—who had organized an exhibition of modern Cuban art for the Centre d'Art—surprised and completely changed me with the enthusiasm that Haitian primitive painting inspired in him (especially the first works of Louverture Poisson, who was then painting on photo-

graphic paper). My eyes were opened suddenly and forcefully, and it took only a matter of days–at most a few weeks–for me to become even more enthusiastic than Gómez Sicre about this type of art.

The whole truth is there. And the other truths proposed or imposed afterward are unimportant. Because it was in fact José Gómez Sicre who was the father of primitivism. For Gómez Sicre, it was essentially a matter of popular art being important, heavy with poetry, with human and Haitian truths, spontaneous expressions of the vision and the lived realities of the people, expressions that should not and could not take shape in any less direct or more ornate ways.

The ascent of primitive art was as rapid as it was unforeseen. This is probably at the source of some of the emotional reactions to the new form, from delirious enthusiasm to blind hostility. It was also the source of a whole range of commercial dealings that, in the long run, opened the door to lies and deceptions and even, to a certain degree, the signing away of the future.

In April, 1945, in the context of a cultural exchange between Cuba and Haiti, an exhibit entitled "Peinture moderne de Cuba" arrived at the Centre d'Art, which had been a huge success at the Museum of Modern Art in New York. Cuban painting had long been considered "modern," and among the artists who participated in the exhibit some, such as Wilfredo Lam and Carlos Enriquez, were already counted among the big names in modern painting. This exhibit created a feeling of helplessness among the Haitian painters, who were already conscious of their deficiencies and of being behind the times. If they were ecstatic as they stood in front of the Cuban paintings, if they were jostling one another to listen to Carlos Enriquez talk about surrealism, if they hastened to follow the advice of Mario Carreño, Roberto Diago, and Cundo Bermudez and blithely borrowed their techniques, it was to better stifle their anguish. Fundamentally, they sensed how dangerous, and even ridiculous, it would be to send an exhibit of Haitian painting to Havana. It was at this moment, as a real sense of panic arose at the Centre, that Gómez Sicre, who had accompanied the exhibit to Haiti, discovered the work by Philomé Obin abandoned in a warehouse. He was seduced by its sincerity, by its wild poetry, and he saw a potential solution to the problem posed by the lack of Haitian work that could be exhibited in Havana. Haiti could mount an exhibit of popular painting that would avoid questions of technique and put the Cuban public in close contact with Haitian popular culture. With difficulty, Gómez Sicre managed to convince Peters of the merits of his idea. The works of ten artists, most of whom had never exhibited before, were selected. Some of these young painters, among them Luckner Lazare and Jean Agnant, had been working since the beginning of their careers to give their art a solid grounding in technique, and were already turning away from purely instinctive approaches with an eye toward opening their work up fully to modernism. Alone among the group of exhibitors, Rigaud Benoît, Philomé Obin, and, with serious reservations, Louverture Poisson, would, after 1946, enter into the category of "primitive" artists.

The success of the exhibit in Havana was great—so great that Peters' remaining doubts crumbled. And then there were more and more exhibits, in Washington, New York, and San Francisco, culminating with a show at the Museum of Modern Art in Paris in January, 1946. At this great exhibit, "Exposition Internationale de Peinture Moderne," organized by UNESCO and involving the participation of more than 40 nations, the painters who represented Haiti were declared the most original.

Thus began the *grande aventure* of Haitian painting, which seemed as if it would never end. In the midst of the general euphoria, however, this adventure would in fact limit and distort the artists' perspectives and circumscribe their potential by creating, ironically enough, a standard of "originality" from which they would not be allowed to deviate. In the end, the movement would cut the artists off from investigations into pure aesthetics and the age-old norms of universal art, sacrificing them to lies, deceptions, self-denial, and self-destruction.

It is by no means our intention to dismiss the Haitian primitive movement out of hand. It is with a profound respect and a great sense of pride that all Haitians should pronounce the names of Hector Hyppolite, Philomé Obin, Rigaud Benoît, Castera Bazile, Louverture Poisson, and all those who between 1945 and 1960 struggled to maintain the quality of their work and to establish the reputation of Haitian primitive painting. It is certainly not primitive painting itself that is to blame for what happened to it, but rather the use to which it was put by the outside world, sometimes without regard for the artists and out of a deep contempt for the Haitian people. When I met José Gómez Sicre in 1964, where he was then in charge of the audiovisual department of the Organization of American States (OAS) in Washington, DC, he did not try to hide his disappointment and anger over the determination of some to isolate Haitian primitive artists in a cultural ghetto, ostensibly to protect the purity of their vision.

Haitian primitive painting was not the deliberate creation of outsiders, meant to respond to some people's whims and the megalomania of others. Nor was it the creation of the Centre d'Art. It imposed itself upon the Centre in response to the many issues introduced by indigénisme, which, unfortunately, found itself abruptly passed by, without ever having understood the possibilities of visual expression and the value that visual arts could bring to the movement. Primitivism originated out of a descent into the depths of a people's soul. Not only was it the vehicle of myths and beliefs, but, above all, primitivism provided a direct, spontaneous visual language that was uniquely capable, through a symbolism of line and of color arranged in powerful and unpredictable harmonies, to enfold and to translate the most intimate national, collective, and individual truths. In its particular way of apprehending the world, primitivism reimagined space and depicted light in ways that broke free from the confines of traditional artistic conventions; painters chose to light their works from multiple sources or, more often, made light radiate from objects themselves. In primitive painting, large shapes are not simply inert and silent; instead, the painters instinctively made them whirl and eddy, all the while creating a sense of equilibrium from the expansive yet contained fluency of a circular arrangement of forms. Primitive painting suggests rather than explains, and like a whispering in the luxuriance of the night, it immerses viewers in the haze of a dream, revealing the absurdity of life.

The value of Haitian primitive art seems therefore to lie in the vigorous rejection of norms, and thus "in a lack of *savoir-faire* [ability] and a lack of *savoir-vivre* [good manners]," (to cite an expression dear to Bernard Dorival). It is, alas, this lack of savoir-faire that first attracted and charmed viewers, and which they then wanted to protect at all costs. And here is the prejudice that would compromise everything, that would poison everything: The Haitian, remaining at the margins of Western culture, beyond the evolution of ideas and cut off from access to the notion that his art might be considered part of a "universal art," could not help but become isolated; if he tried simply to open himself up to other cultures and to investigate them with an eye toward appropriating the achievements of contemporary world art for himself, he was forced back into his innocence and had to cling to the authenticity of his vision. The power and the poetry of Haitian painting were the result of a lack of education and a means of expression that was completely virginal, completely naïve, and completely magical. And in the veritable race after artists that the craze for primitivism occasioned, it was believed that one could recruit people who unconsciously carried artistic talent within themselves from anywhere in the country—in the slums of Port-au-Prince, in the remote countryside, in the farthest reaches of the mountains.

In this game, on which true talent no longer had any bearing, those who were fortunate enough to have some sort of formal training were already sidelined. In *Renaissance in Haïti* (1948) Selden Rodman—buoyed, admittedly, by an ambivalence within Haitian culture—denounced a Europeanized Haiti as specious and vain, lacking any sort of connection to the deep, true African Haiti. He reserved a severe judgment for the sophisticated painting of the elites, who were very open to Western influences.

Thus indigénisme found itself condemned; the only "real" Haitian painting was primitive painting, and any form of painting that was not primitive was destined for a slow death by asphyxiation. Those critics who wanted things this way failed to realize that, despite appearances, all of Haitian art and culture sprang from the same source. Neither did they understand that if primitive painting had effected a return to Haiti's origins, these origins belonged to the nation as a whole. It likewise escaped them that art in all its forms can never be grounded in theories that are divorced from experience without throwing into question the very principles upon which that art is based. The critics certainly did not want to admit that primitive art was simply a stage, a necessary stage but a stage nonetheless, that would soon be left behind. Without a pause to take stock of its unique worth in order to take advantage of it, primitive Haitian painting could not help but exhaust itself, stagnate, and disappear.

This situation led to a violent debate that placed the very existence of the Centre in jeopardy. Sophisticated art was not dead but had been able to capitalize on the contributions of primitive painting and to experiment with redefining line and color, and renew its techniques of composition and *mise en page*. Contact with contemporary Western art proved fruitful. Lucien Price, Luce Turnier, Antonio Joseph, and Max Pinchinat worked without ever losing touch with their Haitian identity to create harmonious and surprising syntheses in which cubism, surrealism, and abstract art were rethought through the lens of Hector Hyppolite's work, or via African masks. Already the young painters Roland Dorcély and Luckner Lazare were getting impatient, discovering in their anxiety, their thirst for recognition, and the freedom to express their ideas the energy of a powerful, unsettling temperament. If exhibits of primitive painting had grown more numerous abroad, the Centre d'Art continued to show the work of modern painters on a regular basis. The public had developed a taste for it, seeming to relate well to these sophisticated pieces. They applauded Lucien Price's "Chants d'Afrique"; they approved of Max Pinchinat's nudes and still lifes; they liked Antonio Joseph's rickety, crooked little houses. The primitive artists and the sophisticated artists saw each other, talked to each other, and sometimes watched each other work. But this atmosphere of competition without outright rivalry—despite a few incidents that were quickly played down—could not conceal a pervasive uneasiness.

The Crisis of 1950

A new branch of the Centre d'Art was created in the United States, The Haitian Art Center, under the direction of the art critic Selden Rodman, a friend of Dewitt Peters. It was in this atmosphere of euphoria that, in 1950, the idea came to Bishop Charles Vogoeli to decorate the interior of the Cathedral of the Holy Trinity in Port-au-Prince with murals painted solely by primitive artists. When, after a stay in the United States, Bishop Vogoeli returned to Port-au-Prince to see the completed work, he was moved to exclaim, "Thank you, God! They have painted [something] Haitian!" The works were certainly of inestimable value, bearing the mark of poetry and of human and Haitian truths. Something very important had happened here that would have a lasting effect on Haitian religious art: the iconography had been nationalized. All the figures were black and the scenes took place in a typically Haitian world where the sacred was integrated into everyday life, and the mysteries of faith, even as they kept their miraculous secrets, became human and familiar.

But 1950 was also the beginning of a major crisis that drew in the Haitian judiciary, divided artists and intellectuals into opposing camps, and almost eradicated the Centre d'Art. We do not intend to go into the details of the crisis here, for some were rather sordid. However, it must be noted that the economic aspects of the crisis have gotten too much attention, while not enough has been paid to issues of aesthetics.

Selden Rodman's book *Renaissance in Haiti* was not unrelated to the crisis. In a rather arbitrary way, Rodman had divided Haitian painters into the categories of primitive and sophisticated in such an extreme way that dialogue between the two groups became impossible. "The very small and exclusive group of intellectuals and painters trained in Port-au-Prince were unhappy about the fact that they were strangers to African Haiti [l'Haïti africaine]," he wrote. "But a century of bourgeois provincialism is hardly something that can be overcome in a night, especially when it concerns an art form like painting, which depends on a clear conscience as well as on factors that are beyond one's conscious control."

Did the administrators of the Centre want to protect the purity of the primitives by separating them from the *sophistiqués*? Since 1947, the problem of the preservation of primitive art had increased. Certain members of the Administrative Committee of the Centre d'Art had argued from the start that primitive painting could only be a stage, and what people called naiveté was merely the result of weaknesses in technique and a lack of culture. Economic considerations aside, it was possible, according to them, to help the primitive artists to progress, to lead them all the way to the stage of great modernist painting.

However, these administrators came up against the inflexible will of the director of the Centre. And, even as Price, one of the founders of Le Foyer des Arts Plastiques, insisted that "drawing is everything! One must know how to draw," his colleagues were making themselves heard: "Your worth resides in your naiveté. If you build a bridge between your technique and the theories of Western art, you are lost."

Could one thus set out to isolate artists in their own best interests? Was this not a way of slowing down the progress of Haitian art? Could one, in 1947 and 1948, still talk about the authenticity of the primitives when the majority of them had already given themselves over to the demands of the marketplace, turning away from the flow of their inspiration, imitating the advanced techniques of painting?

These questions came at a time when almost all of the primitive painters had opened themselves up to the influence of the five greatest painters in Haiti—Obin, Duffaut, Bazile, Benoît, Cédor—because they shared a clientele (a clientele that often, unfortunately, found itself unable to distinguish the best from the worst).

But was the joining of the experience of the primitives with that of the sophistiqués possible without throwing into question the aesthetic values, the particular vision of the world, the whole complex of direct knowledge that the primitives had, which, through the sincerity of their work, permitted them to have a vision of the Haitian soul like nothing anyone had ever had before? Could a people make use of a system of values that remained fundamentally foreign to them? Would Haitian painting risk becoming irrelevant just as it had finally begun to affirm itself, and risk losing itself in the subtleties of technique and become once more a bourgeois pastime? All of these questions are still relevant.

Le Foyer des Arts Plastiques

The board of directors of the Centre d'Art was compelled to dissolve on June 26, 1949. A new council presided over by Maurice Borno was created, from which the members for the most part rather rapidly resigned. Failing to take charge in the climate of uneasiness that grew more pronounced each day, constantly threatening to boil over, the management of the Centre authorized the formation of an Association of Haitian Artists under its own auspices, which was charged with gathering information on the complaints of artists and with defending their interests.

The good feeling that had reigned in the artistic community, and which had created at the Centre during its first four or five years an incredible atmosphere of devotion, cooperation, a lack of self-interest and even a willingness to sacrifice for the cause, had completely disintegrated, giving way to petty rivalries, money-grubbing, and all kinds of sordid little games.

The Foyer des Arts Plastiques was founded on August 11, 1950, in the midst of endless discussions, indictments and self-justifications. The dissident artists who had energetically rejected "all responsibility [for the rupture] in the Centre's leadership" and who had appealed to the judiciary and the Department of Labor, soon realized that not only was power not on their side, but their revolt against the Centre had been interpreted by the Haitian government as a politically subversive act. They could, however, count on the support of the young intellectuals and the goodwill of many members of the press.

A month later, in September, 1950, the *Manifesto of the Foyer des Arts Plastiques* appeared, which stated, among other things, that:

> Haitian art, like art everywhere, cannot develop in a vacuum. It must set out to create something unique, but it would be presumptuous to think that, in order to achieve this goal, it must turn away from the best that the genius and experience of all the ages, and all the races, has to offer. To refuse to introduce the forms of education that are currently available and

that could develop a deepening, a broadening of our means of expression, would be to destine our art to be limited by the ideas of a few.[7]

Housed for a time in a modest space on the rue du Centre, which it finally had to abandon for lack of funds, the Foyer struggled in the beginning with difficulties that were made bearable only by the indomitable strength of the artists themselves. There were certainly desertions and pleas for forgiveness from the directors of the Centre d'Art, but far from discouraging the artists, particularly Lucien Price, this only made them more determined to succeed.

The first aim of the Foyer des Arts was to arrive at an art that, in rejecting intuitiveness and spontaneity, would not follow any of the fundamental tenets developed by primitivism. It would begin with the ideas of Hector Hyppolite and Castera Bazile and rethink them, restructure them, and connect them with an overarching notion of universal art. Immersing the basis of their art in the drama of the Haitian people, they sought above all to find a visual language that was at once Haitian, allowing them to enfold all the horror of the Haitian condition, and yet not be marginalized, that is, not cut off from developments in Western art. The works of art containing this message were quite foreign to the Centre d'Art, in spite of its origins in indigénisme. In the context of the Foyer, the artist was considered a socially and politically responsible being, or at least one concerned with the realities of everyday life. But in order to behave in a truly responsible way, the artist had to have a solid grounding in technique. This was the first difficulty that needed to be overcome.

Art had ceased to be considered an adventure. Among Cédor, Pinchinat, and the writer Jacques Alexis, who followed the new artistic debates very closely, theories were multiplying—they were often awkward and timid, but this showed that the artists were learning what they wanted to do and actively searching for the means of realizing their ambitions. Each painting by Cédor, Vergin, Dorcély, Lazare, Néhémy Jean, Pinchinat, and Elzire Malebranche was the result of passionate research and thinking as they continued to develop their ideas. If the results were not always satisfying, if their real successes were still in the future, important issues were being raised and key challenges were being articulated.

All these experiences would lead to *le réalisme de cruauté* [the realism of cruelty]. After three or four years of solid effort, formerly primitive painters had fully mastered their medium and were capable of executing the most refined techniques. They had taken the distorted forms of Jérome Bosch, Daumier, Goya, Munch, and Bernard Buffet and remade them according to the demands of a uniquely Haitian aesthetic, plunging them into an atmosphere of horror particular to certain Haitian legends, sometimes leaving us with the painful impression that we share in the secrets of zombification. Far from wanting to arouse pity or compassion, le réalisme de cruauté wanted to shock and, in the uproar of scandal that this work occasioned, to provoke indignation and outrage. On many occasions, Cédor had warned his comrades about the dangers of "populism." This tendency to focus on scenes from popular life, wallowing around in misery and filth as a way to try to praise those who had to live with it on a daily basis and to ease one's own conscience, was for him not only antithetical to the whole project of art, but also an odious exploitation of the misfortune of the poor. It was crucial to transcend particular situations and stories in order to get at the very essence of what was going on and to communicate this in the most simple, direct way. Le réalisme de cruauté disfigured its subjects, bloated them, made them into monsters, placing them in a world from which humanity had been banished—a world from which there was no escape, a world without hope, where everything was false, even the light, and which stank like rotting corpses.

All artists certainly were not participating in this realism of cruelty. Some of them were more interested in aesthetics than social issues, investigating, for example, the structural values of primitive painting and the quality of light in cubism, which itself took its basic tenets from Africa, or building a bridge between popular dance and painting, impressing on the latter the rhythms of dance because it seemed that in dance could be found the basis of Haitian identity.

To give Haitian painting back to Haitians—that is, to get the Haitian people interested in their own tradition of painting, to generate a core group of people capable of talking intelligently about painting and of discussing works of art, to encourage artists and to provide a significant market for their work, these were the other goals of the Foyer. In order to accomplish them, the Foyer promised to organize traveling exhibits, conferences, and public discussions of Haitian art. Did the Foyer keep these promises? Perhaps not. Can the best intentions accomplish anything when faced with a lack of means?

After 1957, the Foyer would become only a shadow of itself. La Galerie Brochette had opened, and the best artists had gone there; moreover, the market for art had grown more difficult to penetrate. The situation for artists was much more challenging, and the period during which it was possible to make sacrifices seemed to have ended for the time being.

A la recherche de la peinture perdue

At the Centre d'Art as well, the sophisticated style of painting reasserted itself; having reined in the commercial ambitions of some contemporary critics and other members of the art world, the Centre had quietly decided to maintain a balance between primitive and sophisticated painting. In any event, the concerns of the sophisticated artists dovetailed with those of their former classmates, the founders of the Foyer des Arts Plastiques.

Luce Turnier's and Antonio Joseph's sojourns abroad had greatly benefited their art. They were able to integrate strong, often conflicting influences into works that were bold, to say the least.

They quickly began to produce work that was simultaneously profoundly Haitian, original, and at the forefront of modernism. Refusing cheap indigénisme, they wanted to investigate primitive painting's ideas about space, light, and composition from the perspective of Haitian themes. The results they achieved were both troubling and surprising. Through remarkable syntheses, the works revealed the strong personality of these artists who had studied Kandinsky, Duchamp, and contemporary American painters. Luce Turnier, having come out from under the influence of Wilfredo Lam and certain Cuban painters, had returned to a style of art that appeared less intellectual. Antonio Joseph was using light to organize his compositions rather than spatial perspective. Enguerrand Gourgue had evolved steadily toward a style of solid construction in which references to contemporary Western painting were apparent here and there, a style that seemed in some ways aligned with the realism of cruelty. At the same time, the number of primitive painters was growing.

La Galerie Brochette, which opened in 1957, was for a time the rallying point of the intellectual and artistic avant-garde in Port-au-Prince. The gallery's goal was to continue the work of the Foyer, which had sacrificed its mission to the demands of the marketplace. Remaining true to themselves, and having become calmer and more confident, the artists at the Brochette did not hesitate at times to return to the original source of inspiration of primitive painting, seeking the secrets of the popular soul and, above all, seeking the most profound and specific means of articulating the essence of Haitian identity.

The 1960s were difficult years. A very serious political situation of distrust, repression, and betrayal that grew worse each day kept tourists out of Haiti, and hampered the sale of Haitian art outside the country. The struggle to survive would bring the artists, trapped in an unprecedented economic stagnation and now objects of suspicion like most Haitian intellectuals, toward new reflections and a reconsideration of the purpose of art, and of their own relationship with society.

In the 1960s, La Galerie Brochette vanished, swept away in the general upheaval. Calfou[8] took over its role immediately, nurturing a generation of artists who were less fiery and more inclined to investigations of pure aesthetics. Many artists left the country. Those who remained sensed that they would have to depend primarily on a small sector of the Haitian public that, though lacking the means to really support art and artists, did have its own particular tastes and preferences.

The Haitian public, in fact, had never fully accepted primitive art. It had ultimately accepted Hector Hyppolite, Philomé Obin, and Préfète Duffaut, much more out of snobbery than out of genuine love or pride. Saint-Brice had found favor in their eyes because, according to him, his work created a connection with modernity, and allowed for the interaction of primitivism and abstract art.

First tempted by purely formal investigations, then sometimes adopting a mannered style, the young Haitian artists of this tumultuous period asserted their presence quite quickly. In addition, the exchanges between those who had left the country and those who had remained were many, and these exchanges awakened unexpected curiosities among the artists. The chance to meet foreign artists, the challenges of living in the artistic milieus of New York and Paris, led the expatriates to broaden their vocabularies and made their expressions more forceful and precise. They were obliged to overcome their timidity and free themselves fully from the constraints of a sometimes burdensome traditionalism.

Those remaining in Haiti decided to work towards a more complete inventory of the components of Haitian culture, particularly Vodou, which they perceived not in terms of a religion or an inexhaustible source of stories, but rather as a form of pre-art, a carrier of original forms circulating around a philosophy and linked to a particular symbolism of line and color. Those things that Ramponneau and Pétion Savain had intuited were systematically introduced into the art of Poto-Mitan and Jean-Claude Garoute (Ti-Ga), who worked with emerging artists such as Patrick Vilaire.

Taking into account the trends that were occurring in art both outside and inside Haiti, the works of Bernard Wah, Bernard Séjourné, and Rose-Marie Desruisseaux marked a decisive step in the evolution of non-primitive painting. Haitian painting had been up until then anonymous, in the sense that it refused to express the intimate truths of individual artists, and spoke only of the condition of the generalized Haitian subject. Following Wilson Bigaud, in the paintings of Wah, Séjourné, and above all Desruisseaux one finds the desperate struggle of individuals in conflict with a society that has set itself against them and denied them the right to fully realize their unique qualities and weaknesses.

The Final Throes of Primitive Art

At the end of the 1960s, thanks to a political situation that was a bit more controlled, there was a renewal of tourism in Haiti, which would increase until the beginning of the 1980s when it would crumble under the pressure of a new political crisis. The market for Haitian art began to expand again. Art galleries sprang up in Port-au-Prince, Cap Haïtien, and Jacmel. Many exhibits of Haitian art took place in Europe and North America. Never had Haitian painting been so valued, yet never had it been so threatened. The extensive, uncontrolled local production of art opened the way to a short-lived celebrity for all sorts of artists, some in name only, but it also testified to the force of a Haitian creativity that was constantly renewed.

Responding purely to the concerns of the art market, some supposedly reputable critical publications gave new credence to the old prejudice that insisted that Haitian art was and could only be primitive painting—that is, painting characterized by spontaneity, rawness, and a lack of knowledge and technique. However, even though they had sacrificed their work to commercialism, the first primitive artists—those who were still living—remained aware of their aesthetic responsibilities and sometimes, even without intending to do so, they questioned themselves about what they were doing in their art, and forced themselves to venture off the beaten track. In Cap-Haïtien, the old man Philomé Obin had surrounded himself with students and, impressing his style upon them, taught them that a work of art must be clear, clean, attentive to the smallest detail—that is to say, technically accomplished. And we see this perfectionism and a sense of striving in the work of all his students. The real Haitian painting was not, therefore, those "Paradis terrestres" and "Jungles" that were produced in quantity. It was more noble, rich, more ambitious—but also threatened by an art market that was inclined to substitute false naiveté for the genuine, more difficult-to-grasp Haitian primitivism.

Neo-primitivism was intended as a reaction against false spontaneity, carelessness, and an evident lack of expertise. The works of the neo-primitive artists were meticulously worked, polished, and blatantly seeking approval. They might have succeeded if only they had been touched by a breath of truth; if, avoiding coarse colors and false or forced juxtapositions, they had known how to show fantasies and daydreams without devolving into wild imaginings. It seemed more and more that the primitive movement had reached a dead end and that, except for rare cases of genuine naiveté, the artists were unable to renew themselves in a worthwhile way, and indeed they had nothing more to say.

Fortunately, Saint-Soleil appeared, like an extraordinary swan song.[9] For six or seven years, the village of Soissons-la-Montagne, several kilometers from Port-au-Prince, was the center of feverish activity. Every element of daily life was filled with wonder. For all those peasants who had never been formerly taught to paint to whom Jean-Claude Garoute (Ti-Ga) handed over canvases, paints, and brushes, the act of painting was mystical. In a mute trance, they entered into conversations with the *lwa* and captured and represented their inaudible words. Painting returned to the depths of the sacred like a gift, above and separate from any form of expertise. These paintings revealed a kind of pre-existing harmony of line and color in the stammering stages of infancy, yet filled with a savage poetry that probed the borders of time, signifying the deepest essence of being. And then came a time of stillness and silence, as if these men had been exhausted by the *lwa*, and that the *lwa* themselves, having said everything already, were unable to murmur other songs.

Nouvelle Lumière, Nouvelle Peinture
The success of primitive painting (henceforth referred to as naïve painting) during that euphoric period did not stifle the development of sophisticated painting. On the contrary: the Haitian bourgeoisie had grown, had reaffirmed its interest in art and affirmed its tastes. And if the aversion of the bourgeoisie to naïve art had been somewhat tempered, its sensibility was still taint-

ed by prejudice and suggestibility and its education linked to repressed prejudices. Its exposure to the outside world still did not permit it to appreciate the true worth of naïve painting and to find itself in these rough works, in this form of painting seen by some as concerned only with dreams and celebrations. Even when the bourgeoisie condemned sophisticated painting for being too direct or too brutal, it insisted that this style responded better to its aspirations and its trials.

The Ecole des Beaux-Arts, founded in 1957, had given three or four generations of painters and sculptors a solid grounding in technique before it disbanded. Now that Calfou had been dissolved and a number of the older artists had killed themselves or left Haiti, many young artists would experiment, alone or in groups, with new concepts and approaches. Ernst Louizor and Emmanuel Pierre Charles, among others, talked about Haitianizing impressionism, and revisited the question of light and color, not by conforming to the theories of Monet or Pissarro, as Antonio Joseph, Lazare or Dorcelly had done before them, but by exploring a shivering moment at which the bright tropical sun destroyed the heightened colors of dawn and dusk. Their results were not always successful, but their material was revelatory in its sensuality and in its expressive force, like a self-reflexive language.

The meeting of Simil, Bernard Séjourné, and Jean-René Jérôme at the Ecole des Beaux-Arts in the 1970s was extremely important for the development of Haitian art. They were three artists of different temperaments, of different social classes, of different training, and with different goals, as the future would show. Simil had studied at l'Ecole des Beaux-Arts in Port-au-Prince. Séjourné, who had studied at Calfou when he was very young, had received most of his education in Jamaica and then in the United States after a short stay at l'Ecole des Beaux-Arts. In New York, he entered into the black artistic circles that were at their height. Jérôme was an autodidact who had traveled to the United States where he too had spent time in the company of black American artists.

The meeting between the three was important because it was intended to be a refusal and a rupture. It was a break with the realism of cruelty that, after the stunning, brutal work of Denis Emile, seemed to have become formulaic and lost all touch with truth. It was a refusal, in the name of art, of didacticism, a refusal also of the prejudice that made the artists believe that no work could be worthy if it did not draw its inspiration from the slums. Because these artists were living in a world in which deprivation, ugliness, and human degradation were everywhere, art could have no goal other than to rescue humanity through the introduction of beauty.

Beauty, for those who know how to look, is everywhere, even in the ruin of the poorest neighborhoods. But why persist in searching for it only in ugliness? Why not create beauty out of beauty according to the universal principles that regulate the play of line, and the intrinsic and immutable harmony of color? The beauty of line and color transcends time and space—it existed in the Africa of our fathers, where women knew the joy of sparkling jewels; it existed in the Italy of Simone Martini, of Domenico Veneziano, of Fra Angelico and Botticelli.

It was important to restore the purity and grace of line, and thereby to allow the resurgence of elegant, graceful, harmonious forms. It was necessary as well to renounce raw and exuberant Haitian colors, to create soft, pastel color combinations that faded into gray backgrounds, or to try monochromes of dark browns and blacks upon which appeared delicate, meticulous red or ochre stains. The subject matter also changed radically, focusing on nude female bodies, sometimes veiled or transformed into flowers and shells, but always graceful and ethereal. L'Ecole de la Beauté was born, and developed toward mysticism in search of timelessness, substituting transience and fragility for solid forms.

The Poetry of Despair

Very few artists joined l'Ecole de la Beauté. One of the characteristics of modern Haitian painting was its refusal to conform to just any artistic ideology and form schools. If the aesthetic of beauty had brought them, in a general way, to have a better conscience about their work as artists and to be more discreet and contained in their engagements with society and politics, each followed his own path, dictated by his own temperament, pretending he did not owe anything to anyone.

The work of Célestin Faustin is perhaps the most surprising, the most original, and the most captivating of this period in the 1970s; it is also the work that should contribute most to a rethinking of the fears and prejudices that have hindered the evolution of Haitian painting. It goes to the most profound depths of Haitian culture, connecting with the questions and struggles of Bosch, Gainsborough, and William Blake before locating itself in the midst of a fantasmagoric, macabre world. It depicts nudes that are among the most beautiful in Haitian painting. Heartwrenching, agonized work, it carries with it all the contradictions of Haitian society, torn between an unquenched thirst for the modern world and an indestructible attachment to its traditional ways, a society where Vodou is at once a constraint and a promise of liberty and happiness, where richness is doomed to be accompanied by frustration, anguish, and remorse. One sees the tragedy of a man selected and pursued by the *lwa*, a man marginalized by a society that never could or would look at him directly. It is work that can be measured above all in terms of its aesthetic qualities, and it attests to an incomparable technical facility. Time and space are pushed aside to allow the narrative to unfold without ever compromising the unity of vision. Faustin's work demonstrates how wrong-headed and dangerous is the opinion of those who refuse to admit that there is, in fact, something in particular that can be called Haitian painting and who deny Haitian artists the right to go beyond spontaneity in order to think through and structure their work.

A Time of Courage

Renewed economic and political crises and the negative press around the AIDS issue kept tourists far from Haiti, and weighed heavily on discussions of the future of art in Haiti. Yet once again, Haitian painting was able to continue and to advance. In this sense, the 1980s should be considered a time when the Haitian public and Haitian artists entered into a very intimate dialogue. Most of the great primitive painters had disappeared, and the movement seemed to have nothing more to offer. More and more, the collective gaze turned toward modern painters. We note that the contributions of international art, far from blurring the vision of the world so particular to the Haitian people instead reinforced and enriched it. Artists such as Gesner Armand, Luce Turnier, Lucner Lazare, Michèle Manuel, and Jacques Gabriel experienced a renaissance, and their work had never been so powerful and original.

The realism of cruelty and the aesthetic of beauty were from then on outmoded, and some artists who had remained in the shadows now had the chance to appear. The difficulties of the art market, far from being a handicap to these artists, actually propelled them toward innovations. Haitian painters learned to make surfaces move and to experiment with the most varied kinds of material, even the most humble and unexpected, and to give craftsmanship its due. More and more they turned away from being extremely precise, but contrary to what was happening elsewhere, they hesitated to explore non-figurative styles, discovering perhaps that these were not really compatible with the Haitian mentality. Haitian painting appropriated both old and new styles, restructuring them in ways that never ceased to speak to an underlying Haitianness. It moved from Gérard Hyppolite's geometric forms and Etzer Charles' and Ti Ga's symbolism of revolt to the morbid expressionism of Franck Etienne, the hyperrealism of Franck Louissaint, and the intellectual primitivism of Edouard Duval-Carrié. Painting overflowed the limits of surrealism with rare mastery. The work of Sacha Thebaud contains a sensual and explosive language and that of Marie-Claude Gousse is stunning and electrifying.

Primitive or sophisticated, Haitian painting remains intimately linked to Haitian realities, to the aspirations and the emotions of the Haitian people, and it is still the strongest expression of Haitian culture. The two styles are ultimately impossible to separate, and certain artists, such as Enguerrand Gourgue and Célestin Faustin, have claimed to draw from both. It was wrong to try to place the so-called primitive and the so-called sophisticated art in opposition to one another, as if to say that one was better or worse than the other, for they belonged, essentially, to two different kinds of people living in two separate lands. But ultimately, the difference between naïve or primitive painting and sophisticated painting was not one of nature but one of degree. We do not mean to deny the importance or primitive painting. On the contrary, we think that it is a reference point to which all Haitian painters should continue to return, if they wish to understand their identity as Haitians. But it would be a disservice to the Haitian people to think that naiveté only is its domain, and it undervalues Haitian culture to believe that it could be endangered by contact with other cultures. Exposure to the skills and knowledge that belong to humanity at large can only enrich Haitian culture. Bearing witness to the life, the evolution, the suffering, and the hopes of the Haitian people, and remaining in the service of the Haitian people, sophisticated painting is no less Haitian than primitive painting.

Haiti had an opportunity that other nations perhaps did not have—to return all the way to its source and to capture the most intimate vibrations of the popular soul, in a language that is spontaneous and direct— yes, sometimes perhaps a bit rough and unpolished. This reality should never be taken as an excuse to isolate Haiti in a cultural ghetto.

Notes

1. A note on quotes, references and names of artists: This article was originally published in French and follows different scholarly conventions. Therefore, there are various incomplete bibliographical references and dates. Some of the names of the artists mentioned include only the first letter of the first name and the last name, or the last name. The translators and editors corrected any obvious omissions, but kept the names as they were in the original French text.

Additionally, there are some direct quotes with no attributions. This version of the essay comes from two sources. The section that focuses on art during the colonial period is from a series of articles that appeared between 1981-1982 in the magazine *Haïti-Santé*, which is no longer published. The second part of the essay is extracted from a catalogue for an exposition that took place in France, "Nouveau regard sur les Caraïbes." The catalogue was published by l'Espace Carpeaux, Creolarts Diffusion, Paris. All notes were added by the translators.

This chapter is of crucial importance because it is one of the few essays in English on the history of Haitian art, by one of the foremost authorities on the form. For more information on Haitian painting, see the special issue of *Conjonction: Revue Franco-Haïtienne*, "Histoire d'Haiti vue par les peintres," 151 (May 1981), which features some of Ulrick Jean-Pierre's paintings. See also a documentary from Denmark, *Dreamers: The Painters of Haiti*, dir. Jorgen Leth (2001). Thanks to Ulrick Jean-Pierre and Elmide Méléance for their comments on the translation.

2. A slave who had just arrived from Africa.

3. There are multiple copies of this work, one of which is on exhibit at the Musée du Panthéon National d'Haïti (MUPANAH) in Port-au-Prince.

4. The Second Haitian Empire lasted from August 25, 1849-January 15, 1859. On August 25, 1849, Soulouque, who had been elected president on March 1, 1847, proclaimed himself Faustin I, Emperor of Haiti. His court was organized on the model of that of Henry I. His reign lasted until January 1859.

5. Emile Marcelin, *De l'Enfance à l'Adolescence*, 42.

6. Le Centre d'Art, a key point in the development of Haitian art in the twentieth century, was founded in 1944.

7. *L'Action*, 25 September 1950.

8. Calfou was an art center/cooperative studio founded in 1963 by several artists, including Edouard and Bernard Wah from Le Foyer des Arts Plastiques. Other members included writers and poets such as Néhemy Jean and Max Kenol.

9. Saint-Soleil was founded in 1971 by Jean-Claude Garoute (Ti-Ga). The name Saint-Soleil originates from one of Ti-Ga's paintings. The purpose of the Saint-Soleil movement was to promote artistic creativity among the peasants of Soissons and to create works of art for the sheer beauty of creation. However, the ideology of "art for art's sake" did not last long. For more information about the Saint-Soleil movement, see Selden Rodman, *Where Art Is Joy: Haitian Art, the First Forty Years* (New York: Ruggles de Latour, 1988) and André Malraux, *L'intemporel* (Paris: Gallimard,1976).

Chapter 29

Bicentennial Conversations
An Interview with Ulrick Jean-Pierre

Edwidge Danticat

Born in Roseaux, near the town of Jérémie in the lush southern region of Haiti, Ulrick Jean-Pierre started drawing at the age of 4 and painting when he was 16. "I remember my first sketch looking more like a pig than the horse it was supposed to be," he recalled those early days from his home in New Orleans, Louisiana:

> I had an uncle who was a sculptor; his name was Louius Jean-Louis. Once when I was four years old, I went to his studio and watched him as he drew a horse on the blackboard. Later, when he left to go to an art supply store, I stood on a chair and began sketching next to his horse. I remember being frustrated because I could not draw my horse to look like his, but I did not give up. While I was drawing, I realized to my horror that my elbow had accidentally rubbed off the original outline of my uncle's sketch! My uncle was a very mean person-he would beat us and so after I realized what I did, I ran to my grandmother's house and crawled under her bed, where I hid for several hours. I found out a few days later that when my uncle returned from the art supply store he had found some kids including my twin sister, Claudette, playing in his studio, and he thought they had destroyed his horse. But that was my very first sketch. Since that time the pencil has never left my hand. Even when other children were playing, I was not tempted to leave my pad and pencil.

Another more pleasant childhood memory encouraged him to keep his pencil:

When I was a child, I used to draw on the wall. My parents never expressed anger; instead they bought me paper. They thought what I was doing was so beautiful. Their encouragement gave me a great deal of self-confidence. I used to have a pencil in my hand and drew constantly. My schoolmates would say, "This boy is always sketching nonsense." My parents' constant appreciation and support were the vital forces that motivated my artistic development. They truly believed in my natural talent and always encouraged me. Their appreciative gaze at my drawings gave me the determination to excel. When I was 6 years old, my family moved from Roseaux to Pétion-Ville. There I grew up and continued to develop my drawing skills. Both Roseaux and Pétion-Ville were incubators of artistic inspirations. Jérémie is known for its poets and Pétion-Ville for its varied artistic community. I received positive responses from many people who recognized my potential, especially my older cousins, Lunique and Samuel Lafortune. My childhood was filled with positive influences and pleasant memories. One of my hobbies was reading, collecting, and exchanging comic books with friends who shared my interests. These books had colorful characters such as Blek le rock, Mike le ranger, Zembla roi de la jungle and Robin des bois. I used these figures in my drawings to practice humans in motion. I never ran out of real human models; I grew up among six sisters and one brother. I used to make my own comic books using my sister Claudette and the other siblings as the featured characters. I considered everyone and everything in my surroundings as subjects of my creative world. When I would go to the movies, I would draw everything that I saw along with the movie's dialogue.

At the age of 16, after years of experimenting alone, Ulrick Jean-Pierre produced his first paintings in collaboration with a young art dealer and another artist.

At this time, I was in high school and had not yet received the academic discipline of painting. My curriculum included science, geometry, and principles of drawing. My work had earned me quite a reputation in my neighborhood. It was in this manner that the young art dealer invited me to take part in his project. Dr. and Mrs. Adrien Raymond, passionate art lovers, commissioned this project. They thought they were dealing with three artists. In fact, there were only two of us artists and the art dealer; the art dealer craftily acted as if he were an artist. In the presence of the commissioners, he acted as if he directed the proceedings. The subject matter was taken from *Vogue* and *Paris Match.* I remember how nervous my two collaborators were when they learned that the commissioners were on their way to inspect the painting. I, on the other hand, was anxious for constructive criticism from these art connoisseurs. I was hoping they would approve a second painting, which was already conceived in my fresh creative soul; just like a volcano, it was ready to erupt upon my canvas. When Dr. and Mrs. Raymond finally assessed the painting, they acted as if they were impressed. These two sophisticated art lovers and supporters did not want to discourage our naïve expressions. They gave us a warm smile, patiently examined our work, and kindly offered suggestions. In fact, they gave us the approval to execute other paintings. My apprehensive partners were now exuberant with a new sense of confidence. Their initial insecurity and intimidation dissolved when the commissioners enthusiastically showed us two paintings they had produced. I thought that they were two masterpieces. I then realized that I had a lot to learn from them. Their selected subject matter was mainly figurative and required basic skills in the drawing of human anatomy and proportions. At that time, my skills in human anatomy and proportions were limited. The artist collaborator was only capable of painting birds and leaves, a style influenced by his father. The other acting artist did not know how to draw and paint; he only played the role to impress his patrons. Since I could not rely on their abilities, I had no choice but to produce most of the expected paintings. After the completion of the project, we disbanded. My determination drove me to expand my natural talents. After high school, I decided to engage in the academic study of art.

After high school, Jean-Pierre met prominent local artists with whom he worked closely. They encouraged him to enroll at the Foyer des Arts Plastiques in Port-au-Prince, where he fashioned his first paintings. In 1976, the Haitian Cultural Society of Philadelphia was founded by art patrons Marie-Thérèse Jérôme and her husband Dr. Yves Jérôme as an effort to establish a bridge of communication between artists in Haiti and their compatriots in the United States. Soon after graduating from the Foyer, Ulrick was invited to the United States in 1977 by the Haitian Cultural Society and Drexel University in Philadelphia. His collection of new work was featured as a one-man exhibition at Drexel University. He attended classes at the University of the Arts (formerly known as the Philadelphia College of Arts). He was impressed by the wealth of Haitian historical documents that he found at the Jérômes' home library. During that same year, he received his first commission from the Haitian Cultural Society to paint a series of historical paintings on Haiti. He also painted some illustrations for children's books, and representations of vèvè. He has been painting professionally ever since.

I have visited Ulrick Jean-Pierre in his New Orleans home studio many times. Over the years, I have always been struck by Ulrick's tremendous artistic vision. Though his work is more than grandiose—and I mean that in the best sense—he certainly is not. In fact, he is very humble. He pours all his energy into his painting, sometimes bypassing food and sleep. You sometimes have the impression that Ulrick is daydreaming even as he is speaking or listening to you. No matter what else he is doing, you can also see a spark in his eyes that says something magnificent is forming in his head.

Edwidge Danticat: What do you convey through painting?

Ulrick Jean-Pierre: For me, painting is liberty; it is an open window of exploration into the infinite world of imagination. Painting is a universal language of self-expression; it describes and captures the essence of time and emotion in a concrete reality. My artistic creativity and expression is a charismatic force and a radiant energy in my life that electrifies my hopes and dreams. And it upholds the secret wisdom of love, peace, and harmony. My daily experience is a limitless spiritual exploration and a challenging emotional inspiration. The challenge is the powerful vehicle that makes the need to constantly create so exciting.

ED: I know exactly what you mean. Sometimes this need to create is as urgent as physical hunger; however, it can also be so thrilling. I can see it in your work, this urgency to bring something to life, not just to create, but also to recreate pieces of ourselves, fragments of dreams, memory, history that we might otherwise have lost. You are primarily known for your depiction of important moments in Haitian history. When did your interest in Haitian history start?

UJ-P: My fascination with Haiti's history began in my childhood, as early as I can remember. Haitian history was one of my preferred subjects in class because learning Haiti's glorious history was inspiring. I was always proud of being the son of a great history and culture. My early introduction and exposure to this unique history led me to investigate more in depth my own history, to uncover its essence and crystallize it upon my canvas. In 1977, when I emigrated from Haiti to Philadelphia, I was exposed to a treasure of historical documents on Haiti. I was able to live in a fertile environment that was the genesis of my historical art.

ED: So, you were lucky enough to have your love of Haitian history fed both inside and outside of Haiti. Some people leave Haiti and lose interest in Haiti due to lack of access and exposure to their culture in the United States. It seems like you found yourself even deeper in your study of Haitian history while living in Philadelphia.

You often write historical descriptions and sometimes poetry to accompany your paintings. I am thinking particularly of the poem you wrote for the Mother figure in your painting "Crucified Liberty." It states: "Since I won my crown of liberty, my dignity as a nurturing mother has been victimized." Do you see text or words as a way to develop or elaborate on your visual subjects?

UJ-P: A painting is often so profound that it makes it necessary for the artist to further elaborate its significance in writing.

ED: I like the way you elaborate through your images with words, as you say, without limiting the interpretation of others. I am curious: How do you choose the titles for your paintings? For example, "Crucified Liberty" seems to hint that you want the viewer to come away with a certain perspective after seeing this work. Do you want your paintings to have an educational as well as an aesthetic quality?

UJ-P: The titles of my paintings are always based on the captured subject. Since the title depicts an historical event of great significance, it embodies an educational as well as an aesthetic quality.

ED: As far as historical events of great significance, the historical figures in your work range from a portrait of the Taino Queen Anacaona to a depiction of Christopher Columbus's landing in the New World to the portrait of an African princess found on one of the album covers of the Haitian singer Carol Demesmin. How do you choose your subjects? Or do they choose you?

UJ-P: I would say that the subject matter chooses me. The vibrant spirits of my ancestors are exhibited through my entire being and select me as a spokesperson to paint the images of their greatness and of the subjects inspired through them.

ED: What about the more recent images from Haitian life? Would you say the same about them? Can they be made into art?

UJ-P: My contemporary subject matter originates from the depths of my consciousness, and is inspired by an urgency to communicate messages to the world, exposing reality's nakedness. As an artist, I sometimes find perfect beauty in the midst of life's imperfections. These effects, synthesized by extremes, often ignite my creative responses. Oftentimes, in an effort to capture the spirit of that beauty in another dimension, I venture beyond my perceptions to clarify its substance as a universal message. I have come to realize that I, as a product of life's imperfections, am perfectly imperfect. Human imperfection is the open gate to the logical path of life's experiences and challenges, and these often lead stimulated minds of various disciplines to great discoveries that contribute to the advancement of mankind. In the creation of my contemporary figurative subjects, my ultimate objective is to capture the simplicity of life as well as the essence of sincerity in the innocent smile of a child. My art is a tribute to Nature's unconditional generosity to mankind.

ED: What was it like for you to live and work in New Orleans, a city that, like the rest of Louisiana, has such strong historical and cultural connections to Haiti? I am thinking in particular of the Louisiana Purchase and the Haitian Revolution and its aftermath, which brought many Haitian slaveowners to Louisiana. For many Louisianians who are of Haitian descent, Vodou has been embraced as an important part of their culture, even if in an occult, sensationalized way. In fact, you were featured on the PBS documentary series "Voodoo in New Orleans." In that context, you were-considered an artist from New Orleans as well as a Haitian artist. How did living in New Orleans inspire your work?

UJ-P: New Orleans was not only an exciting place to live but also a constant source of inspiration for a Haitian-born artist. There is a well-known link between the revolutionary period of Haiti and the socio-political development of Louisiana, especially New Orleans. In my research, I have learned that a multitude of links exist between Haiti and Louisiana that many historians have still not addressed in their work. I am currently working on a series of paintings that depict historical and cultural connections such as those inscribed in the Louisiana Purchase, the inspiration that the Saint-Domingue uprisings had on slaves in the U.S. south, and even the styles of architecture common to the two places. I lived in Louisiana for ten years. There is a personal connection between my past and Louisiana history. It would take volumes to develop this particular subject. Suffice it to say that every day, every minute, and every second that I have lived in this magical, diverse city has reminded me of my beloved homeland. Ayiti cheri! *Bèl fanm kreyòl mwen.*

ED: How do you explain the fact that Haiti, this "Bèl fanm kreyòl" who has suffered so much, with so little material means, has produced so many great artists such as yourself?

UJ-P: As you know, there is a difference between the spiritual and the material. It is true that Haiti has so little material means. However, her magnitude of historical references and her cultural richness are profound and sacred treasures that inspire greatness. The fidelity of my unconditional love for Haiti is one of the energetic forces that has produced the consistency in my depiction of Haiti's history for the past two decades. Even though I have been living outside of Haiti during those decades, my spiritual flame of inspiration has never permitted my creative soul to forsake the zeal of liberty that my ancestors engraved upon the history of humanity. Haiti's cultural richness is infinite. It has a magical beauty, as well as an open door of generous inspiration to life and all sensitive souls. Therefore, sincere artistic inspiration expressed in music, painting, sculpture, poetry, theater, dance, and so forth are purely spiritual, and not related in any way to the material.

ED: In reference to material, in the "tools" sense now, as in painting tools, how is your working process? How long does it take you to work on a painting, especially large works such as "Ceremony of Bois Caïman I" and "Slave Uprising I" that involve so much movement on a single canvas and the depiction of so many people?

UJ-P: The subject that chooses me takes me on a journey that involves many days, weeks, and even months of extensive research. Thereafter, I concentrate on all the information that I have gathered. Then, I project myself across the bridges of the past to relive this particular moment and incarnate the personalities of the characters in question. It is like stepping into a different time and space; my body is removed from the present. When my soul bears the fruits of this journey, it explodes in color upon my canvas. It is as if I am a part of the subject matter, and my brushes are guided by an invisible hand that is the essence of the spirits of my ancestors.

It has been over two decades since I created these two favorite paintings of mine, "Ceremony of Bois Caïman I" and "Slave Uprising I," which depict the 1791 Revolution of Haïti (Saint-Domingue). I still treasure the vivid memories of the many mysterious experiences I had while I was creating these paintings. My emotional experience and frame of mind sailed beyond the scope of logic, capturing these memorable events from the past. No words can accurately describe the flames of my emotions projected in these paintings. Working on these pieces was a labored, spiritual, and fulfilling odyssey. For a period of ten months, I would paint from seven in the morning until the next day. Nature required only that I stop to shower, eat, and sleep for three hours. Haiti has been, and will always be, my endless fountain of sacred inspiration and energetic excitement to thrive and to create. Such commitment did not allow me the opportunity to relax enough and sleep for long hours. It was a passionate dedication driven by overflowing rivers of inspiration. There were times when I would be transported into the painting to witness these events. I experienced living during a different time period. My body, no longer affected by gravitational force, floated weightlessly across the canvas.

One day, as I was working on "Slave Uprising I," I observed a furious facial expression on one of the figures depicted in the painting. I was so transfixed in the trance of the moment that I could not obey my most urgent needs. I just continued to paint for hours, unable to put down the paintbrush. Finally, I ran to the bathroom. There, I was astonished by my outlandish expression in the mirror. I thought I was looking at another person through me. I became conscious that I was emotionally monopolized by the most profound concentration and inspiration. That expression in the mirror was the vehicle that transported my state of mind back to the reality of the present.

ED: When you are immersed in a painting in the way you just described, do you ever dream the scenes in the paintings? Some of your paintings are so dream-like. I am thinking, for example, of your painting "Haitian Refugees II," which depicts the Statue of Liberty with the boat people. In that painting, it is almost as if the reality is too much to bear so it can only be seen through a surreal, dreamy gaze. Can you elaborate on the role of dreams in your creative process?

UJ-P: Dreams have a significant impact on my art. Sometimes historical figures reveal themselves to me to relate things such as the secret codes for names and particular objects, and the date, time, and exact location of the occurrence of certain events. At my home and art studio in New Orleans, I was visited by events that took place in 1840. These dreams occurred when I was immersed in the serene domain of meditation, therefore at the gateway of the stars. The world of imagination is an infinity of inspiration for sensitive and inspired souls. As an explorer of the imaginative world, observer of reality, and part of everyday life on earth, I am inspired by various sources that influence the natural rhythm of our heartbeats. I am also inspired by the essential forces that govern life: wind, water, fire, thunder, magnetic forces of gravity, sound, motion, infinity of space, and light and darkness. My constant awareness of the importance of these things leaves me in awe and makes me appreciate all of God's creations, whose star-dusted trail is the fertile garden of endless inspirations. Every painting is different. Oftentimes, the scenes in my paintings are revealed to me in my dreams. Therefore, I endeavor to capture the essence of my dreams in my process. Some of the symbolic paintings are translations of messages originated from dreams and interpretations of my philosophy of life. Allow me to elaborate on the painting depicting Haitian refugees struggling to keep their boat afloat with the Statue of Liberty in the background. The painting vividly captures a horrific moment for people who seek freedom at all costs. I was appalled by the unfair treatment and legislations against Haitian refugees. I took pains to display the courage and determination of men, women, and children to survive against all odds.

ED: Your painting "General Toussaint Louverture Issuing the First Constitution" is becoming one of the many iconic depictions of the renowned leader. In some ways, it has become not an interpretation but a representation of Toussaint. How much do you study other portrayals of famous historical figure, or of well-known historical moments before you produce your own?

UJ-P: My research and study of General Toussaint Louverture took me five years. Based upon his physical descriptions by historians visiting and residing in Haiti (then Saint-Domingue) during the time he was alive, I gathered a composite anatomy and physiology. I started by sketching a skeleton and muscles, and clothed the body in the military garments of the period. And then, as if by magic, the painting gained a life of its own to become what it is today. On the days I did not paint, one would find me at the Philadelphia Public Library or at the Temple University Library researching the varied subjects of my paintings.

ED: Other than your portrait of "General Toussaint Louverture Issuing the First Constitution," which you just described, I know that you have two other paintings of Toussaint Louverture. Is this a way of ensuring that the significance of his achievements is not forgotten?

UJ-P: I think it is important to invoke our Haitian collective consciousness and willingness and courage to preserve our ancestors' inspiring legacy. What made Toussaint Louverture memorable as one of Haiti's greatest leaders was his unselfish vision of equality and justice. At the dawn of the slave revolt of 1791, Toussaint Louverture recognized that it was imperative to provide military training to the revolutionaries, men and women alike, to defend their liberty and dignity. Toussaint's ultimate dream was to ensure that prosperity would continue to flourish in Haiti and its people would always be self-reliant, living in peace, liberty, and dignity, inspiring present and future generations to control the ultimate potential of their destiny. Toussaint recognized that the education of all the people was essential in order to build the society he had envisioned.

ED: Much like your "Toussaint Louverture," your "Marie-Jeanne Lamartinierre" is another very stunning image, as well as an extraordinary representation of a strong Haitian heroine. In your crowd scenes, there are always women. In "Key to Freedom," a female angel offers hope to a hard working peasant. You just referred to Haiti as a Bèl fanm kreyòl. How do you see the role of women in your depictions of Haitian history and Haitian life in general?

UJ-P: For me, women represent the roots of humanity, as well as the tree of life that gives fruits of hope to the continuity of life and survival. But unfortunately, only a few women have been credited for their accomplishments. One must not ignore the central role that spirited and dedicated women played in the birth of our nation. It is a well-known fact that many men who became recognized as heroes for their contributions to the history of Haiti would not have succeeded if it were not for the courage and support of many valiant Haitian women, my heroines.

ED: Your work has been compared to that of Eugène Delacroix and Jacques-Louis David, Michelangelo Buonarroti and Leonardo da Vinci. Are these artists whose work you have studied or admired?

UJ-P: During my years in art schools, studying the proportions and anatomy of the human body and of animals, geometry (perspective), composition, physics, chemistry, and so forth was required as part of the academic discipline of art. In my anatomy courses, I studied Leonardo da Vinci and Michelangelo Buonarroti. I never studied Jacques-Louis David's and Eugène Delacroix's paintings, although a similarity between their paintings and mine is relatively evident. The similarity is based upon the fact that we all depict men and women revolutionaries in military uniforms. The artists who influenced my work at the very beginning of my career were Haitian artists such as Louverture Poisson, Enguerant Gourge, Rosemarie Desruisseaux, Kesnel Franklin, and René and Lavorancy Exumé. Lavorancy Exumé became my first teacher. He had the greatest influence on my life as an artist. When I was offered a scholarship at the prestigious Foyer des Arts Plastiques in 1973, it was Exumé who convinced the administrators to accept me on a tuition-free basis because of his strong conviction that I had much to offer.

Lavorancy Exumé was one of the greatest Haitian masters of impressionism. He was widely respected for his sophisticated academic style of painting. He was also a very well known muralist. I learned a lot from him: theories of color, painting techniques, and composition perspectives as well as drawing techniques and anatomy. He was a dedicated teacher whose charisma inspired all those who were learning the art of painting. His twin brother, René Exumé, was one of the administrators of the school. His meticulous attention to detail in the study of human anatomy had a significant influence on me. He was known for his academic principles and was also a well-admired teacher of Le Lycée de Pétion-Ville. I feel fortunate to have had the opportunity to admire up close the paintings of these national treasures. This experience was the additional key to the development of my artistic inspirations. I was awed by the magical colors and the intense expressions reflected in their work. I felt as if I had miraculously fallen into a barrel of honey in the garden of paradise.

ED: Are any of your paintings in public collections, in museums, in Haiti? I remember once reading an editorial in a Haitian newspaper that said your work should be in Haiti, belongs in Haiti. ("Son encre a été trempé dans notre histoire," it said.) What are your feelings about that?

UJ-P: Due to the irregularity of my travel to Haiti, I cannot accurately answer this question. To my recollection, the first time my historical paintings were exhibited was in 1980 at Le musée national, in Port-au-Prince; in 1981, they were exhibited at the French Institute in Port-au-Prince, and at Le musée du Panthéon National; in 1985, there was an exhibit at Le musée colonial Ogier-Fombrun located at Moulin-sur-Mer in Haiti. I know for a fact that one of my favorite paintings, "Général Jean-Jacques Dessalines à l'assaut" is part of the Musée colonial Ogier-Fombrun collection. To completely answer your question: I do believe that most of my historical paintings belong in Haiti, where they could be accessible to the public, particularly to young Haitians and schoolchildren.

ED: How did you get the opportunity to paint the portrait of former American President Jimmy Carter?

UJ-P: I was selected by the Haitian Cultural Society of Philadelphia and Audience of America, an association in Philadelphia that promotes art and culture, in 1978 to produce that portrait of President Jimmy Carter. It was a way to honor the president for his views on foreign policy, which affected many small countries around the globe. The portrait is a part of the collection of the Jimmy Carter Presidential Library and Museum in Atlanta.

ED: I know that you have painted other non-Haitian subjects such as the portraits of Reverend Dr. Sarah Porter and the two portraits of "Louis Armstrong (Satchmo)," for which you received the first prize as part of the centennial of Louis Armstrong's birthday celebration in New Orleans in 2001. Are you moving towards more non-Haitian subjects? How do you become inspired by a particular subject?

UJ-P: Every day on earth is an endless garden of inspiration that is constantly blooming with sacred ideas to be expressed or captured. Therefore, as an artist, my creative soul is totally exposed to the magnetic force of natural, universal inspiration and expression. But Haiti has my soul, and she will always be the focal point on the canvas of my existence. And furthermore, my strong determination will never allow me to deviate from my sacred mission as a portrayer of Haiti.

ED: Your historical painting series also suggests, and encourages, a constant acknowledgment and celebration of a collective Haitian memory. How important is this acknowledgment since Haiti has commemorated the bicentennial of its independence?

UJ-P: To pay tribute to this commemoration of our independence, poets, writers, scholars of various disciplines, historians, art historians and museum curators, ethnologists, Vodou priestesses and priests, and myself have gathered in the circle of harmonious collective spirits to mark this event with images and words. Publishing this book illustrates and certifies the importance of collective efforts and acknowledgment, which Haiti needs every day from me, from you, and from us—all Haitians. It is the way to inspire the youth of Haiti, and future generations.

ED: After 200 years of independence, I feel that it is important for us to pause and reflect on where we are now. If that Toussaint you paint so beautifully came back to life today, what would we tell him? What would we tell the Dessalines of your "Général Jean-Jacques Dessalines à l'assaut"? Have we not failed our ancestors? Have we not failed the Boukman whom you celebrate so beautifully in your "Ceremony of Bois Caïman" and the fighters in your "Slave Uprising"?

UJ-P: My canvas is an open window of constant celebration that allows me to travel into the depths of the past, to bring pride to the present, as well as hope to the future. In 1804, our ancestors, the unified people of Haiti, officially declared our independence from France, giving us the distinction of becoming the first black republic of the world. This symbolic event was achieved through collective efforts of solidarity, harmony, fraternal love and singularity of purpose. All those involved shared the common objectives of liberty, prosperity, and dignity. Our nation has joined the body of nations and sculpted its place in history. Our foremothers and forefathers comprehended the importance of solidarity and unity. This was instrumental to the success of the revolution from 1791 to 1804. Their collective strengths begot our Haitian identity. I remain hopeful of our national slogan: "L'Union fait la Force [In Unity, There Is Strength]. I believe that the spirit of pride incarnated in patriotism will prevail to rebuild our shattered union, reform its paralyzed institutions, and restore stability and liberty as our fragile democracy gathers strength.

The primary purpose and ultimate objective for the creation of historical paintings of Haiti is to crystallize and immortalize the importance of our heroines and heroes who have sacrificed their lives for our liberty and collective identity. These paintings are an homage to the proud people of Haiti. They are also dedicated to people around the world who love Haiti and to those countless souls who contribute to making a difference in Haiti. Most important, my historical paintings are a tribute to all Haitian children. I sincerely hope that the essence of pride and accomplishment embodied in these paintings will inspire their love for Haiti as her future leaders. To achieve the dream of our ancestors, we should plant the seeds of posterity in the vibrant stream of education for all Haitian children, regardless of socioeconomic status. With the encouragement of a free and stable environment, they will apply themselves to the various tasks that the nation requires. Haitian art is a mirror image of its colorful society. It reflects the essence of its soul, its sensual magic, its joy, its sorrows and its hopes. The artist captures in a rather dramatic manner themes that make Haitians unique and special. Art will continue to evolve and present significant events that may forever change the course of Haiti's often-troubled history. The artist is, in effect, a fearless visionary inspiring the population to engage in purposeful struggles for a free, safe, and industrious society, resurrected from the catacombs of poverty, lawlessness, and despair.

ED: Your work does a great job of balancing the bitter with the sweet, the triumph and the pain. There is a popular saying, "History is little more than a picture of human crimes and misfortunes." In Haiti, history certainly seems to constantly be repeating itself, not always in the most positive way. You have always portrayed the best of Haiti, without shying away from the crimes and misfortunes. How have you managed to do that?

UJ-P: In an atmosphere saturated with psychological remnants of colonial crimes and unfortunate circumstances, when I paint, I carry a flame of hope in the subjects I depict, which is a way to revive the consciousness of greatness that has been idly forgotten. In one of my paintings, I depicted Christopher Columbus, the notorious character who introduced crimes to Haiti—slavery and brutality that have percolated a poison throughout our history.

ED: That is what I mean. There is Columbus the criminal in your work. But there are also rainbows, angels, and children. With all the echoes of the past that haunt us, there is still a future to tend to. There are the children to think about. We can never forget them. Is that all part of your broad and complex view of current Haiti?

UJ-P: Yes—depictions of children and a sense of hope captured in my paintings are a reflection from the mirrors of our past reality, which in turn reflect an essence of hope through my optimism for a better tomorrow in Haiti.

ED: How do we carry that essence of hope into the future?

UJ-P: This is my prescription for the future. To carry the continuity of hope in Haiti, first of all, the rights and the importance of every Haitian citizen must be equalized and acknowledged. All Haitians must assume a sense of responsibility as citizens. We must become conscious of self-inflicted wounds, and learn from them. We should not buy into the mentality of blaming everyone except ourselves for our problems. In addition, blaming every current problem on the past is a waste of time; it takes away our ability to do something in the present. It is also imperative to acknowledge that our greatest enemy is disunity. Thus self-analysis and auto-criticism should be the reference point and frame of mind of any individual who is committed to the betterment of Haiti.

We must also put a greater emphasis on education for all Haiti's children as a national priority. The key to the solution of Haiti's chronic problems is in our hands—in education. We must have in place a structured system that will empower positive changes.

Our deeply rooted divisions have made us weak and have consequently produced opportunistic criminals running Haitian citizens' lives through fear. However, we must learn to forgive one another. It is the only way to find peace, love and inspiration within ourselves so that we may move forward to a promising future for Haitian children. Most of us Haitians are proud of our unique legacy. We must transform this energy of pride into concrete action. It is absolutely necessary to remind ourselves that taking action to build a prosperous, united Haiti will be one of the best examples for our children to follow as Haiti's future leaders. The children are our witnesses, our listeners, and the best recorders of our actions. They are tomorrow's artists, musicians, writers, sculptors, poets, and painters. They are the storytellers, the teachers, and the historians who will give a full account of what we have done for our country.

Sa nou plante nan jaden listwa peyi nou se sa pitit-pitit, pitit nou tou pral rekolte demen.

[What we have planted in the garden of our country's history, our great-grandchildren will harvest.]

Chapter 30

Conclusion
Ayiti se tè glise

Cécile Accilien

> *Ayiti se tè glise.*
> Haiti is a slippery land.
>
> *Dèyè do se nan Ginen.*
> We left Africa [Ginen] a long time ago, but we have not forgotten it.
>
> *Ou pa janm konen kote dlo pase pou li antre nan kokoye.*
> You never know how water gets through to the inside of the coconut.
>
> –Haitian proverbs

From the time Columbus landed in 1492 and instituted slavery, through French colonization, American occupation, dictatorships, political and economic instability, military coups, and on and on, Haiti's endurance, strength, and power have been extraordinary. Haitians and non-Haitians alike are skeptical about Haiti's ability to achieve complete sovereignty, considering its current economic and political situation. Yet Haiti has survived so much adversity and so many vicissitudes: international economic sanctions and embargos, high debts to developed countries such as France, exploitation at the national and international level, and the loss of an endless number of its children through massacres, deaths, and exile. The capacity of Haiti to remain a nation is beyond simple understanding.

Haitians who have been forced into exile—economic, social, religious or political—and who desire to see Haiti move forward, should not have to choose their country of exile over Haiti. In *Le pain de l'exil*, Marc Christophe elaborates on this complex choice. He writes:

> If one must choose
> Between Anacaona and Ovando
> Between the Negro and the Slave-ship
> Between the Planter and the Slave
> Between Dessalines and Pétion
> Between France and America
> Between Péralte and Caperton
> If one must choose
> Between the Cross and the Vèvè
> Between the Cathedral and the Hounfor
> Between Creole and French
> Between Palm Tree and the Conch
> Between Union and Power
> One must
> Choose
> Above all the passions
> Above all the doctrines
> All the methods
> All the prejudices
> And the preferences
> One must
> Always
> Choose
> Haiti.[1]

This volume is a way of celebrating Haiti's past, present, and future because we believe that it has a future. There are still thousands of Haitians and non-Haitians with visions for Haiti, visions that include community, equal rights for all Haitians including equal access to education, resistance through non-violence, and racial solidarity and pride. Through his visually arresting paintings, Ulrick Jean-Pierre captures histories of the amazing land that is Haiti—a "slippery land."

> Ayiti cheri
> There is hope for you–
> When you fought for freedom

You were covered by the mantle of the spirits of Ginen.

The spirits are still there, they have not left you–you must seek them as you did at Bwa Kayiman, and they will come to you.[2]

Notes

1. My translation of Marc A. Christophe's poem entitled "S'il faut choisir," included in *Le pain de l'exil* (Washington, DC: Garnett Publishing, Inc., 1988) 61. The original follows:

S'il faut choisir

Entre Anacaona et Ovando

Entre le Nègre et le Négrier

Entre le Planteur et l'Esclave…

Entre Dessalines et Pétion…

Entre la France et l'Amérique

Entre Péralte et Caperton

S'il faut choisir

Entre la Croix et le Vèvè

Entre la Cathédrale et le Hounfôr

Entre le Créole et le Français…

Entre le Palmiste et le Lambi

Entre l'Union et la Force,

Il faut,

Choisir,

Au-dessus des passions

Au-dessus des doctrines

Des systèmes

Des prejudices

Et des préférences

Il faut

Toujours

Choisir

Haïti

2. Poem by Cécile Accilien.

SECTION VI

Paintings

Paintings

Section I - Beginnings of the "New World"

Section II - What Is Freedom?

Section III - Forgotten Women of Haitian Liberty

Section IV - Legacies of Vodou

Section V - Behind the Mountain Are More Mountains

Map of Pre-Columbian Haiti.

Christopher Columbus's First Landing (December 6, 1492). Oil on canvas, 50" x 72", 1980.

Caonabo. Oil on canvas, 24" x 36", 2005. Collection of the artist.

Indian Revolt (1505). Oil on canvas, 30" x 40", 1994-2005. Collection of the artist.

Bohechio (Indian Chief, 1492). Oil on canvas, 20" x 24", 1992.
Collection of Dr. Jean C. Brierre, Shreveport, LA.

Queen Anacaona (Native Haitian) I. Oil on canvas, 24"x30", 2004.

Exchange of Culture (Between Indians and African Maroons). Oil on canvas, 24" x 30", 2005. Private collection.

François Makandal (1750s). Oil on canvas, 36" x 48", 2003-2005. Collection of the George and Leah McKenna Museum of African American Art, New Orleans, LA.

Unknown Maroon Announcing the Uprising (1791) (Tribute to Albert Mangonès). Oil on canvas, 34" x 52", 1994. Collection of Picard and Sharon Losier, Esq., Philadelphia, PA.

Slave Uprising I (Revolution of Saint-Domingue, Haiti, 1791). Oil on canvas, 44" x 72", 1979. Collection of the artist.

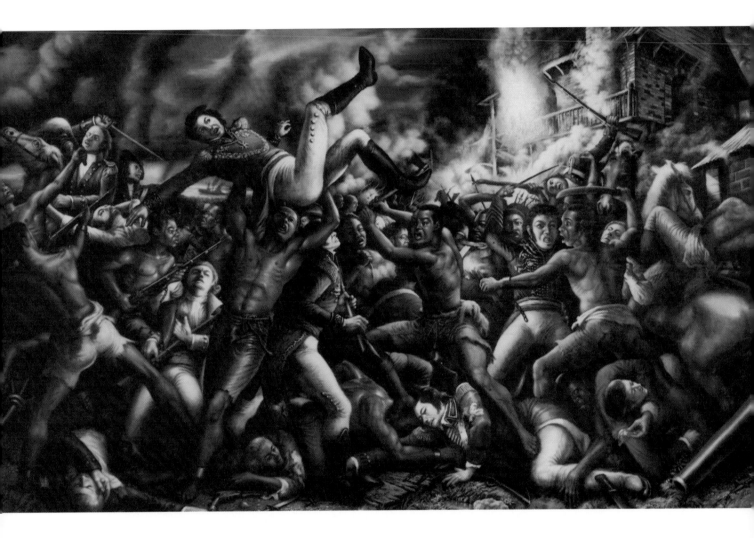

Slave Uprising II (Revolution of Saint-Domingue, Haiti, 1791). Oil on canvas, 34" x 52", 1992. Collection of Dr. and Mrs. Daniel J. Mompoint, New Orleans , LA.

General Toussaint Louverture (Issuing the First Constitution of Saint-Domingue [Haiti], 1801).
Oil on canvas, 65" x 89", 1986-1987. Collection of the artist.

The Last Meeting of Toussaint Louverture and Jean-Jacques Dessalines. Oil on canvas, 24" x 36", 1994. Collection of Dr. Fritz Fidèle, New Orleans, LA.

Creation of the Haitian Flag (1803). Oil on canvas, 54 " x 72", 1980. Collection of the artist.

General Jean-Jacques Dessalines (Commander-in-Chief of the Revolutionary Army, Saint-Domingue [Haiti], Presenting the Flag, 1803). Oil on canvas, 24" x 36". Collection of Dr. and Mrs. Daniel Bouchette, New Orleans, LA.

Général Jean-Jacques Dessalines à l'assaut. Oil on canvas, 36" x 60", 1991. Collection Musée Colonial Ogier-Fombrun Moulin-sur-Mer, Montrouis, Haiti.

Battle of Vertières I, Haitian Revolution (November 18, 1803). Oil on canvas, 34" x 68", 1990-1994. Collection of Dr. and Mrs. Ludner Confident. St. Petersburg, FL.

Battle of Vertières II, Haitian Revolution (November 18, 1803). Oil on canvas, 48" x 60", 1995.
Collection of Dr. and Mrs. Michel Joseph Lemaire, Plantation, FL.

General Boisrond Tonnerre (Secretary of the Revolutionary Army, Saint Domingue [Haiti] Issuing the Declaration of Haiti's Independence, 1804.) Oil on canvas, 30" x 40", 2003-2004. Collection of Dr. Fritz Fidèle, New Orleans, LA.

President Alexandre Pétion Reading Bolívar's Letter. Oil on canvas, 24" x 60", 1992. Collection of Dr. Fritz Fidèle, New Orleans, LA.

King Henri Christophe and his Architect (Henri Barré, 1811). Oil on canvas, 36" x 48", 1997. Collection of the artist.

King Henri Christophe and his Citadelle. Oil on canvas, 48 " x 60", 1993. Collection of Dr. and Mrs. Alix Bouchette, New Orleans, LA.

Le Caco (During the American Occupation in Haiti). Oil on canvas, 30 " x 40", 1986. Collection of Mrs. Marie Thérèse Jérôme, Philadelphia, PA.

Key to Freedom. Oil on canvas, 40" x 60", 1981. Collection of Picard and Sharon Losier, Esq., Philadelphia, PA.

Queen Anacaona II (Native Haitian). Oil on canvas, 36" x 48",
1992. Collection of Dr. Jean C. Brierre. Shreveport, LA.

Belle Congo. Acrylic on canvas, 24" x 30", 1997. Collection of the artist.

Cécile Fatima (The Manbo of the Ceremony of Bois Caïman, 1791).
Oil on canvas, 18" x 20", 2004.

Heroine Maroon Slave. Oil on canvas, 18" x 24", 1998. Collection of Picard and Sharon Losier, Esq., Philadelphia, PA.

Zabeth. Oil on canvas, 48" x 60", 2001-2002. Collection of the artist.

Marie-Jeanne Lamartinierre (Haitian Revolution, 1802).
Oil on canvas, 22" x 28", 2000. Collection of Judge Marie Bookman, New Orleans, LA.

Catherine Flon (May 18, 1803). Oil on canvas, 34" x 48", 2002. Collection of the artist.

Défilée la folle Carrying Dessalines' Body. Oil on canvas, 36" x 48," 2005. Collection of the artist.

Sacred Instruments. Oil on canvas, 30" x 40", 1997. Collection of Picard and Sharon Losier, Esq., Philadelphia, PA.

Boukman Invoking the Spirit of Freedom. Oil on canvas, 36" x 48", 1997. Collection of Picard and Sharon Losier, Esq., Philadelphia, PA.

Ceremony of Bois Caïman I (Revolution of Saint-Domingue, Haiti, 1791). Oil on canvas, 40" x 60", 1979. Collection of Dr. and Mrs. Jean-Phillipe Austin, Miami, FL.

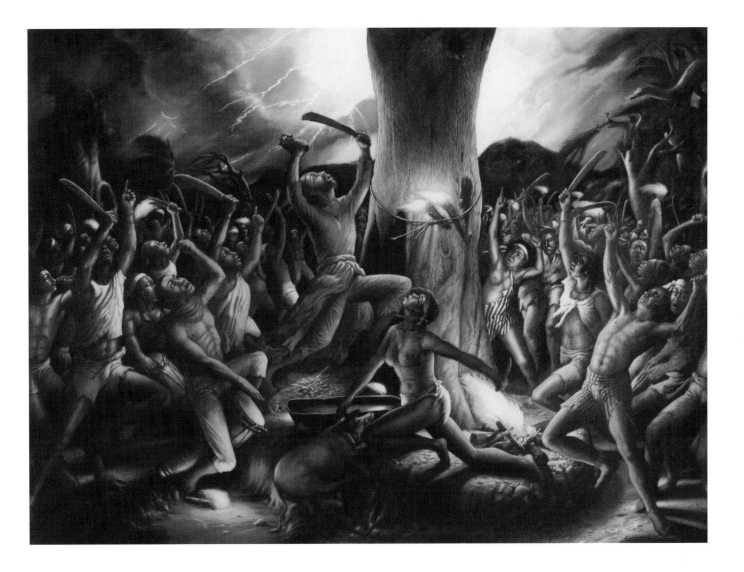

Ceremony of Bois Caïman III (Revolution of Saint-Domingue, Haiti, 1791).
Oil on canvas, 40" x 60", 1995. Collection of Drs. Edna and Farère Dyer, New Orleans, LA.

Marie Laveau (Invoking the Spirit of Love). Oil on canvas, 60" x 70", 2003. Collection of the George and Leah McKenna Museum of African American Art, New Orleans, LA.

Zaka. Oil on canvas, 18" x 24", 1983. Collection of Mrs. Marie Thérèse Jérôme, Philadelphia, PA.

Commodification of Religion. Oil on canvas, 24"x30", 1990. Collection of Dr. Jean Claude Compas, New York, NY.

Gingerbread House. Oil on canvas, 36 ' x 52", 1981. Collection of Mrs. Marie Thérèse Jérôme, Haitian Cultural Society, Philadelphia, PA.

Awareness of Exploitation. Oil on canvas, 20" x 30", 1996. Collection of Dr. and Mrs. Robert Nerée, Miami, FL.

238

Haitian Refugees I. Oil on canvas, 30" x 40", 1994. Private collection.

Haitian Refugees II (Denied Liberty). Oil on canvas, 48" x 60", 2004. Collection of the artist.

Crucified Liberty. Oil on canvas, 48" x 60", 1998. Collection of the artist.

Liberty Palm Tree. Oil on canvas, 24" x 48", 1977. Collection of Mrs. Marie Thérèse Jérôme, Philadelphia, PA.

Appendix 1

Glossary

Ayibobo. A cry of joy that can be translated as Hooray!

Bois Caïman, Bois Kayiman, Bwa Kayiman. The term, which has several spelling variations (Cayman, Caïman, Kayiman, Kayman, Kayiman), refers to the 1791 Ceremony of Bois Caïman leading to the Haitian independence. Bois Caïman refers to the location where the slaves gathered and revolted against the colonial ruler, France.

Houngan, hougan, oungan, ougan, gangan. Considered the equivalent of priest or master of the *lwa*; in daily usage, people sometimes use the diminutive "gangan."

Lanbi, lambi, corne de lambi. A conch shell. The lanbi plays an important role in Haitian history and memory. It is at once a sacred and political instrument. It is used to announce important events such as birth and death, as well as in ceremonies. It is also used to call the ancestors and the *lwa* or the gods. During the Haitian revolution, the lanbi was used to call slaves from the hills.

Lwa, loa. (Lwa is the preferred spelling of this term in Haitian Kreyòl.) Refers to a deity or a spirit. During a Vodou ceremony, the manner in which the lwa is manifested in the individual is based on the patron saint the lwa represents. For example, a person who experiences the lwa of a docile saint will behave as such during the experience; similarly, if the lwa is angry, the possessed individual will exhibit anger during the time the *lwa* inhabits the person's spirit. Individuals may experience lwa because the "lwa possesses them," or because they actively seek the *lwa*.

Manbo, mambo. A Vodou priestess.

Ogou, ogun, ogu, Ogu/Ogou. The term refers to a deity; it is important to note that there are varieties of this deity: Ogou Ferraille (Feray), Ogou Petro, Ogou Shango, and Ogou Yansan, etc. Ogou is considered the lwa of war, and thus a dangerous lwa. Ogou is associated with the color red.

Vèvè. A geometric figure that is drawn on the ground, usually with a flour-based substance. The color used depends upon the ritual being celebrated. The vèvè has been called the signature of the gods. It concentrates energies of a spirit in order for that spirit to reveal her/himself to a particular devotee. For that reason, a vèvè should not be carelessly drawn; the initiated person draws it with the intent that the *lwa* come.

Vodou, vodu, vodun, vaudou, voodoo, voodoo. Vodou is the most common spelling among Haitians. Vodou refers not only to a religion, but to a way of life. Vodou is reflected in one's daily activities: eating, dressing, interacting with others and spending time with oneself. For example, with regard to eating, one does not consume a type of food just because it exists, but rather because it is essential for the body. Dressing is as important as eating in that one's attire reflects the individual's state of mind. One's interaction with peers is essential because it reflects the fundamental principle of Vodou: being harmonious with others and with the self in order to create balance on Earth.

Wanga, ouanga. A spell, an intentional act of magic to bring about changes to an individual's life or attitude. The change may be directed toward a person, issue or event, for example, and it can be positive or negative.

Appendix 2

Suggested Reading

Sources in English

Alexis, Stephen. *Black Liberator: The Life of Toussaint Louverture.* London: Ernest Benn Limited, 1949.

Armstrong, Karen. *The History of God: The 4000-Year Quest of Judaism, Christian and Islam.* New York: Alfred A. Knopf, 1994.

Arthur, Charles, and Michael Dash, eds. *Libète: A Haiti Anthology.* Kingston: Ian Randle, 1999.

Beard, John R. *The Life of Toussaint Louverture: The Negro Patriot of Hayti: Comprising an Account of the Struggle for Liberty in the Island and a Sketch of its History to the Present Period.* London: Ingram, Cooke and Company, 1853.

Bellande-Robertson, Florence. *The Marassa Concept in Lilas Desquiron's Reflections of Loko Miwa.* Dubuque, IA: Kendall/Hunt, 1999.

Bellegarde-Smith, Patrick. *Haiti: The Breached Citadel.* Boulder: Westview Press, 1990.

Bryan, Patrick E. *The Haitian Revolution and Its Effects.* Kingston: Heinemann, 1984.

Carpentier, Alejo. *The Kingdom of this World.* Trans. Harriet De Onís. New York: Alfred A. Knopf, 1957.

Candler, John. *Brief Notices of Haiti.* London: Thomas Ward & Co., 1842.

Chancy, Myriam J.A. *Framing Silence: Revolutionary Novels by Haitian Women.* New Brunswick, NJ: Rutgers University Press, 1997.

Christensen, Eleanor I. *The Art of Haiti.* South Brunswick, N.J.: A.S. Barnes, 1974.

Clark, B.C. *A Plea for Haiti with a Glance at Her Relations with France, England and the United States for the Last Sixty Years.* Boston: Eastburn Press, 1853.

Cleaver, Carole, and Selden Rodman. *Spirits of the Night: The Vaudun Gods of Haiti.*
Dallas: Spring Publications, 1992.

Cosentino, Donald, ed. *Sacred Arts of Haitian Vodou.* Los Angeles: UCLA Fowler Museum of
Cultural History, c1995.

Crosley, Reginald. *The Vodou Quantum Leap: Alternate Realities, Power and Mysticism.*
St. Paul, MN: Lewellyn Publications, 2000.

Danticat, Edwidge. *Krik? Krak!* New York: Soho Press, 1994.

-----. *Breath, Eyes, Memory.* New York: Soho Press, 1994.

-----. *The Farming of Bones.* New York: Soho Press, 1998.

-----, ed. *The Butterfly's Way: Voices from the Haitian Dyaspora* [sic] *in the United States.* Soho,
2001.

-----. *After the Dance: A Walk through Carnival in Jacmel, Haiti.* New York: Crown, 2002.

-----. *The Dew Breaker.* New York: Knopf, 2004.

Dash, J. Michael. *Haiti and the United States: National Stereotypes and the Literary Imagination.*
New York: St. Martin's Press, 1988.

-----. *Culture and Customs of Haiti.* Westport, CT: Greenwood Press, 2001.

Deren, Maya, dir. *Divine Horsemen: The Living Gods of Haiti.* Ed. Teiji & Cherel Ito. New York:
Mystic Fire Video, 1985.

-----. *Divine Horsemen: The Living Gods of Haiti.* New York: Thames & Hudson, c1953.

Davis, Wade. *Passage of Darkness: The Ethnobiology of the Haitian Zombie.* Chapel Hill: U of
North Carolina P, 1988.

Dayan, Joan. *Haiti, History and the Gods.* Berkeley: U of California P, 1995.

Desmangles, Leslie. *The Faces of the Gods*: *Vodou and Roman Catholicism in Haiti.* Chapel Hill: U of North Carolina P, 1992.

Desquiron, Lila. *Reflections of Loko Miwa*. Trans. Robin Orr Bodkin. Charlottesville: U P of Virginia, 1998.

DuBois, W.E.B. *The Suppression of the African Slave Trade to the United States of America 1638-1870*. New York: Schocken, 1969.

Dunham, Katherine. *Island Possessed*. Chicago: U of Chicago P, 1994.

Dupuy, Alex. *Haiti in the New World Order*: *The Limits of the Democratic Revolution.* Boulder, CO: Westview Press, 1997.

Farmer, Paul. *The Uses of Haiti, 3rd ed.* Monroe, ME: Common Courage Press, 2006.

Fick, Carolyn E. *The Making of Haiti*: *The Saint-Domingue Revolution from Below.* Knoxville: U of Tennessee P, 1990.

Fouchard, Jean. *The Haitian Maroons of Liberty or Death*. New York: Edward W. Blyden, 1981.

Gaspar, David Barry, and David Patrick Geggus, eds. *A Turbulent Time: The French Revolution and the Greater Caribbean.* Bloomington: Indiana U P, 1997.

Geggus, David P., ed. *The Impact of the Haitian Revolution in the Atlantic World.* Columbia: U of South Carolina P, 2001.

Glissant, Edouard. *Monsieur Toussaint.* Washington, DC: Three Continents Press, 1981.

-----. *Caribbean Discourse.* Charlottesville: U P of Virginia, 1989.

Hall, Gwendolyn Midlo. *Social Control in Slave Plantation Societies: A Comparison of Saint-Domingue and Cuba.* Baltimore: Johns Hopkins U P, 1971.

-----. *Africans in Colonial Louisiana: The Development of Afro-Creole Culture in the Eighteenth Century.* Baton Rouge: Louisiana State U P, 1992.

Hassal, Mary. *Secret History: Written by a Lady at Cape François to Colonel Burr.* Freeport, NY: Books for Libraries, 1971.

Heinl, Robert, and Nancy Gordon. *Written in Blood: The Story of the Haitian People, 1492-1995.* 2nd ed. revised and expanded. Lanham, MD: U P of America, 2005.

Hoobler, Dorothy, and Thomas Hoobler. *Toussaint L'ouverture.* New York: Chelsea House Publishers, 1990.

Hunt, Alfred N. *Haiti's Influence on Antebellum America: Slumbering Volcano in the Caribbean.* Baton Rouge: Louisiana State U P, 1988.

James, C.L.R. *The Black Jacobins: Toussaint L'Ouverture and the San Domingo Revolution.* 3rd ed. New York: Vintage, 1989.

James, Cynthia James. *The Maroon Narrative.* Portsmouth: Heinemann, 2002.

Janson, H.W. *History of Art.* New York: Harry N. Abrams, 1995.

Kédar, Daniel. *Haiti: Reflections.* Port-au-Prince: Shiboumba, S.A., 1999.

Kumar, Chetan. *Building Peace in Haiti.* (International Peace Academy, Inc., Occasional Papers Series.) Boulder, CO: Lynne Reinner Publishers,1998.

Laguerre, Michel. *The Military and Society in Haiti.* Knoxville: U of Tennessee P, 1993.

-----. *Voodoo and Politics in Haiti.* New York: St. Martin's Press, 1989.

Lawless, Robert. *Haiti's Bad Press.* Rochester, VT: Schenkman, 1992.

Maguire, Robert, ed. *Haiti Held Hostage: International Responses to the Quest for Nationhood 1986-1996.* Providence, RI: Brown University, Occasional Paper # 23, Thomas J. Watson Jr. Institute for International Studies, 1996.

McAlister, Elizabeth. *Rara! Vodou, Power and Performance in Haiti and Its Diaspora.* Berkeley: U of California P, 2002.

McCarthy-Brown, Karen. *Tracing the Spirits: Ethnographic Essays on Haitian Art.* Seattle: U of Washington P, 1995.

-----. *Mama Lola: A Vodou Priestess in Brooklyn.* Berkeley: U of California P, 1991.

McKissack, Patricia C., and Frederick L. McKissack. *Rebels Against Slavery: American Slave Revolts.* New York: Scholastic, 1996.

Michel, George. *Charlemagne Péralte and the First American Occupation of Haiti.* Trans. Douglas Henry Daniels. Dubuque, IA: Kendall/Hunt, 1996.

Montejo, Esteban. *The Autobiography of a Runaway Slave.* Ed. Miguel Barnet. New York: Pantheon, 1968.

National Coalition for Haitian Rights, www.nchr.org.

Nicole, Christopher. *Black Majesty: The Seeds of Rebellion.* London: Severn House, 1984.

Pamphile, Leon D. *Haitians and African Americans: A Heritage of Tragedy and Hope.* Gainesville: U P of Florida, 2001.

Renda, Mary A. *Taking Haiti: Military Occupation and the Culture of U.S. Imperialism,* 1915-1940. Chapel Hill: U of North Carolina P, 2001.

Rey, Terry. *Our Lady of Class Struggle.* Trenton, NJ: Africa World Press, Inc., 1999.

Ridgeway, James, ed. *The Haiti Files: Decoding the Crisis.* Washington, DC: Essential Books/Azul Editions, 1994.

Rigaud, Milo. *Secrets of Voodoo.* Trans. Robert B. Cross. New York: Arco, 1969.

Rodman, Selden. *Renaissance in Haiti: Popular Painters in the Black Republic.* New York: Pelligrini and Cudahy, 1948.

-----. *Haiti, the Black Republic.* Old Greenwich, CT: Devin-Adair Co., 1973.

Ros, Martin. *Night of Fire: The Black Napoleon and the Battle for Haiti.* New York: Sarpedon, 1991.

Rotberg, Robert, ed. *Haiti Renewed: Political and Economic Prospects.* Washington, DC: Brookings Institution Press, The World Peace Foundation, 1997.

Roumain, Jacques. *Masters of the Dew.* Trans. Langston Hughes and Mercer Cook. Oxford: Heinemann, 1978.

Shacochis, Bob. *The Immaculate Invasion.* New York: Viking Penguin, 1999.

Smart-Bell, Madison. *All Souls' Rising.* New York: Pantheon, 1995.

-----. *Master of the Crossroads.* New York: Pantheon, 2000.

-----. *The Stone that the Builder Refused.* New York: Pantheon, 2004.

Trouillot, Michel-Rolph. *Haiti, State Against Nation: The Origins and Legacy of Duvalierism.* New York: Monthly Review Press, 1990.

-----. *Silencing the Past: Power and the Production of History.* Beacon Press, 1995.

Webb, Barbara. *Myth and History in Caribbean Fiction.* Amherst: U of Massachusetts P, 1992.

White, Dale, ed. *Dialogue and Medicine.* Nashville: Abingdon Press, 1967.

Wucker, Michele. *Why the Cocks Fight: Dominicans, Haitians and the Struggle for Hispaniola.* New York: Hill and Wang, 1999.

Sources in French

Alexis, Jacques-Stéphen. *Compère Général Soleil.* Port-au-Prince: Éditions des Antilles, 1993.

-----. *Romancéro aux étoiles.* Paris: Gallimard, 1960.

Ardouin, Beaubrun. *Etudes sur l'histoire d'Haïti.* Port-au-Prince: Dr. Dalencour, 1958.

Ateliers des Droits Humains du Centre de Recherches et de Formation Economique et Sociale pour le Développement (CRESFED). *Haïti: Jamais Plus! Les violations des Droits de l'Homme à l'époque des Duvalier.* Port-au-Prince: Imprimerie Henri Deschamps, 2000.

Benoît, Max. *Cahier de folklore et des traditions orales d'Haïti.* Port-au-Prince: Haïti, Agence de Coopération Culturelle et Technique, Imprimerie La Phalange, 1970.

Bloncourt, Gérald and Marie-José Nadal-Gardère. *La peinture haïtienne.* Paris: Nathan, 1986.

Buch, Hans Christoph. *Le mariage de Port-au-Prince.* Trans. Nicole Casanova. Paris: Editions Grasset & Fasquelle, 1990.

Camille, Roussan. *La multiple présence, derniers poèmes.* Port-au-Prince: Editions Caraïbes, 1978.

Centre pour la libre entreprise et la démocratie (CLED). *Haïti 2020: Vers une nation compétitive.* Port-au-Prince: Imprimerie Henri Deschamps, 2003.

Césaire, Aimé. *La tragédie du roi Christophe.* Paris: Présence Africaine, 1963.

Charles, Christophe Philippe. *Trajectoire III: Perspectives 2004/vers un nouvel ordre culturel en Haïti.* Port-au-Prince: Éditions Choucoune, 1984.

Charles, Jean-Claude. *De si jolies petites plages.* Paris: Stock, 1982.

-----. *Manhattan Blues.* Paris: Barrault, 1985.

-----. *Ferdinand je suis à Paris.* Paris: Barrault, 1987.

Clarkson, Thomas. *Haiti ou renseignements authentiques sur l'abolition de l'esclavage et ses resultants à Saint-Domingue.* Paris: Hachette, 1835.

Corvington, Georges. *Port-au-Prince au cours des ans: La ville coloniale.* Port-au-Prince: Henri Deschamps, 1975.

-----. *Sous les assauts de la révolution.* Port-au-Prince: Deschamps, 1975.

-----. *La métropole haïtienne du 19ème siècle, 1814-1888*. Port-au-Prince, Deschamps, 1974.

-----. *La métropole haïtienne du 19ème siècle, 1888-1915*. Port-au-Prince: Deschamps, 1976.

Dépestre, René. *Hadriana dans tous mes rêves*. Paris, Gallimard, 1988.

Des Rosiers, Joël. *Théories Caraïbes: Poétique du déracinement*. Montréal: Les Éditions Triptyque, 1996.

Dorsinville, Roger. *Jacques Roumain*. Paris: Présence Africaine, 1981.

-----. *Toussaint Louverture ou la vocation de la liberté*. Paris: Collection Temps Modernes, 1965.

Drot, Jean-Marie. *Journal de voyage chez les peintres de la fête et du vaudou en Haïti*. Genève: Éditions d'art, Albert Skira, 1974.

Étienne, Gérard. *Un ambassadeur macoute à Montréal*. Montréal: Nouvelle Optique, 1979.

-----. *Une femme muette*. Montréal: Nouvelle Optique, 1983.

-----. *La reine soleil levée*. Montréal: Guérin, 1988.

-----. *La pacotille. Montréal:* L'Hexagone, 1991.

Eugène, Grégoire. *Mes adieux à l'exil*. Port-au-Prince: Les Éditions Fardin, 1988.

Fouchard, Jean. *Les marrons du syllabaire*. Port-au-Prince: Deschamps, 1974.

-----. *Plaisirs de Saint-Domingue*. Port-au-Prince: Imprimerie de l'État, 1955.

-----. *Les marrons de la liberté*. Paris: Éditions de l'école, 1972.

-----. *Le théâtre à Saint-Domingue*. Port-au-Prince: Imprimerie de l'État, 1955.

Gouraige, Ghislain. *Continuité noire*. Dakar-Abidjan: Les Nouvelles Editions Africaines, 1977.

-----. *La diaspora d'Haïti et l'Afrique*. Québec: Éditions Naaman, 1974.

Hamdani, Amar. *Rites et secrets du vaudou. 2nd ed.* Farigliano, Italie: Editions Magellan, 1994.

Hurbon, Laënnec. *Dieu dans le vaudou haïtien.* Port-au-Prince: Editions Deschamps, 1987.

Laferrière, Dany. *Comment faire l'amour avec un nègre sans se fatiguer.* Montréal: VLB éditeur, 1985.

-----. *L'odeur du café.* Montréal, VLB éditeur, 1991.

-----. *Pays sans chapeau.* Montréal: Lanctôt Éditeur, 1996.

Lahens, Yanick. *L'exil: Entre L'ancrage et la fuite.* Port-au-Prince, Haïti: Imprimerie Henri Deschamps, 1990.

La Selve, Edgar. *Le pays des nègres*: Voyage à Haïti. Paris: Hachette, 1875.

-----. *Histoire de la littérature haïtienne depuis les origines jusqu'à nos jours.* Versailles: Imprimerie et stéréotypie Cerf et fils, 1875.

Leconte, Frantz Antoine, ed. 1492: *Le viol du nouveau monde.* Montréal: Editions indépendantes/CIDIHCA Presses, 1996.

Lemoine, Lucien. *Douta Seck ou La tragédie du Roi Christophe.* Paris: Présence Africaine, 1993.

-----. *Le veilleur de jour.* Dakar: Les Nouvelles Éditions Africaines, 1980.

-----. *Onze et un poèmes d'amour.* Paris: Seghers, 1966.

Lerebours, Michel-Philippe. *Haïti et ses peintres de 1804 à 1980: souffrances et espoirs d'un peuple.* Port-au-Prince: Imprimeur II, 1989.

Louverture, Toussaint. *Mémoires du général Toussaint L'ouverture écrits par lui-même.* Port-au-Prince: Les Éditions Fardin, 1982.

Madiou, Thomas. *Histoire d'Haïti, 1492-1846. Tome I-Tome VIII.* Port-au-Prince: Imprimerie Henri Deschamps, 1989.

Manigat, Leslie. *Eventail d'histoire vivante d'Haïti: Des préludes à la révolution de Saint-*

Domingue jusqu'à nos jours. Port-au-Prince: CHUDAC, 2001.

Métraux, Alfred. *Le vaudou haïtien.* Paris: Gallimard, 1958.

Paillière, Madeleine. *Saint-Brice en six tableaux et un dessin.* Port-au-Prince: Henri Deschamps, n.d.

Moïse, Claude. *La croix et la bannière: la difficile normalisation démocratique en Haïti.* Montréal: Editions du CIDIHCA, 2002.

Péan, Stanley. *Zombie Blues.* Montréal: La Courte Échelle, 1996.

Placoly, Vincent. *Dessalines.* Fort-de-France: Les éditions de L'Autre Mer, 1994.

Roumain, Jacques. *Gouverneurs de la rosée.* Fort-de-France: Désormeaux, 1977.

Salgado, Antoine. *Hauts-lieux sacrés dans le sous-sol d'Haïti (1947-1980).* Port-au-Prince: Ateliers Fardin, 1980.

Thoby-Marcelin, Philippe. *Panorama de l'art haïtien.* Port-au-Prince, 1956.

Victor, Jean-André. *Bouqui et malice: Ainsi parla l'autre (Tome I).* Port-au-Prince: 1993.

Sources in Haitian Kreyòl

Apollon, Marlène Rigaud. *Haiti Trivia.* Coconut Creek, FL: Educa Vision, 1998.

Castera, Georges. *Konbèlann.* Montréal: Editions Nouvelle Optique (s.d.), 1976.

Deyita. *Kont nan jaden peyi Ti Toma.* Port-au-Prince: L'imprimer II, 1991.

Frankétienne. *Dézafi.* Port-au-Prince: Editions Fardin, 1975.

Kazimi/Casimir, Jean/Jan. *Pa Bliye 1804.* Souviens-toi de 1804. Delmas, Haiti: Imprimerie Lakay, 2004.

Konstitisyon Repiblik Ayiti. Pòtoprens: Palè Lejislatif, 1987.

Moriso-Lewa, Feliks. *Teyat Kreyòl*. Haiti: Editions Libète, 1997.

Paillière, Madeleine. *Insèlbadjo*. Port-au-Prince: Henri Deschamps, 1978.

Trouillot, Michel-Rolph. *Ti difé boule sou istoua ayiti*. New York: Koleksion Lakansiel, 1977.

Sources in Spanish

Aniquila el Batalon Fijo de Santo Domingo. Boletin del Archivo General de la Nación. Ciudad Trujillo, no. 2, 1938.

Arrendo y Pichardo, Casper de. "Memoria de mi Salida de la Isla de Santo Domingo, 1805." *Clio* (Ciudad Trujillo), no. 82: 1948.

Bastien, Rémy. "Jacques Roumain en el décimo aniversario de su muerte." *Cuadernos americanos juillet-août 1954*.

Cumont, Franz. *El Egipto de los astrólogos*. Bruselas: [n.p.],1938.

Del Monte y Tejeda, Antonio. *Historia de la Isla de St. Domingo*. Ciudad Santo Domingo, [n.p.],1853.

Erman, A. *La religión de los egipcios*. Paris: Payot, 1937.

Fortunado, René, dir. *Trujillo: El Poder del Jefe I*. Santo Domingo, R.D.: Videocine Palau, S.A. videocine@codetel.net.do.

L. de Gérin-Ricard. *Historia del Ocultismo*. Trans. Sylvia Suárez. Barcelona: Luis de Caralt Editor S.A., 1961. (Trans. of *Histoire de L'occultisme*. Paris; Payot, 1939.)

Guillén, Nicolas. *Prologo a "Gobernadores de rocio"* (*traduction en espagnol du roman Gouverneurs de la rosée*). La Havana: Presse Nationale, Université Centrale de La Villas, 1962.

Pattee, Richard. Haiti: *Pueblo Afroantillano*. Madrid: [n.p.], 1956.

Prestol Castillo, Freddy. *El Masacre se pasa a pie*. Santo Domingo, D.N.: Ediciones de Taller, 1998.

Rodriguez-Demorizi, Emilio. *Invasiones hatianas de 1801, 1805, y 1822.* Ciudad Trujillo: [n.p.], 1955.

Rogmann, Horst. "Realismo mágico y negritude como construcciones ideológicas." *Journal of Hispanic and Luso-Brasilian Literatures*, no. 2:10 (septiembre-octubre)1979.

Rozo, Luz Stella. *El Poder Milagroso de los Salmos.* St. Paul, MN: Llewellyn Español, 2002.

Appendix 3

Selected Chronology of Ulrick Jean-Pierre's Work

"My belief is that it is most important for an artist to develop an approach and philosophy about life—if he has developed this philosophy he does not put paint on canvas, he puts himself on canvas."
—Jacob Lawrence to Josef Albers, 1946

The work of Ulrick Jean-Pierre can be divided into five major themes: the social life series, the historical series, the vèvè series, the surrealist series, and the portrait series.

Social life was Jean-Pierre's first series and constitutes the bulk of his work. These paintings comprise a powerful and heartwarming depiction of Haitian social scenes.

Jean-Pierre is better known for his impressive collection of Haitian historical paintings that he created in Philadelphia and in New Orleans, many of which are featured in this book.

The vèvè collection is a series of still-life compositions of Afro-Haitian religious artifacts. These are filled with mystical fantasms, rigorous linearity, and meticulous precision and detail. The surrealist series combines dreams, visions, and abstract concepts in complex compositions. These works represent a natural expression of the fantastic realism which permeates the culture of the Caribbean and has nothing to do with the European surrealism movement.

Jean-Pierre reveals his multidimensional quality as a painter in his mastery of the difficult art of portraits. Beyond routine technique, he manages to bring humanity, pride and dignity to his numerous subjects ranging from beauty queens to presidents. His paintings hang in private and public collections and in museums, galleries and universities in the United States, Haiti, Canada, Africa, and Europe. His work has been featured in a number of publications including: *ARTS Quarterly Catalog of the New Orleans Museum of Art; Haitians in the Diaspora (Directory Book of Haitian Artists Living Abroad)* by Emile Viard; *D'or du bicentennaire* by Jean-Paul Lafitte, *Journey Towards Freedom: A Bicentennial Celebration of the Haitian Revolution,* and *Mystérieux dans la gloire (catalogue et exposition commémorant le bicentennaire de la mort de Toussaint Louverture)* by Fritz Daguillard; *Haitian Artists in America* by Shubert Denis, Emmanuel Dostaly Patrice Piard, and Patrick Wah; *Haïtiens d'aujourd'hui* magazine; *Audience Magazine; Dialogue des anciens:*

Toussaint. What sets Jean-Pierre apart from other contemporary Haitian historical painters are the metaphysical, spiritual, and cosmic dimensions that he gives to historical subjects. His passion for Haiti's history has been a constant part of his work, his philosophy, his mission, and his life. For him, creating art means documenting Haitian history for future generations as well contributing to it. His work seems to say, "It is important to remember the past in order not to repeat its mistakes."

Selected Exhibits

2004

"Dèyè mòn, gen mòn: A Celebration of Haiti's Bicentennial in Art, Music, History and Spirit: Unveiling Haiti's History through the Art of Ulrick Jean-Pierre," Portland State University, Oregon

"The Haitian Revolution: Celebrating the First Black Republic," curated by Charles L. Blockson, African-American Museum, Philadelphia, Pennsylvania

"Celebrating Haitian History and Diversity," Tams Talk Artist Museum, Port Arthur, Texas

"Celebrating the Haitian Bicentennial of Independence," Black World History Museum, Saint Louis, Missouri

"Madness and Creativity," Maharry College of Medicine, Nashville, Tennessee

2003

"The Impact of the Haitian Revolution," New Orleans Municipal Auditorium

"From a Legacy of Freedom to an Explosion of Culture: May 1803-May 2003: Commemoration of the Haitian Flag," African-American Research Library and Cultural Center, Fort Lauderdale, Florida

2002

"Of Revolution and Peace," John A. Logan College Museum, sponsored by Southern Illinois University, Carbondale, Illinois

2001

"A Tribute to Satchmo," Louis Armstrong Centennial Art Exhibit, first prize. Mayor's Office of Tourism and Art and French Quarter North and South Art Guild, New Orleans, Louisiana

"Haitian Contemporary and Historical Paintings," Barrister's Gallery, New Orleans, Louisiana

"Public Art," City of New Orleans Arts Council, New Orleans, Louisiana

2000

"Creolization in the Academy and the Community," gallery exhibit and symposium, Tulane University, Center for Scholars and the Interdisciplinary Scholars' Network, New Orleans, Louisiana

"A Great People of World History," National Association of Haitian Physicians annual meeting, Fort Lauderdale, Florida

"A Bicentennial Celebration of the Haitian Revolution," Organization of American States, Washington, D.C.

1999

"Revelations," Moving Spirit Gallery, Atlanta, Georgia

"Inspirations," traveling group show, Southern University, Hammond, Louisiana; Contemporary Arts Center, New Orleans, Louisiana

"Ulrick Jean-Pierre's Haitian Historical and Contemporary Paintings," Barrister's Gallery, New Orleans, Louisiana

1998

"Of Revolution and Peace: Paintings by Ulrick Jean-Pierre," Birmingham Civil Rights Institute, Birmingham, Alabama

"The Art of Haiti," group show, Contemporary Arts Center, New Orleans, Louisiana

"Commemoration of Vertières," Haitian Association of Atlanta, Spelman College, Atlanta, Georgia

1997

"Ulrick Jean-Pierre Salutes Hurston," Zora Neale Hurston Museum of Fine Arts, Eatonville, Florida

"A Celebration of World Culture," The Louisiana International Art Exhibition, Southeastern Louisiana University, Hammond, Louisiana

"Essence Festival Art Exhibit," Ernest Memorial Convention Center, New Orleans, Louisiana

"Contemporary Expressions of Haitian Art" group show, Heritage Gallery, Philadelphia, Pennsylvania

Index